The Zinzan Brooke Story

The Zinzan Brooke Story
with Alex Veysey

rugby publishing limited
Auckland, New Zealand

Acknowledgement

The author and publishers wish to thank all those photographers and organisations who have contributed to this book, notably Andrew Cornaga, Peter Bush and rugby statistics by Geoff Miller.

©Alex Veysey, Zinzan Brooke
First published in 1995 by Rugby Publishing Ltd
67-73 View Road, Glenfield, Auckland, New Zealand.
Reprinted and revised statistics 1997.

Typesetting/design by Sportz Graphics Ltd, Glenfield, Auckland.
Printed through Colorcraft Ltd, Hong Kong.

Rugby Publishing Ltd is a member of the Medialine Group of Companies. P.O. Box 100-243, North Shore Mail Centre, Auckland 10, New Zealand.

ISBN 908-630-54-9

Contents

Dedication

To my family – Mum and Dad, Naera, Margaret, Martin, Robin and Simon – and to Ali. I owe them everything.

Foreword

When I took the decision in 1985 to abandon Auckland and move 'across the bridge' to join the fledgling North Harbour union, I had never heard of Zinzan Brooke. Or Michael Jones, for that matter.

They were promising colts on the way up, their rugby careers just beginning to unfold. I was just breaking into the All Blacks and more concerned with Murray Mexted who appeared to have a mortgage on the No 8 jersey at the time.

It wasn't to be too many years before Zinzan Brooke...and Michael Jones, of course...began to make their mark at provincial and international level.

In 1987, Zinzan made his All Black debut and by 1989 he was my understudy with the All Blacks, first in the queue for test selection at No 8, as I had been for so long behind Murray Mexted.

A year later I was out and Zinzan was in, and despite all those loyal supporters who waved 'Bring Back Buck' signs, I never did regain my All Black jersey. Zinny was the man.

So naturally I've followed his career with great interest. I certainly didn't, as some people have suggested, harbour any resentment that he displaced me from the All Blacks. It was the selectors, not Zinzan, who made that decision.

Zinzan was an exciting footballer from the start, quite different as a No 8 from the traditional players like Brian Lochore, Murray Mexted and myself. He broke the trend because he possessed so many skills, skills the rest of us simply didn't possess.

He could kick with either foot, throw skip passes, sidestep, dummy and, as the English players witnessed with such astonishment in the World Cup in South Africa, even drop-kick goals from 45 metres!

I certainly never attempted a 'pot' in my first-class career, and I'm sure Brian Lochore and Murray Mexted weren't audacious enough to either. I would like to record here, however, that I *have* dropped a goal, as a lock when I was playing college rugby back in 1973. Maybe if someone had encouraged that skill I, too, could have chalked up a few three-pointers for the All Blacks!

Drop-kicking was one of the multitude of skills that Zinzan was blessed with, and he possessed enough confidence to utilise these talents in any circumstances. The important thing is that he possessed enough natural talent to get out of any situation if something went wrong.

I respected him for his skills and his ability. I hope, in return, that he respected me for the footballer I was. I didn't sidestep, or slam away left-footed touchfinders, or feature in too many sweeping backline moves, but I hope I might have taught Zinzan something about forward drive and commitment and leadership from the front, which I believe were my best qualities as a rugby player.

The sadness of Zinzan's career is that New Zealand audiences, certainly those beyond Eden Park, saw too little of the genius of the man at top level. Injuries and fluctuations in form – not always his fault, for often the All Black pack simply wasn't performing – meant for a couple of years he and Arran Pene were sharing the All Black No 8 jersey, and it wasn't really until 1994, for the domestic series against the Springboks, that the best of Zinzan was produced consistently at test level.

He thoroughly deserved the New Zealand Player of the Year award for 1994. And if he didn't manage to produce world class performances year in, year out at international level, he remained nevertheless a great player. I'd always have him in my side. He and Michael Jones together at their peak represented just about the ultimate in a loose forward pairing.

Zinzan's rugby in 1994 was the best I'd seen him play since the 1988 New Zealand Maori team's world tour when Eric Rush (as the openside flanker), Zinzan (blindside flanker) and myself combined most effectively.

Everyone was super fit and with Maori rugby not being so tight, it allowed the loose forwards to cut loose. Zinzan was absolutely dynamic, even though he was out of position. I have to say that after that tour I believed blindside flanker was Zinzan's best position, but I must concede he has done a great job as No 8.

Wayne Shelford, September 1995

Introduction

Since this book was started much has happened to change the face of rugby. The revolution through which the players set out in frustration to decide their own destiny was both inevitable and a trauma for a game which has thrived on the traditions created by great players playing great matches. In many ways the atmosphere of rugby in New Zealand was the atmosphere of the past, a sport still able to capture the senses through legend…the deeds of the 1905 team, the 1924 team, the Kiwi Army team, the 1956 team, the 1967 team, the 1987 team and of players whose names weave as much magic now as they did long ago.

However history judges the events of 1995 and their aftermath, whatever rugby's traumas and convulsions, the names of players who have taken the public imagination in the years of change will stand with those of the distant past. Among them will be the name of Zinzan Valentine Brooke, a back-country kid who brought his range of natural skills to the city and became a great rugby player.

The Zinzan Brooke story is inspirational first because it shows that young people disadvantaged in material things can, by the warmth of family spirit and by their own determination to succeed, overcome what a distressing number of youngsters see to be insurmountable handicaps and, so, submit themselves to life on the streets.

There may never have been a more competitive sports person than Brooke. He competed as much with himself as with his opponents on the field. He set himself standards beyond the reach of most and on achieving them he set higher ones and went out after those. People speaking of him as a rugby player almost invariably come back to his remarkable skill level – a forward with a huge pass off either hand, with handling and kicking skills beyond the reach of many backs and with a defence which searched out the courage of those on the receiving end of it. All of these qualities were sown when, as a scrap of a kid, he had no toys other than a football and competition with his brothers and sister on the farm ran red-hot.

The Brooke family drew their collective strength from the struggle to eke out an existence from the family farm at Ahuroa, in the hinterland behind Puhoi. Two of the boys were to become All Blacks – Zinzan and his younger brother Robin – and a third, Marty, established himself as an Auckland representative and might well have become an All Black before taking his ability to France and Japan.

As a 14-year-old Zinzan could handle and shear 300 sheep in a nine-hour day and he welcomed the dogged pain in his shoulders and back at the end of it as proof that it had to be good for him. At that time all he ever wanted from life was to be a shearer, but not just any shearer, a Golden Shears champion.

He played his first first-class match for a New Zealand Marist XV in 1985 and at the end of the 1994 season had played 229, scoring a phenomenal 132 tries. In 46 Ranfurly Shield matches he scored 43 tries and in 115 matches for Auckland, 83, breaking records along the way. He scored four tries in a match five times, three four times and two 21 times. Some of his tries were memorable demonstrations of his extraordinary skill and strength and of his instinctive feel for a scoring chance. Instinct and the philosophy that it is acceptable to take a risk to reap a profit was in his try against South Africa at Johannesburg in 1992 when, with New Zealand presented with an easy chance for a Fox penalty goal, he raced in, grabbed the ball, tapped, ran and dived for the try.

Against Waikato in the 1987 Ranfurly Shield match he scored a try which encouraged Don Cameron, the New Zealand Herald writer and one not given to inflated praise of players, to call him "this astonishing young man". Covering the fullback, Lindsay Harris, about the Auckland 10-metre line, he beat Waikato backs Kevin Putt and Ian Foster to the ball and pushed it ahead. Another Waikato back, Warren Jennings, raced across to go down on the ball and as he dived on it Brooke tapped it under his body, hurdled Jennings and sprinted to it only a few metres from the line. With two defenders converging, Brooke scooped up the ball at full pace and dived over for the try. It was a matchless demonstration of high skill, superb athleticism...and the unerring instinct which separates the great from the good.

It was recognition of the "something extra-special" he had in Brooke that gave his Auckland coach, Maurice Trapp, the confidence to give him the space and the freedom, while conforming to the basic team patterns, to play it as he saw it and felt it. Trapp calls the Auckland approach "fingertip rugby; having the ball do the work" and Brooke fitted almost instinctively into it. Should Brooke suddenly produce a dropkick or unleash a raking touchfinder with left or right foot it came as no surprise to Trapp..."I wanted someone superbly skilled. The bonus was in the physical presence of the man. He could make a huge tackle, be on his feet again, tackling again and on his feet again. If that was in 1987 the players he tackled would still be showing-off their bruises in 1988. He could run on the shoulder of the wing, drive close, drop-kick from half-way – the ultimate competitor for 80 minutes."

Together with Alan Whetton, Brooke marshalled Auckland's close defences superbly, says Trapp, always thinking, communicating and then by the sheer velocity of the defence – "offensive defence" – throwing back an attack.

Between 1987 and 1991, the period when Trapp and Bryan Williams coached Auckland, Brooke's try-contest with the very fast winger Terry Wright was a constant source of entertainment and wonder. In 74 games Brooke scored 75 tries and in 77 Wright scored 61.

It was when Brooke was a young New Zealand seven-a-side representative in Hong Kong that the noted Welsh rugby writer and former international player Clem Thomas judged him to be the finest young player he had ever seen. Sevens were close to Zinzan's heart for they gave him the freedom and the space to express his skills and he was heartened by the encouragement he received from his Auckland coaches to take those skills and the free-thinking into the15-a-side game.

Persuaded by Sean Fitzpatrick, the New Zealand coach Laurie Mains broke a stand-off between himself and Brooke by giving the player much the same licence and it was that recognition of

11

what Brooke had to offer which saw him have one of his greatest seasons in 1994. Twice a New Zealand Rugby Almanack player of the year he was voted New Zealand rugby personality of the year in 1994, a season in which he also led Auckland to the National Provincial Championship for the second successive year.

It had been Brooke's ambition to be part of a New Zealand World Cup squad which would erase his own memories of 1991, a year when, he says, the All Blacks judged themselves to be bigger than the game and when team spirit was secondary to self-interest. When he was seriously injured in a 1995 World Cup preparation match he was emotionally shattered. The story of his recovery, Mains' perseverance with him and his participation at the World Cup is told here – as is his honest appraisal of his ability to perform at the Cup tournament. His drop-kicked goal against England, he says, could not disguise that he was playing below his capacity when fully fit.

Mains says Brooke's skill level and natural ability are inspirational to the whole team. But beyond that he had a sharp practical intelligence about the game…"his anticipation of changing circumstances and his ability to communicate under pressure are a crucial part of the All Blacks' defensive strength. All these things have been developed from his great natural competitiveness whether it is tossing coins, spinning balls, playing cards or playing rugby – he has to win."

Having to win was as much a part of the Brooke make-up when he was a stripling as when he was a seasoned All Black. When he was 17 he entered a gravel-shovelling contest promoted by Auckland's Radio i on the premises of a hardware merchant in Henderson. Brooke's opponents, about 100 of them, were mostly massive men from the heavy-duty areas of New Zealand industry, timber-workers, road-builders, body-builders. It was no place for a 17-year-old apprentice plumber with an eye to making a quick thousand dollars. But the boy among men won it in a canter. "It was a fascinating sight," says Phil Gifford, one of the presenters of the contest. "Fascinating and quite unbelievable that this determined kid with an unlikely name could outshovel those big hairy guys with muscles on muscles and tattoos on tattoos."

Of Brooke's achilles injury and the extent of its recovery for the World Cup Laurie Mains says, "Knowing the ability he has and the incredibly hard work he put in I was confident he would

12

be right for the crucial games. The England semi-final showed that at the level of recovery he had achieved he was again a powerful influence in the team. What is not generally known is that in the final against South Africa he took a very, very hard blow on the leg early in the game. He showed in the Bledisloe Cup match in Sydney why he is still such an integral part of the All Blacks and the way we play the game."

Mains says of the Brooke-Brewer-Jones loose forward combination that each was inspirational to the other "and history will record with regret that they didn't more often play as a trio."

Brooke says he did not want to have a book which squeezed the joy out of the playing of the game, not a book which concentrated on the game's politics to the exclusion of its capacity to entertain and cross all cultural and political divides. But nor did he want to avoid the controversies within the game because he felt much that had been swept under the carpet or glossed-over had to be aired because the rugby public deserved to know.

Alex Veysey
September, 1995

Zinny – by Ali

I was a seventh former with braces on my teeth, stars in my eyes, a whole beehive of ambitions buzzing around in my head and no secure notion about how I should go about pursuing any one of them. Dancing had been my life from the time I had my first ballet shoes at the age of five. Classical ballet, jazz, aerobic dancing…what I knew was that, in whatever form, dancing was my past, present and future.

So here I was in 1986, all braces, stars and ambitions, auditioning for what was a new concept for New Zealanders in sports entertainment: cheerleading. What New Zealanders knew about cheerleading was what they had seen in American movies, with college gridiron teams surging this way and that while beautiful blondes with long legs and jazzy military uniforms strutted their stuff and twirled their batons and batted their eyelids on the sidelines.

The Auckland rugby cheerleaders were to be something else, a professional troupe choreographed to a whole variety of dance-forms for the entertainment and, hopefully, the appreciation of the crowds and, stretching the imagination a little further, the inspiration of the players. For Auckland was at the beginning of its wonderful Ranfurly Shield era and there was a growing awareness of the need for big rugby occasions to offer other entertainment. Those cheerleading days were to be the beginning of professional dancing opportunities for many of us.

As an up-front display of player-interest in the concept the Auckland Rugby Union arranged for five players to attend the auditions. Among them, standing at the back, was this big guy

Ali Imm and Zinzan.

and I thought he was not at all bad. Just a school-girlish perception, of course, but no, not bad at all. Purely by chance, I swear, I started to see more and more of him at a distance, like in the newspapers. He was a sevens star with an unlikely-sounding name and it seemed whatever paper I happened to be reading he happened to be in it.

Zinzan! Really? That's his real name? Well, OK. Finally I met him and spoke to him through my braces at a function for the players to meet the cheerleaders and that was the beginning of a relationship and a partnership which has changed my life. Being a part of Zinny's life has rescued me from the danger of concentrating my life between narrow boundaries. My whole life was dance. Zinny's was rugby. If you confine yourself tightly into one activity or perhaps one vehicle of artistic expression you can lock yourself out of broader enjoyment of life. What we have both found, what we have discovered through each other, is that life is richer than rugby or ballet.

Now I have mixed with people of two different worlds and have found there is much to take from both. I think, too, I have brought something into Zinny's life he might otherwise never have experienced. He has, for instance, developed a love of classical music and, given the mood, can become lost in it.

I kept my career moving along. After the World Cup of 1991 we went to Italy where Zinny was to play out the season. In Rome I taught 13 classes a week in aerobics and from there spent a year in London dancing. It was one of those buzzing ambitions I might not have fulfilled had there been no Zinny and no rugby.

I love rugby. Its physical dynamics, even the contest body against body are refreshing, invigorating things outside my working world of choreography, dancing and modelling. But I am also able to appreciate the grace in the game. Even in dynamics there may be grace. Watching rugby in slow motion on television I have been quite taken aback by the beauty of much of the body movement, the leaping in the lineout, the swerve and fend away from a tackle. I can see value for rugby players in the flexibility-training ballet dancers have. Beyond all else the muscular flexibility of the male ballet dancer is his greatest asset. I am sure rugby players would benefit from it if it became part of their training from a young age. As it is they have muscles pinging here and pinging there and that indicates the need for greater flexibility rather than greater strength.

Zinny and I have been together for more than eight years. I feel as privileged as he does to have been involved in the great eras of Auckland and New Zealand rugby. There is a wonderful sisterhood of wives and partners in rugby. I think it happened first as some sort of defensive mechanism because they were omitted from all the social functions and celebrations of the game. Once it was as if they did not exist or, at least, existed to wash jerseys and socks and to rub bruises and ease the pain of a loss in a big game.

Some fine women quite aggressively pioneered the new acceptance of wives, partners and girlfriends and, when you come to think of it, they are a vital part of the game in the sense that now they can share fully in the triumphs and sadnesses and become so involved rather than being the irrelevant sidekicks they were once considered by the administrators.

Woman's place in the game has become more and more important as the players have had more and more pressure placed on them for their time and commitment to rugby while not seeing adequate material return for the professional time and attitudes demanded of them. Women are able now to understand the stresses involved and help deal with them.

I have found there is much more to fulfilment in the game than the sense of achievement being a good All Black brings. To be great, players have to love the game not merely play it well. Zinny's love of the game is so intense, runs so deeply - as it does for his brother Rob and for many of the players I know. With Zinny it is total commitment or nothing. He will not accept anything else in himself or in others. But within that commitment there is this clearly tangible pleasure in the expression of his own sense of freedom which is so much a part of his game. Free expression is a quality I know something of and which I can recognise in others from my background in dancing. It is the essence of Zinny's character.

He does have low times. I think of the state of mind immediately after the World Cup loss to Australia in 1991. There was a low, low period of soul searching but once he had come to terms with what he identified as the problems of that period he bounced back - as did most of the players. We all went to Italy for John Kirwan's and Fiorella's wedding and the occasion was just a marvellous recuperation for the players. Had there not been that sort of gathering together in celebration their recovery from

17

the World Cup loss would have been much more painful.

I still laugh over Michael Jones and Inga playing the DJ role and I still feel the emotion as John and Fiorella danced and all of us linked arms around them, swaying to the music and singing *You are so Beautiful*. I could feel the magic of those moments bonding the players together – an experience I will never forget.

Obviously I have great pride in Zinny's achievements as a rugby player but perhaps even more in what he has done in creating a successful life for himself out of nothing. When I say "nothing" I exclude his family from that because the qualities the Brookes as a family gave him are the most basic reason he has "discovered" himself in business. Zinny did not do particularly well at school and I think he has probably had a chip on his shoulder because of that. He knows that had he spread his interest more evenly between the sportsfield and the classroom he could have done very much better.

His intentions for his own children are clear. He will ensure they have a better understanding of the need to take a full part in their own education. Zinny has set out with great determination to establish himself and has revealed a natural aptitude in the field he chose to be the base of his financial security: residential property. He is a great reader of books on investment.

I need the sort of person Zinny is around me, someone with ambition, someone who sets goals and then resolutely sets about achieving them. He sets his rugby goals and his personal goals radiate from those. His resolution and his competitiveness are unbelievable. I cannot envisage anyone else tackling his achilles injury before the 1995 World Cup as he did. It was his own personal contest and although success came with the assistance of others his dedication was immense. I know what he went through when he went down with the injury. I know what I went through for him. He could see it all ending there, his career broken just as he was preparing for what he wanted to be his personal compensation to New Zealand for 1991.

The Brooke family is really quite exceptional. The warmth, the closeness and what they have achieved as a family after weathering terribly difficult times says much for the character of the parents, Hine and Sandy, and for six kids, Naera, Margaret, Marty, Zinny, Rob and Simon, who, with so little of material things, achieved so much that is truly worth while. I want six kids just like them.

1

In Failure, Success

I wanted my book to gallop along on the back of a World Cup-winning performance by the All Blacks. More than anything I have wanted in my life I wanted to be part of a team which would wash away memories of another World Cup when players judged themselves to be bigger than the game and paid the price.

That may seem an odd basis for ambition but to an extent it has been a driving force behind my rugby since 1991 when I was part of an All Black team which, in focusing on self-interest, effectively kicked the rugby priority to touch and with it any chance of glory. The 1995 World Cup team was different in every way, with a single-minded but free-thinking coaching philosophy and a group of players, young and older, bonded by a spirit the team of 1991 could never comprehend.

When, at Ellis Park, Johannesburg, June 24, 1995, this team failed by the margin of a dropped goal to bring back to New Zealand the William Webb Ellis Trophy a team with similar qualities had first won in 1987, it was so distressed by its failure and by the circumstances of it that it lost sight of its success. To the players at that time everything that had gone before did not exist. Everything that mattered was buried in Ellis Park.

It was not until we became caught up in the response of New Zealanders to the style of rugby we had played through our Cup programme that we fully understood that within failure there can be success. Traditionally, New Zealanders are harsh and unforgiving judges in rugby failure. The All Blacks are their personal possessions. When the All Blacks lose, all of New Zealand loses. When the All Blacks win all of New Zealand basks.

Here, a team New Zealand confidently expected to win the World Cup had been beaten on the post. In other days that soaring expectation followed by a bad result would have brought swift retaliation. New Zealand would have swung an axe over the necks of selectors, coach and players and happily watched the blood spurt.

Some of the blood would have been mine. Wasn't I the guy who dropped the ball? That colossal up-and-under of Joel Stransky's which I had covered when it left his boot, covered on its upward flight, covered at its peak and covered on its long fall into and through my arms? This was my sort of "take". It was my sort of skill – the sort of skill I had when I was a little kid and which I had polished until it was second nature. I did not drop the high ball. I caught it and kicked it unerringly to touch or cosily wrapped it up with the other forwards and delivered it to the backs. Always. Nearly always.

More than halfway through the 20 minutes of extra time in the World Cup final I dropped a ball which, nine times out of ten, I could have taken one-handed while singing. If I took my eye off it for a split second it was to judge that time was on my side, that I would be under the ball without too much pressure from the advancing South Africans. But I spilled it and when my brother Rob tore in to grab the loose ball it was as if he was desperately trying to retrieve the Brooke family honour.

When the referee called the scrum I forced the error into a distant corner of my mind. The South Africans set themselves with three options: Andre Joubert up to the left for the stab down the blind; Stransky deep behind for the "pot" or to run the same sort of try they scored against Australia – the No 8 feeding the halfback who runs wide and turns it back into Stransky on the burst and in the gap. I told Graeme Bachop I would cover the blind and the Stransky run. It was, of course, the drop-kick, superbly hit by Stransky and, God knows how, threading the needle between Bachop and Andrew Mehrtens charging hard and close.

Now, how would New Zealand judge us? Amazingly to us, New Zealand judged us on what we had given it in the matches leading up to the final. It judged us not only on Jonah Lomu and Glen Osborne, on Andrew Mehrtens and Josh Kronfeld, on Ian Jones and Robin Brooke, on Walter Little and Frank Bunce, on Graeme Bachop and Jeff Wilson but on the whole. It judged us on the second-strings who showed that first-strings were never safe. It judged us on Laurie Mains for his pursuit of a vision. It judged all of us on a style which was embraced with eagerness. New Zealand was not alone in this. Other countries, and notably the Home countries, judged the style of the All Blacks as being the style of the game's future. It was not all flawless, at times far from flawless. Inevitably in a game of such movement and, at times, audacity there would be error. But the seeds were well and truly sown. The call is clear in England, the staunchest bastion of rugby conservatism, for a rethink which would restore its attack-capable backs to their rightful place in the game. That may be the greatest victory of all for what is now freely labelled "the New Zealand game".

When we came home New Zealanders went out of their way to show us that losing the final was less important to them than what they had taken from the rest of the campaign. At that great welcome at Auckland's Aotea Centre a little girl named Gemma showed me all was forgiven by holding up a placard saying, "Welcome home, Zinzan". That really hit the heart. I did not know seven-year-old Gemma until just before the World Cup. She wrote a beautiful little letter to me when my future was in the lap of the gods. I rang her and we had a yarn about cabbages and kings and achilles tendons. Two of Ali's friends were standing near Gemma at the welcome and signalled to me to throw a ball to her. Someone beat me to it and then I was under pressure to drop-kick mine, anyway.

Which reminds me. About that drop-kick against England. The team is now quite familiar with how it was done. I have told them as a team and as individuals many times because it is important they should not forget. I will be giving them refresher courses on it from time to time when we get together for games, training and after-match functions and at our 25th and 50th reunions.

For the sake of accuracy in the book I will confess to readers what I would never confess to the players. It was an ugly kick. Like, *ugly*. It looked much less ugly on television than it really was. It was from broken play. Will Carling had to clear for touch and I reckoned I was in just about the place he would find it. I had a quick look out to my left to see whether our backs were lined up for a long pass from me and a push down to the corner. So Will, usually-unflappable Will, miskicked. I think it must have been something to do with his groin because he certainly looked very pained. I was behind halfway when the ball came down and I was waiting for it to roll toward me. But when it hit it bounced straight up in the air and I was running into it. That's when I thought, "Hey, Zinny, there's a droppy on here." I was on the run when Grimm Bachop, behind me, suddenly realised what I had in mind. He was screaming, "No, Zinny! No, Zinny! Don't! Run it, Zinny!" And just over my shoulder Bruiser Brewer was muttering, "Oh, shit, Zinny" and all around the paddock All Blacks were putting their hands over their eyes. I laid into it. After it left my foot it sort of swooped down toward the ground. Then for no reason I could guess at it gained height but was heading for the corner-flag. Then God thought, "Zinny has seen enough of trouble and strife", gave it a puff and it slewed back toward the posts still rising and at the end looked a ripper of a kick.

An English reporter described it as "a handsome stroke from a player who places no limits on his skills", which was nice of him but not very perceptive. Another used it to bash the English attitude to rugger: "Where in all the land, even in our dreams, would we find a forward who could contemplate drop-kicking a goal from 45 metres let alone have the audacity to actually do it in a test match?" A quick interview with Bach or Bruiser might have brought him back to earth.

At the parliamentary reception when we came home a guest came up to me and said, "Ah, about that drop-kick. I was sitting there watching it on telly. When you kicked it I put my head in my hands and groaned, 'My God, Brooke, what a bloody idiot you…are…*oh-great-kick-Zinny!*'"

You may think I have gone on long enough about the drop-kick. The players would say you have got off lightly. They may even say jokingly they expect never to hear the end of it. But they don't know how right they are. My Marist clubmates in Auckland will vouch for my persistence. Two years ago in the club championship semi-final, blocked to the right, I turned and drop-kicked a goal with my left foot. It will be some years before I let them forget that. About the year 2025 I would think.

By now it will be clear I do, as Keith Quinn is given to saying, fancy myself as a kicker. But that goes back a long way, right back to when kicking a ball with either foot, barefoot or fully shod, was the natural thing to do – and when dropping a high ball was never a possibility…

2

The Puhoi Kid

I t's a wet day in Puhoi. Out of the river it's dry. Dry enough to kick up dust and hurt your heel when you dig up dirt for a shot at goal. But in the river, where the ball and I happen to be, it's as wet a day as I can remember anywhere. Every kid should have a game of footy at Puhoi. It's where the real heart of New Zealand rugby beats.

There are Puhois all around the country going by other names. Little rural communities with footy grounds naturally fertilised by what ever happened to be grazing on them the day before. My Puhoi browses, 55 kilometres north of Auckland, just a five-second flash of Rod Seymour's pub and the store and the church and the library if you're dumb enough to drive through it without stopping.

Anyone who hasn't stopped at the Puhoi Pub for a pint of draught or to splash his boots or get lost in the museum which hangs all over the walls or just talk a bit of footy with Rod Seymour has missed out on one of life's warmest experiences. Rod's a north-of-Auckland man through and through and the unsung benefactor of more kids than Barnado's.

The Puhoi Pub has made it to the pages of Bateman's New Zealand Encyclopaedia and that has to mean it's famous. But Bateman's Encyclopaedia doesn't know the half of it.

Across the bridge opposite the pub there's the Puhoi footy ground. A big green bank of lush native bush to one side, the river piddling along amiably on the other. A bunch of kids chasing the ball, some getting to handle it, some hoping they might get to touch it and some hoping like hell they don't have to. When you

Aged 11, captain of Rodney Sub-union team, receiving ASB Roller Mills Shield from Sid Going.

play from right to left facing the bush a good right-foot hook will carry the ball unerringly into the river. As rivers go it's no big deal though it can flush up to a pretty respectable torrent given the weather for it. I'm in it because the ball's in it and we kids are not yet up to understanding the wisdom of "Bugger the ball, let's get on with the game".

It's just another day in Puhoi. We got there from our farm at Ahuroa, about 20 kilometres off the main road and into the sticks, with dad driving the 1967 Holden Kingswood Special with the holes in the floor and toadstools growing in one of the back corners. There's Marty, me and Rob in order of seniority. Our big brother Naera has gone off to play in Whangarei. He's driven the old tractor 20 kilometres over rough roads to where he gets his lift. Margaret, our elder sister, has to get to Warkworth to play netball and Simon, the squib brother, comes along for the ride.

Through the holes in the floor we watch the tyres whipping up the creamy-coloured dust, spurting it up into our faces so that when we get to Puhoi we're Maori bros with white eyebrows, lashes and hair. We reckon that's pretty neat. On the way we've driven past the property where this joker used to breed ferrets. One bad year he went bust and with malice towards none and

24

The Kingswood Special...holes in the floor, toadstools in the corner and full of Brookes.

out of kindness to the ferrets he set a whole bunch of them loose. His nearest neighbour was a thriving poultry farm. Suddenly, from a healthy position, the poultry farm went bust, too. Every time we drive past dad starts laughing.

This day we get to Puhoi in time to play the game. Sometimes we don't quite make it because the farm chores have to be done and we regret that but we aren't bitter about it. It's a fact of life when the family's struggling to make a crust and, anyway, working around the farm is what we like most next to rugby.

Farming has been all we know. Not farming of the country-squire kind. Farming of the work-till-you-drop-or-you-go-under kind. The mortgage hung over the farm like a shroud and it must have worried the life out of my mother and father but they never let their worries spill over on to us. We knew what work was about because it was a family farm in every sense and we were a family in every sense. For me, even as a little kid, it was more than that. I had farming in my soul. I loved working with the animals, rounding up stock from horseback, getting in to help with the shearing and even the brucellosis testing and weeding in the giant vegetable patches where we grew acres of spuds and cabbages, corn and tomatoes and melons as a sort of jumbo-sized family survival kit.

I need to talk about the family life on the farm and the way we amused ourselves, the ways we set out to make an extra buck or two to help things along because it is the essence of what I became as a rugby player and what I became as a man. Those days were the foundation of my life; the freedom, the confidence mum and dad had in us kids and the way they pulled us all in so that even if they were deprived we were never made to feel it. There were times when we couldn't buy food at the store because we were a small fortune over the credit line, times when I could sense real worry in my mother. I have seen her, quietly desperate, waiting for the next mail delivery, finding a cheque in it, kissing the cheque and saying, "Thank you, Lord."

If we lacked the usual sort of things kids have to amuse themselves we didn't know it. Summers were not summers as so many city kids would understand them. No holidays away with the family or even holidays to do what you liked with. We spent our summer holidays cutting scrub and gorse or doing whatever needed to be done around the farm. Every day was another day's work, but we missed nothing.

There were no toys as most kids understand toys. Rewards were simple and rare but when we got them it was like Christmas…a Crunchie Bar or a Topsy ice-cream with a jelly tip at the end of a week of scrub-cutting, a swim when we finished weeding those endless acres of vegetables. These were our luxuries. To us getting a Crunchie Bar was some other kids getting a bike. But there were always footballs. We were born and bred to be footballers.

My father, Sandy, and my mother, Hine, knew all about rugby and about farming. Dad had farmed a property near Pukekohe, south of Auckland, and he'd locked the scrum for Patumahoe. Mum was from farming stock, too, and her uncles, Pat Whiu and Paki Matene, played rugby for New Zealand Maoris and so did her cousins, Huirua Whiu, Joe Whiu and Brownie Cherrington, who was also an All Black. Our grandmother, Sybil (Zinzan) Brooke, and our grandfather, Martin, were very special to us, always there for us with clothing and with home-cooking. My grandad, my friend, a veteran of Gallopoli, died last year on his 103rd birthday.

Mum and dad loved rugby with passion. There was no way we were going to be ballet dancers, though dad reckons that when Rob was the little kid in the team, spindly and younger than the

With my grand-dad and great supporter, Martin, on his 102nd birthday.

rest, he skirted around the edges of the scrums like a ballet dancer protecting her toes and if he was shoved out on to the wing he performed with all the conviction and coordination of a spider caught in a downpour. Rob's come some way since then.

For a lock dad might not have been as big as you would expect. But he's a surprisingly big guy for a little guy, physically very strong and rawboned. At Patumahoe he and Dick Brewer, father of Mike, locked the scrum. When he moved north he played for Grafton and had a lot of games for the Barbarians, locking the scrum with players like Richard (Tiny) White and Morrie McHugh and in teams with Freddie Allen, Johnny Simpson, Bob Scott, Ponty Reid. I remember him telling us how Peter Jones came down from North Auckland to play with his gear in a sugar-sack and how his boots only just fitted into it. We drew pictures in our minds of Peter Jones tearing around the paddock in boots like punts and we all went, "Geee!" and "Whee-ew!" and "Hoo-eee!"

The farm at Pukekohe was 120 acres and dad wanted to get to a bigger place so he mortgaged himself to the eyeballs and bought the Ahuroa farm with a couple of thousand breeding ewes and three or four hundred breeding cattle on it before we moved into fattening bulls and steers. When we went on to the farm wool was 130 pence a pound. Two weeks later it was 32 pence. That hit mum and dad between the eyes but they battled on and took the little battlers with them.

The front lawn was about 30 acres with totara trees all over the place. Our favourite game was to take a footy ball each and run around the section kicking the ball so that it hit every totara tree plus a few other targets like gates and posts. First to hit the front gate was the winner. We all developed kicking skills both with left and right foot and we became intensely competitive. Probably I became the most competitive of all. No matter what we were doing it was a contest and I hated losing. In later years I would reject playing in friendlies, whether touch-rugby or basketball or a bit of a hit around at cricket. If it wasn't played seriously and at 100 miles per hour I didn't want to know for it was from that sort of competition I took my enjoyment.

Through the years we played just about everything – badminton, cricket, basketball, softball, swimming, athletics – and losing was something I would never contemplate. I was an all-rounder and, with a decent sense of anticipation and hand-eye

Digging to survive – with Dad.

co-ordination, reached good standards in most of the sports we played and most athletic events. Good but not great, master of none. Not like Rob who held national age-group records in both track and field events and still holds school records. He broke just about every record in the books and was potentially an open sprint champion.

Sean Fitzpatrick has called me the ultimate competitor but I'm no more competitive now than when I was a ragged-arsed kid on the farm kicking a ball at the totara trees. Those trees played an important part in my education other than in rugby. There was the one by the middle gate. I was under strict instructions never to pee on it…"Don't you dare pee on that tree, Zinny, or it will bite you back." Bite me back! I might have been just a kid but one thing I did know was that trees didn't bite, not when you kicked a ball against them, not when you climbed them, not when you peed against them, not ever.

Well, you know what it's like out on the farm. If you need to pee, you pee. It seemed pretty unreasonable to me that I could pee on any other tree but not on this one. So there was this time I ran up the drive to open the gates ahead of the old car. When I got to the middle gate with the forbidden tree I felt like a pee. So I had one against the tree. Things were going pretty normally when, as kids do, I started to spray around a bit, testing for height

29

and distance. Suddenly there was a flash and a bolt of something shot back up the stream and hit me where it hurt like hell. Pee splashed 27 startled Hereford bulls ten paddocks away, I went a surprising shade of white and fell into the car in a loud state of panic, pain and outrage.

It was practical education at its best. In one blinding flash of enlightenment I had learned all about the reaction of electricity to a jet of water and that trees do not actually bite. It is the electric fences behind the trees that bite.

We were scrawny kids, I suppose, but we grew quickly. To this day I envy Naera, Marty, Rob and Simon their extra two or three inches. Boy, could I use that at the back of the lineout. But I blame myself. I had played one year in the ASB Roller Mills schools tournament for Rodney sub-union and was determined to play in the next but knew I would have a weight problem. So I played around with starvation for a year. Sometimes, as a gesture to mum, I'd eat what was put in front of me but then I'd get outside and work till I was absolutely stuffed to get rid of it. I deliberately cut back on everything – an 11-year-old going all anorexic so he could play a few games of footy. Crazy.

Three weeks before the weigh-in I went to the store and weighed myself at 55 kilograms. The limit was 52. So I went into full starvation mode for three weeks, then off to the weigh-in. Make yourself light, Zinny, make yourself light. Toilet first, that'll help. Hop on the scales, hardly touch them, hop off. Spot-on, Zinny, you're in. Now go and eat.

Half-a-dozen hot dogs and a couple of hamburgers later you're nicely stuffed and well over the weight limit. A professional foul. Mum says that starving through that year at a crucial age for growth stunted my progress in later years compared with Marty, Rob and Simon. Marty grew something like 20 centimetres in one year about that time. Look at my brothers now: Marty 6ft 6in, Rob and Naera 6ft 5in, Simon 6ft 4 1/2in. Zinny (shortarse) Brooke, 6ft 3in. I hate that.

Sometimes when we reflect on those days it is with disbelief that we were able to achieve what we did. We talk about the year of the flash-flood which wiped out all the vegetables which were to feed us for months. And we think about carting firewood down to Takapuna or even Remuera at 20 bucks a load less the ten it cost us to get there and back, selling farm-meat to the school teachers, me shearing my little flock of black sheep and selling

Robin competes…a great all-round athlete.

the wool to the music-teacher who was a spinner. These were all dollars in the family kitty. It was hand-to-mouth stuff.

I couldn't get enough of shearing. By the time I was 14 I was up to 300 in a nine-hour day and all I ever wanted to be was a shearer. I love the oily smell and feel of the wool and the battle with full-sized rams and cranky-minded ewes and the look of a clean shear, the companionship of men and even the stink of the yards. An All Black? It never occurred to me. But a Golden Shears champion? Yes! I never did match my cousin Hamatona Tewhata who was a Golden Shears champion but I did compete in my grade at the Shears.

I started at home doing the crutching, then some shearing in the little two-stand shed and then one year we couldn't afford to have shearers in so we did it all ourselves after school and at weekends. Later, at school-holiday time, we joined our cousins in a shearing gang down the East Coast.

Talk about a Brooke family benefit. Naera was head pressman, Margaret, Marty and I were roustabouts. Then they let me shear one side of a sheep, then the first sheep of the run and then I was into real shearing, 120-130 when I was 13 and feeling the deep back and shoulder pain you know is never going to go away but which, eventually, does and leaves behind a layer of hard muscle. Footy training without the footy training.

We were making dollars I could never have dreamed of. One year I went home with 800 bucks in cash strapped inside my shirt against my belly. It felt good there, as if it belonged. Eight hundred bucks was a lot of puha, a treasure for a family with nothing but a farm mortgage, a clapped-out car and a black-and-white television which went sometimes. When we went into the house and I ripped open my shirt to show mum her face made the whole show complete. That payday bought us a car without holes in the floor or toadstools in a back corner.

Dad coached us at rugby and for a long time mum was team manager. It was not so easy filling teams in a little place like Puhoi. Dad says he had to shake all the tea-trees on the side of the road and play anything that dropped out. We were told by our mother that enjoyment in anything was as important as achievement. That has stayed with me in my sport and my life. The test of it for me is that I still play my best rugby when I allow myself to cut loose naturally, play with freedom and instinctively. My competitiveness and my hatred of losing does not change that.

Graciousness in defeat was another of mum's messages. I can still live with that, too, but only when I know I have given the game everything and that the team has, too. Graciousness is not in my make-up when a performance has been half-hearted but if a team has given 150 per cent a loss sits more comfortably with me.

That is why I took huge satisfaction for the team from the Bledisloe Cup match against Australia in 1994, the match of the magical second spell when the New Zealand players to a man gave everything there was to give and then some more. There was such pride in that 40 minutes, such self-motivated inspiration that when we lost I was able to weigh defeat against performance and say, "OK".

On the other side of the coin I felt nothing but despair and anger at the depths to which the New Zealand rugby character sank in the lead-up and loss to the Aussies in the 1991 World Cup semi-final, an event I will write about more broadly in this book.

Dad was great with the kids. He demanded nothing from them but that they play the game with enjoyment and as best they could. No sideline-screaming father-coach here, just a warm-natured encourager. He says parents who assail their kids from the sidelines are indulging in a form of abuse he finds obscene because all the kids are doing is trying to enjoy a game. He calls it "the strange, angry society of rugby parents".

On the morning of tests in Auckland the All Blacks go through their lineout drills on the ground just opposite our home-base, the Poenamo Hotel. After it, we watch the kids playing their Saturday morning footy. So many parents create a battleground out of a game and it is destructive for the kids and destructive for rugby because the kids come to hate it and are lost to it. It's hard enough for children to understand what the game's all about, anyway; they're bewildered by it all and an aggressive dad and mum on the sideline add to their confusion and their anxiety.

Back in the school days I would play anywhere as long as it was close to the action but then it was mostly as a prop or hooker and it was as a prop that I had my first major age-group representative games. When dad had the Rodney Sub-union under-17s he played Marty, who was to become a top lock, at centre. But dad knew which side was up. When there was a lineout he had Marty running in to take the jumping spot in the middle, winning the ball (which he always seemed to do) then tearing off back out to create havoc through the centres. An innovator, my dad.

There was, of course, school. School was not my best subject. I never quite absorbed the principles of education which was surprising, I suppose, because my mother was a trained teacher. I was happy to view school as a big sports ground where all sorts of games were played but with too many boring pauses when you were whisked off the fields and into a room so a teacher could tell you sport wasn't everything and mathematics and English analysis was very good for you. I never found their arguments convincing.

To try to define my attitude to the classroom I point you to our footy matches against Wellsford. When the big bad Brooke boys faced up to the bros from Wellsford there was a whole new meaning to chicken-shit. They came through with their afro nonhaircuts and they had "no mercy" carved into their hearts. When you stared at them they didn't quickly look away and that was a bad, bad signal. They glared right back and tossed their hair and pawed at the ground. It was the bull-ring and no place to be but, on balance, I would rather have played an hour against the Wellsford bros than spend 10 minutes tussling with an algebraic equation.

Not surprisingly, I left Mahurangi College at 15. The others were more academically inclined.

I have had regrets I did not become a farmer but realistically the time was not right, the money-well too shallow. As my life has unfolded I have come to accept that my time to be a farmer will be the right time and that it will happen. Farming is still my heritage, my first love, my free existence. Every kid should experience it, even in poverty.

I get so bloody frustrated when I see the young lives wasting away on the streets of the cities, the juvenile dead-beats, their brains scrambled from glue-sniffing, mugging for money and mugging for fun, exiles from their families whether forced out by abuse, encouraged out by neglect or pandered out by false images of what is cool and what is uncool.

So many families seem fractured now. It's not cool for kids to be with their parents but it's real cool to get into your Michael Jordan boots, shove your head into a back-to-front baseball cap, hunt in a gang-pack, act out the violent fantasies of television and accept sub-human living as the cool image, man.

I resent that so many of the street-kids are Maori when by culture the Maori family is an all-embracing unit. My mother is Maori and she brought to our family all that is best of the qualities which create mutual affection and respect. Her great regret is that through all the stresses of trying to eke out a living there seemed no time to educate us in Maori language and culture. But the dignity and pride with which she carried her Maoritanga rubbed off on all of us.

So where are street kids headed with their minds bent by what they take to be acceptable in violence and abuse? Mt Eden? They're not headed for a footy club, they're headed for trouble. Maybe the real contest for their minds is between guys who play rugby in black jerseys and guys who beat-up and kill on the little box in the corner, but that contest has to be won early before their parents lose interest in them let alone their love for them. I wish there was a way to get through to them that, even in poverty, what we had as a family is for everyone provided the will to have it is in the parents.

When the All Black World Cup squad went to Te Aute College in 1987 two or three hundred Maori students did the haka. The

All I ever wanted to be was a shearer.

Mum and Dad and all the kids...me, Simon, Robin, Naera, Marty and, in front, Margaret.

solid, pounding warrior rhythms reverberated and my hair stood rigidly to attention. It was a shivery, bristling sort of pride and it pulled all that was Maori in me to the surface. It was, in its way, much the same sort of pride I wanted to share when I saw Maori street kids in Auckland.

So much of Maori youth gets lost along the way. I know that when I left school I searched hazily for direction through a sort of no-man's land. What was I going to do, a country kid like me? That I found direction and purpose was entirely due to my family background, to my sporting affiliations and the security that was always there through both. If there is a family breakdown, as clearly there is with most of these young people in the streets, I would hope for personal pride to pull them through.

Sport and membership of any sports club is an anchor kids should look to when they feel themselves drifting. There were some brilliant young rugby players in the schools last year and this. I wonder what percentage of them will stay in the game and what percentage will be sluiced away aimlessly. It should be part of rugby's quest to guarantee its future that it moves among the schoolboy players, encouraging and advising and pointing the way not just in rugby but in lifestyle.

3

My Name Is Zinzan. OK?

There was this traffic cop. And there was this other traffic cop back in the car. Two traffic cops, two guns. When you go to Australia for the first time it hits you with a jolt that those holsters strapped to the side of cops are gun holsters and inside are real guns and real bullets. The Australians have come a long way from the PC Plod image of Mother England where cops are fair game for villains with guns but don't have the advantage of having something to shoot back because that wouldn't be fair and, as every English rugby writer will tell you, England always plays fair.

So this Queensland traffic cop was looking at me very suspiciously and I was looking at his gun-hand very suspiciously because it seemed to be creeping toward the holster. "Honest," I said. "It really is, isn't it guys?" And I turned to the car-load of Marist footy players who, to a man, yelled stuff like, "Don't believe him ossifer" and "Shoot him" and "Lock him up". They were, of course, pissed as parrots.

We were the Marist sevens team. We had won the Taupiri tournament in New Zealand and this very day had beaten the top Fiji Police team, winners for four successive years, in the final of the Redcliffe Sevens over in the land where cops wear guns. As designated driver I had done no drinking and you know what it's like when you're sober and everyone else is raving and everything they say is very loud and hilariously funny to them. Your mouth gets tired from laughing along because you feel you should and you keep looking at your watch and wishing you were back at the hotel. But you know that when you get back to the hotel and have a few drinks you'll just be coming right when the rest of them are falling over unconscious.

With this lot in the car I was driving along unfamiliar roads when I came to an intersection and on the other side was a stationary car with its lights on full beam. So I flashed my lights at it a few times, turned left on to the main drag and shot off. A couple of ks down the road I looked into the rear-vision mirror and through the alcohol fumes noticed this car with flashing lights. It seemed to be following us but I thought maybe it was on its way to an accident or something so I pulled off down a side-street, turned a few corners, looked again and it was still there.

So I stopped. One cop came over to the car and told me to get out. Licence? No, sorry officer, not here.

Registration papers?

Um, no, sorry.

Where have you been?

We're a New Zealand team and we've just won the Redcliffe Sevens.

The what?

You know, rugby.

No, I don't know. What's your name?

Zinzan...

And it was then his hand moved.

What name?

Zinzan.

Look, sonny. I've gone along with you so far but don't give me that bullshit. Now what's your name?

Honest. Zinzan.

And his lips sort of tightened and he started to look real shitty and the guys in the car were yelling, "Nah; don't believe him. He's having you on, ossifer; he's a bloody crook..."

He took some convincing and he wasn't a happy copper. And he wasn't the first to disbelieve the name is real and he won't be the last. Me? I like it. I was born in Waiuku on St Valentine's day, 1965. Waiuku is over there near Pukekohe where dad had the first farm. I was christened Murray Zinzan Brooke but when I went to school at Ahuroa there was a whole bunch of Murrays in the class and the teacher asked if any kids wanted to change their names. "Just call me Zinzan," I said. "Zinzan?" she said. "Zinzan," I said.

My mother says I wasn't just given the name Zinzan, it was

"bestowed" on me by the matriarch of Zinzan descendants, Aunty Joy Montgomerie, nee Zinzan, my dad's aunt and the mother of John Zinzan Montgomerie, the New Zealand tennis representative. Also descendants of the first New Zealand Zinzan were the Harris cricketing family of Canterbury - Zinzan and his son Chris both New Zealand representatives.

It seems the Zinzan family name – it is originally a surname – came from Italy where there were several derivations…Zinzeino, Zenzano, Zinzano. Hannibal Zinzano went to England and in 1514 was farrier to King Henry VIII, lessee of the Manor of Hatfield and Keeper of the Parks. Robert Comport Zinzan, a surveyor and apothecary, emigrated to New Zealand in the 1830s and my exchange with the Queensland traffic cop 150 years later was the direct result of that.

My name was changed by deed-poll from Murray Zinzan to Zinzan Valentine, Valentine for the day of my birth, and now I hope I have convinced everyone that Zinzan is my name and especially, if he reads this, the Queensland traffic cop who left the scene shaking his head in disbelief.

I was Zinzan, really, from the time my teacher needed to call me something other than Murray and it was as Zinzan or Zinny that I swam in the Puhoi River to save the ball from drowning. And I was Zinzan when I arrived late for my first senior club match at the age of 15, said I was sorry and scored three tries for Warkworth against Kaipara Flats. So, just for the record, Zinzan is not some sort of California-wild nickname or a name pinched from the zany old family cat. Zinzan is my name. OK?

Memories of those early days of rugby are just of the sheer thrill of playing, of accepting that I had certain natural-born skills with the ball and taking every opportunity to show them off. I don't think I did it in any brazen sort of way. It was just doing the things I could do best, loving to beat players with a sidestep or a swerve, kicking with either foot and kicking goals. And I played just wherever they wanted me to play which often was prop, so often that it seemed that would be where my future as a player lay.

It was as a prop that I played for the North Island under-16s against South and then the New Zealand under-17s against Australia at Lancaster Park. I did not think of propping as some deep technical exercise I had to master. It was a position on a rugby field. Not my favourite position, but through it I got to play rugby. Playing rugby as a prop meant bending my back for the scrum and getting stuck into rucks and glaring at the joker opposite me. This meant I had less time to get out and do the sort of things I would do if I was playing loosie, centre, wing or fullback. This, I know, will be seen as some sort of sacrilege. Richard Loe might read this and think it confirms everything he ever suspected about me. But even then I needed that hands-on involvement to feel I was playing the game as I knew I could play it best. Even in the Puhoi days I got to play halfback, and sometimes first-five or fullback, but mostly they shovelled me into prop.

I know it would be doing the right and accepted thing to say that first experience of wearing the New Zealand jersey in the under-17s brought out this great surge of pride in the black with the silver fern. Just about every other player I know reckons he experienced this soaring sense of inspiration from the traditions of the jersey he put on. I'm not sure whether I should be ashamed to say that when I put mine on it felt just like a footy jersey. Different colour. Same game. And more important than the jersey was the game. I was happy about being selected for New Zealand but I can't say I had this magical spiritual thing which made me play like ten men. It was a game of footy and I played as well as I could as one man.

At that time the family had sold up the Ahuroa farm, moved to a 110-acre property at Warkworth and posted me off to Carrington Polytech to study horticulture. It seemed like a good idea, too. The plan was to grow kiwifruit, grapes and strawberries and make a fortune selling them on-site. Then the bureaucrats got a sniff of the scheme and told us we couldn't erect wires on the property because it was adjacent to the satellite station. That put the Brookes in some sort of limbo. Again.

I went down to Auckland and lived in a Maori Affairs boarding hostel while I studied plumbing, like my big brother Marty. The year before, in 1981, I had been in the North Auckland under-18s against Counties and we had been hosted in transit by the Ponsonby Club which fed us like kings on soup, sausages and spuds. That seemed a good enough reason for dad to suggest I play for Ponsonby when I moved to Auckland. I thought if they fed a bunch of strangers like that I might even get steak and eggs as a fully-fledged club-member. Food was a big thing in my life.

But I never did play for Ponsonby. I had been in the North

Island under-18s as a lock – and in those days if you were looking for somewhere to play which was more suffocating than prop, lock would be first choice and only choice. In that team was an Auckland Marist player named Eddie Kohlhase. The day I was to have my first training run at Ponsonby he rang and said it would be nuts to play for Ponsonby when, clearly, Marist was the best club around. I said OK, Marist sounds cool.

Then this cool kid with blond hair and a blue Holden with a surfboard on the roof picked me up and took me to training. He said his name was John Kirwan. How do you spell that? I said. I had a second year in the North Island under-18s as a lock after I had captained Auckland in the same age-group. In that team was a serious kid named Jones. Gidday, he said. I'm Michael Jones. I knew how to spell Jones. And then this same kid went out and played like a rocket in the North Island team and scored two tries while I locked-up the scrum with Rob Gordon.

It was Eric Kohlhase, Eddie's father and coach of the Marist third grade team, who decided I shouldn't be either a prop or a lock. That was a great relief. He turned me into a blindside flanker. I knew nothing about running lines or any of that sophisticated stuff. I chased the ball. If anyone came at me I tackled him. When I got the ball I ran with it or kicked it. That seemed to me to be the right way to play loose forward. And they let me kick the goals, too.

In fact, I had a great year with the boot. Which brings me to one of the great frustrations of my life. From the time I was little I could kick goals from all over the place. Once when I was in the third form and playing for Mahurangi College against Orewa I lined up a shot from halfway. One of the touch-judges, a schoolteacher, was very reluctant to take the long run down to the goalposts. He stared at me and shook his head and said something about bloody Barry John. When I kicked it through the middle he shook his head again, but faster.

Later, I enjoyed kicking sessions with Grant Fox after Auckland training and when I was playing in Italy our kicker was terrible so I told the coach we needed the points we were missing from bad goalkicking and wouldn't it be a great idea if I found a better kicker. Like me. He shook his head, too, but as my Italian wasn't the best I took that to mean "yes". So I grabbed the ball and kicked the goals with a higher success ratio than Naas Botha who was also playing over there.

41

Now when I watch John Eales kicking for Queensland and Australia I wonder whether Laurie Mains is really aware of the little treasure he has hiding modestly behind a No 8 jersey. Eales has a beautiful relaxed style for a big man. If you are short in the leg, like Foxy, you have to punch the big kicks but Eales flows through them with that long leg, just a pendulum-swing...like a golf club, letting the club-head do the work.

It was with the Marist club that I started to play sevens. To me it was just a game where you got the ball, ran and scored a try if you were lucky enough, fast enough or knew you could run through a tackle. It was not until I became involved with guys like JK, Terry Wright and Bernie McCahill who had been in the Auckland side that I realised what a wonderful game it was. Here was the game for me. In sevens I could do all the things I'd done naturally as a kid. Here was the chance to run like mad forward, backward and sideways, dummy, sidestep, scissors, jump, turn somersaults, do cartwheels. Free expression gone nuts and all of it together in one game.

I first played sevens in the Taupiri tournament about 1985 and it was a magic experience. They named me player of the tournament which surprised me because all I did was enjoy myself doing the things I did best because I did them naturally. This little halfback-sized guy with a pointy face came over to me afterward and said, "Would you like to be in the Auckland sevens team?" It just might be the silliest question John Hart ever asked. John Hart! Glenn Rich, Mark Brooke-Cowden, Terry Wright, JK...me! The little Maori kid from Ahuroa who still walked down Queen Street looking up at the buildings with his mouth wide open.

It was the beginning of a six-year love-affair with sevens, five of those with the New Zealand team. At my first tournament with Auckland the occasion and the stature of the players around me got to me and I pulled back, like into a shell. A bloody hermit crab playing sevens. I was scared that if I opened out I would do something wrong. These days it would be called being politically correct. I was limiting myself and stifling my instinct for the game. Opening night nerves. JK grabbed me and said this was no different from Taupiri. "Don't give a stuff who this guy is or that guy. They're just names, Zinny, just names. You play your Taupiri game." So I did and I found it fitted naturally into the team game that sevens is.

First year of my love affair with sevens, 1986. On the run against Fiji with Buck in support.

We beat North Harbour in the final of the regional sevens and, thanks to JK, by then I was having a party with this sevens game. Every game was like a celebration of all the things I loved about playing rugby. In 1986 the New Zealand sevens team went to Australia and the first game was against Tonga. I had been told about these Tongans – cement-blocks on wheels, watch or they'll take you right out of the game, airborne across the Tasman and home. We played at Concord Oval in Sydney and early in the game I was running on to the short ball from Craig Green, doing a bit of a flashy cutback for my own ego, sprinting away and scoring. I was away on a high. Hey, this wasn't skyscraper Sydney,

43

Australia. This was one-storey Taupiri, by the Waikato River just up there from Ngaruawahia.

We beat Australia in that final then went on to the matchless Hong Kong Sevens and cleaned out the French Barbarians in that final. It was the first of five Hong Kongs for me and with every one New Zealand took another step forward in the understanding of what sevens rugby can be. That first year we had Bill Freeman with us. He had been a very successful Wellington coach and was now on the New Zealand Rugby Union. I remember reading a newspaper interview with Freeman after we had won both those tournaments. In it, he slotted the skills of sevens rugby into the 15-man game. It stirred me because it seemed to fit perfectly into my feeling for the sevens game and what could be taken from it.

He said it was vital coaches should take exciting young players and encourage their skills rather than squeeze them dry of excitement. The sevens victories had exposed New Zealand rugby players to the world as exciting and attacking. Skills, he said, did not change from the sevens game to the 15, but attitudes did. Winning test matches did not mean confinement to rolling forwards and kicking five-eighths. The sevens players had showed by scoring tries through speed, evasion, support and ball-skills that there were so many options for players of skill if coaches would embrace them.

And then Freeman pinpointed the forwards in the sevens because, he said, they showed what could be done in the running skills which seemed to be almost a forgotten art in New Zealand forward play. It made so much sense to me and I have remembered it. It is a message which should be circulated to coaches at all levels of rugby.

Only a short time ago a schoolboy said to me he didn't like rugby much any more because the coach had told the forwards playing with the ball was not their business. They shouldn't run with it or kick it. They should give it to the backs who were the real ball players. I told the boy I wanted to meet his coach and have a talk with him. If every schoolboy coach is telling his nine- and ten-year-old forwards not ever to run with the ball we're going to have a bloody awful game to watch in ten years or so. My dad was a great coach for kids. He told us to go out there and have heaps of fun, run with the ball, score tries, kick it, slide around in the mud, dodge the other kids, get yourself dirty and be happy.

Marist had introduced me to first-class rugby through their

Third leg of 1986 sevens treble. On the way to winning Sport Aid title at
Cardiff, Scotland's Eric Paxton in contention. New Zealand had already
won the Hong Kong and Sydney (world) titles.

President's XV in 1985 and the same year John Hart whistled me into the Auckland team as a reserve and I had four games for the New Zealand Colts. In 1986 they made me captain of the New Zealand Colts and I had my first game for Auckland against Fiji.

The 1986 Colts' experience was both educational and humbling – like peeing on an electric fence. We had a couple of convincing wins against weak teams and then were thrown in against Wellington at Athletic Park. They always say you should take advantage of the wind in Wellington because it has a habit of drifting away in the second spell. As captain I was expected to be a thinker and I thought a young team like the Colts needed 15 or 20 minutes to settle down in the big-match atmosphere of a major stadium. That left only 20 minutes to take advantage of the wind and score your points. So I gave Wellington the wind.

We kept them within reasonable bounds for 20 minutes and I thought, as a thinking captain, we'd keep them to 20 points at halftime and then, with the wind, swallow them up. Unfortunately it didn't quite work out that way. Suddenly they were away, stretching out to 40, and the wind we needed so badly gave us the fingers in the second spell and disappeared out into Cook Strait somewhere.

Wellington went on to win the national championship and we went on to lose to a great Australian Colts' team 35-11. Their outstanding player was a bouncy little joker named Ricky Stuart, now my pick as the gun player in Australian league. We had Daryl Halligan, who kicks all the Canterbury Bulldogs' goals over there now. This game was my introduction to Sam Scott-Young, who later won international renown for the blinding speed of his mouth compared with his brain – a rarity among loose forwards.

Having made the New Zealand Colts team the players anticipated something extra-special in coaching and advice. It was, after all, a national team comprising young players who must have been judged as having something significant to offer the future of New Zealand rugby. It would not be stretching it to say we were all looking for something quite inspirational from a big-name motivator. What we got was neither. We got what we already knew. It was basic, it was boring and it was old-fashioned, something the New Zealand Rugby Union should never have contemplated for young players who wanted to be fizzing.

It was also in 1986 that I had approaches from Hugh McGahan's Eastern Suburbs league club. I had become interested in league more because of the way Graham Lowe's Wigan team was playing the game. In fact, I called Graham and told him I wanted to play for his team. It was not that I had been switched off rugby. It was that league looked to me to be a game I could play well. Graham didn't leap through the phone to make me an offer I couldn't refuse. He said he would keep an eye on me, which sounded like "don't ring me, I'll ring you" and didn't do much for my self-esteem. Then Hugh McGahan talked to me and numbers were tossed about, but not from the telephone book. I think it was about $20,000 a season plus a job and a house.

I was really just toying with figures and testing the water and it massaged my ego to see stories in the papers headlined "Zinzan For League?" "League Offer Imminent for Zinzan", "Aussies Chase Zinzan with Big Dollars". I played on the rumours a bit but it was more the business of shameless self-promotion than of serious intent to play for pay.

More serious by far was my Manly flirtation and courtship before I jilted them at the altar in 1990, an affair which fired the imagination of the media and inspired more guesswork and wild rumour than anything outside Buck Shelford's much-vaunted fistfight with Foxy the same year. I still fall over laughing when I picture Foxy dealing to Buck. So does Foxy. And so does Buck. I don't laugh so much over the death-knock decision not to go to Manly with Matthew Ridge, but I'll deal with that later.

That happening season of '86 was cultural trauma for me. Marist had started it the year before when I had my first senior club season but the Auckland regime really forced me to think of my future in the big city. Should I stay and wear a tie I didn't know how to knot, a dress pullover, a blazer, trousers with creases, shoes the right colour and socks? And a coach who drilled you with his eyes and made undue demands, like "Zinzan, you've got to make some tackles"? Or should I just throw up my hands and go back to Warkworth, a sweatshirt and jeans and a pint before, during and after the game? Some choice. I learned to tie a Windsor knot.

In 1986 I owed much of my rugby to the Cavaliers, the rebel All Blacks who were so pissed-off by the cancellation of their tour of South Africa that they organised their own. Had Alan Whetton been around I'd have had the best part of another season on the bench. As it was I played my Auckland debut game against Fiji in Suva. It was a bizarre build-up. Our flight from Nadi to

Suva was cancelled so they put us in a bus. Roads on the route were badly broken up. The trip became a stop-start four-hour marathon, and all this the day of the game.

I still didn't know how to play the blindside, but that's where I was, and it was raining and there were all these giant jet-black people with giant jet-black haircuts all over the place. They were lovely people, the Fijians. They laughed and laughed all the time and they laughed hardest when they called for your blood at the footy. It was a difficult game in the rain and we held on to win 15-10 after a big Fiji comeback.

At team meetings Harty was intense. Even if he wasn't naturally that way, you could understand his stresses. He had lost Grant Fox, Andy Haden, Gary and Alan Whetton and Steve McDowell to the Cavaliers. He was trying to mould a team from the leftovers. He made every individual conscious of his responsibility to the team. You came out thinking, "My God, I'd better not stuff this up." But he was also sensitive to the young players trying to find their feet in what for them was a huge step out of club football into a representative team like Auckland. He also knew how to stir a young man up. Later in the season when we played Taranaki and were not playing well, he marched on to the paddock at halftime, aimed his eyes at me and said, "Make some tackles, Zinzan, make some bloody tackles."

If he had cut my throat it couldn't have irritated me any more than being told to tackle. I have always had this big thing about making tackles and making them stick. The Taranaki guy who fielded our second-spell kick-off just as I arrived should not have sworn at me. He should have sworn at Harty.

But for the Fiji game, conscious it was my first and of my uncertainty about the blindside, Harty told me there was no pressure on me; just tackle around the fringes, get the basics right and you'll find your way. So I did. And I also got a couple of good kicks away because it seemed the right thing to do at the time.

The following week we played New South Wales at Eden Park and won 34-15. The pace of the game, its switches and crackling changes of fortune exhilarated me as a player. Far from Suva and the rain, I felt with it, part of it. Quick throw-ins to the lineout, quick tap-kicks...so this is representative rugby, Zinny. This is really Auckland. I can live with this. This is my sort of game. I don't mind wearing a tie, sir.

4

The Puhoi Kid Strikes Back

It's a funny old game, rugby. Funnier than cricket, which is hilarious if you get off on a game which can last for five days and end in a draw. I've got nothing against cricket. Some of my worst friends are cricketers. But I have never been able to make a lot of sense out of a game which is alive for three days and stone dead for two and at the end you clap politely, call it a "tame" draw and can't wait for the next one, which is likely to end the same way. Sometimes they even play for a tame draw deliberately. I need to know if there's a wild draw. You know, "The cricket test between Australia and New Zealand ended in a wild draw at Eden Park yesterday after Australia batted all day for 76 runs. It was saved from being a tame draw when Shane Warne whacked Ken Rutherford between the legs with the camera stump…"

I said all this to a cricketer mate once and he called me a philistine. If I'd known what a philistine was I'd have whacked him between the legs with the camera stump or any other stump which happened to be handy.

I say rugby's a funny old game because you never know what it's going to turn up. Richard Loe and David Kirk. A guy who talks to his tractor and calls his sheep Gladys and Fred and a guy who knew what a philistine was when he was three – without looking it up. It was a funny old game when a penalty-goal was worth as much as a try and a dropped-goal worth more than either of them. It was a funny old game when a team was given a penalty, kicked it into touch and then conceded the throw-in to the team penalised. And even when they have sorted those things out it can still be incredibly funny if you happen to be an Australian and a bunch of magnificent Irishmen suddenly go slightly mad in the final minute and hand you a crucial World Cup match which they had as good as won.

So in its way rugby is as eccentric as cricket. Rugby turns up in some funny places, too, like on the roof of a house, which is where I was, hammering away, earning my daily crust, when rugby caught up with me one day in May 1987. I was just a young loose forward, still wet behind the ears, making a reasonable fist of finding his way in the big world of representative rugby. Hammering on a roof was my excitement for that particular day.

Then there was a phone call for me. So I complained a bit, drove in a few more nails, clambered down the ladder and took the call. The man said he was from the Auckland Rugby Union and would I possibly be interested in being a Black Team reserve for the New Zealand World Cup trial at Whangarei on Saturday. As this was Tuesday it did occur to me that I was something of an afterthought, a tailor-made emergency-reserve who would be a bum on a seat and cost bugger-all to get there.

I could cope with that provided I was able to get back to captain Auckland for the first time, against Canterbury in a South Pacific championship match on the Sunday. My appointment as captain had been shock enough for one week even in the certain absence of a bundle of Auckland players who would be selected for the World Cup team. The new coaches, Maurice Trapp and Bryan Williams, obviously thought anyone who had played so much of his rugby in Puhoi must have leadership quality.

Anyway, what the hell? Whangarei was just up the road and think of the company I'd be keeping.

So there I was. Zinzan and Brian Lochore and Grizz Wyllie and John Hart and Andy Dalton and Buck Shelford and John Gallagher and Warwick Taylor and Alan Whetton and Murray Pierce and Joe Stanley and Stevie McDowell and JK and Craig Green…great company for a struggling plumber.

What I was doing there was a mystery to me and probably to a lot of people, even in the absence with injuries of Jock Hobbs and Mike Brewer. But there I was and, sitting in the Okara Park sun, I watched Foxy slotting 19 points, Buck scoring two tries and Andy Dalton's team taking Andy Donald's team to the cleaners. And I drank in some Michael Jones miracles and watched how he worked with Buck and Alan Whetton to form a great loose-forward unit. And occasionally I drifted off and dreamed a bit about how I would captain Auckland against Canterbury the next day. Captain of Auckland! The Puhoi Kid strikes back.

That night in the Grand Hotel there was a formal dinner, or as close to formality as you can get with 40-odd rugby players faced with unlimited quantities of food and drink. Well, not just drink. Moet. And not just footy fodder either. Seafood crepes, lamb satay on saffron rice, beef Wellington, duchess spuds. Just like Sunday lunch back on the farm at Ahuroa. Tension was on the menu, too, a lot of tension disguised as small talk and loud laughter.

Formality there might have been at the top table where Russ Thomas, the chairman of the New Zealand Rugby Union, was king, but out there in real-life land, nervous tension ran high and so, increasingly, did some of the players who gave themselves no show of making the squad, anyway.

A group of the reserves and no-show players drifted out into the lounge to play some cards. Some of the calls were pretty flakey which meant that a few of those who reckoned they had no show might just have thought, just maybe, there was a chance. Me? No pretence. I knew I had no show. Just a bum on the reserve seats to make up the numbers. Alan Whetton and Joe Stanley stuck their heads in and told us the cup squad would be announced in a few minutes. We played a few more hands, very casual, very cool, and drifted in to the dining room. I sat down opposite Andy Earl and Brett Harvey. Brett had played that day, one of those rangy elbows-and-knees country loose forwards who had been one of the Baby Blacks in 1986. He had good reason to be confident.

The odd thing was that until Russ Thomas stood up to announce the team I felt quite remote from the show, more focused on Canterbury the next day. But suddenly I had butterflies and clammy palms, as if by some error of judgement there might be some sort of chance. I didn't realise that every player in the room had butterflies and clammy palms. I was staring at Brett Harvey when my name was read out. I lowered my eyes. I couldn't look at him. If I was there he wouldn't be. I had this embarrassed feeling, nothing of elation for myself, but that some sort of injustice had been done to Brett.

People were shaking hands. Strangers came to me and said words I couldn't hear. I looked around and saw Arthur Stone in distress. I saw Warwick Taylor comforting Dean Kenny. I saw

All Black tyros, selected for the NZ World Cup team, 1987.

Brent Anderson, who had been locking Andy Dalton's scrum with Murray Pierce, sitting stunned and sweating, the only player in that team not to make the squad. Yet he had played so well.

And then I remembered my mother saying to me before the trial, "Good luck, son. I hope you make the team." She didn't understand I had no chance at all of making it. Suddenly I had to get out of there, had somehow to release some of the jubilation which was building up as it sank in that I was an All Black. Out of nowhere I was an All Black. From being a bum filling a reserve's seat I was an All Black. I grabbed my mate Bernie McCahill and we took off outside into the street and shouted to the stars. Yes!

The newspapers and the commentators got it right. I was a shock selection. It took a man in a white coat at Eden Park the next day to bring me back to earth. From the day of selection the World Cup squad was wrapped in cottonwool so I didn't get to captain Auckland against Canterbury. But we went to watch. We were swamped by people who wanted to congratulate us. They made us feel like royalty. We had tickets to sit outside the stand but it was too hot. So royalty hopped up into the shade of the stand. The man in the white coat wanted to know who the hell we thought we were...

"If youse jokers want to sit there it'll cost you two bucks." Royalty looked sheepish and got kicked out.

When I went into camp with the squad I was still wide-eyed in the company I was keeping. I was still very much the country boy. I still had this overwhelming feeling of disbelief, of unreality. Hell, I had flown for the first time the year before. And that was in an aeroplane. Now that I know the importance of being an All Black I feel the pressure of it. In 1987 there wasn't room for pressure, just disbelief. When you're a kid everything seems to happen so quickly. Events you should cherish whisk past you and are gone. You don't capture the moment. There is no perspective. Buck Shelford is not as big as you but in your view of him he's much bigger, a giant. A man as to a kid.

You get this issue of clothing and gear. They want you at least to look like an All Black. Laundry? You mean you want my underpants and my dirty gear? Why? You're thinking "gee-whizz" all the time. This is the same little Zinny who not much longer ago than yesterday was carting wood for miles to get a couple of bucks, opening the gate for grandpa for five cents, testing the vacuum-cleaner in the goldfish bowl, picking mushrooms to sell to the Chinese restaurants, crutching a dirty-tempered perendale…this is *that* Zinny? Well, in a lot of ways it was.

And what did I think of Grizz and Harty? I didn't think about them much at all. Following events in 1990-91 people have asked me whether I could tell away back then that they were an unlikely pair. In 1987 I didn't care. Rugby politics? I didn't even know politicians played rugby. To Zinzan, 1987, they were just a couple of jokers who seemed to bounce off each other with what seemed goodwill, one firing rapid-fire pistol-shots and the other firing a trench-mortar. Easier to judge was Brian Lochore, who stood out as a quietly strong, honest man with dignity, who immediately commanded respect. If I sensed anything at all about the trio it was that Lochore was clearly in charge. Whether someone else wanted to be did not occur to me. I didn't learn about rugby politics till later.

Hart was the co-ordinator of the backs and Lochore and Wyllie the forwards. Lochore in his quiet way was the pilot, the mediator, the sort of father-figure who, to a man, the whole squad related to. He was deliberate, thoughtful, and always positive. Had a buffer been needed between a man as mercurial as Hart and one as blunt and agricultural as Wyllie he would have coped with that on his ear. But I was not aware in those days that a buffer was necessary. Hart I knew. He talked with me about my game, guided

The McCahill-Brooke consortium watched over by a benevolent Ilaitia Savai, Fiji. South Pacific championship, 1987.

me along. Wyllie was big and bluff and aggressive, a forward of the old Canterbury school who ate Lions for breakfast.

Training was at test-match tempo; everyone was switched-on. The requirement was for 100 per cent effort at 100 miles an hour, 100 per cent accuracy at speed – crisp, precise. As three men they were not satisfied if they did not get it.

I was told quietly that the Southpac game between Auckland and New South Wales had moved the selectors to pull me in and that it had done Bernie McCahill no harm either. That was the match when we came back from 3-18 down to win 19-18, a ripper of a match for us. My main memories of the Southpac that year were of JK and especially his performance in the 43-18 stoush of Queensland when he scored one of the greatest tries I have ever seen, beating Brendan Moon, Michael Lynagh and Greg Martin in a blistering run from inside our 22.

In its way it was a better try than the spectacular one he was to score against Italy in the opening World Cup match which I watched in total awe from the grandstand. Seventy-pointers against Italy and Fiji were the wake-up call to the world that these All Blacks were something special and as one of the party I bristled as I watched and felt the coming-together of great players who would take the New Zealand game beyond the reach of other countries. But as one of the wet-nosed pups of the squad I was hungry to be part of it, not as a dirt-tracker, but as a player out there where the contest was real. I wanted in.

They gave me my first test in the next match against Argentina at Athletic Park in Wellington, June 1, as openside flanker. That meant some heavy tuition on positioning and running lines. So much to do and only three days to do it. Then 24 hours before the game they called me in and said, "Zinny, there's no Buck, no Steve, no Frano. You're the only Maori and we want you to lead the haka." "Yeah?" I said. "Great. No probs. Beauty." I walked out of the room, slapped my hand against my forehead and said, "Oh, shit." Lead the haka? I didn't even know it. It's easy to do the haka when you're following someone. But all the preliminary stuff out the front? With the cameras watching? Oh, shit, Zinny. Here you are going into your first test in the wrong position and leading a haka you don't know.

Fake it? Everyone else in New Zealand knew the haka, the 30,000 at Athletic Park and the hundreds of thousands in television land. So I went to Buck and Stevie. After some haggling they agreed it would be a fair thing to coach me for free. I practised in front of a mirror, which was not a pretty sight but I convinced myself if I could get the haka right I would get the game right.

It was not till the morning of the game that I felt tension. I woke and watched the sun come up. I rolled out of bed at 6 o'clock and knew I needed to get out in the air, jog, walk, anything. I hadn't played the game in my mind but I knew the first thing I wanted was the ball in my hands. I love the feel of a rugby ball. Soccer players laugh about its peculiar shape for a ball but if you love rugby the thing you love most about it is the way the ball fits into your hands. It's like an easy friendship. It had never been any different for me.

So I wanted the ball in my hands early and I wanted to make a big tackle early. There is something very settling and very satisfying about making the first tackle, making it a big one, feeling the contact. It is like, then, complete involvement in the game.

My first game, my first try, for the All Blacks, v Argentina, World Cup 1987, Wellington.

Never fear, Foxy's near. Pincered v Argentina, 1987.

There is a sort of security in it, a feeling of confidence that you're master of your own destiny in the game. It is as if by carrying the ball and making the tackle you are putting your mark on the game.

Sometimes you may daydream about the things you will do in a game, about the try you want to score, the one that's much better than JK's against Italy. But here I just didn't want things cluttering up my mind. No daydreaming about tries, just getting out there and playing the game as well as I knew how – not as well as the opposition would let me; that would have been conceding something before the contest.

The time between 6 o'clock and the match passed like a flash. We may have been treated like kings everywhere else but the Athletic Park dressing-room made peasants of us all. It was back to the cowshed on the farm, but not as big. A cold and gloomy dungeon with 21 big guys in it. I had given my hamstring a bit of a tweak at training the day before and it was wrapped in a bright blue bandage, which I thought would photograph very well. At a rough estimate I peed ten times in 35 minutes before the kickoff, or ten times in 33 minutes before the haka. The haka was my first

**The captain who was and the captain who wasn't: David Kirk and Andy
Dalton, 1987.**

hurdle. It seemed to go smoothly enough and the noises coming
from the other jokers behind me seemed to be happening in just
about the right places. But it was not a Buck haka. Buck was the
greatest haka-leader of them all. He meant every word of it and
he made every word and gesture stick by the way he played the
game.

Many of the Argentine players had been part of the 21-21 draw
with the All Blacks in 1985, when Hugo Porta dropped four goals
and kicked three penalties. I was conscious that Porta was one of
the greatest of all first-fives, but not over-conscious. I wanted to
play him for what he was in this game or, preferably, what I could
force him to become. As the pressure mounted, he did not respond
well and as the game went on his own performance and that of
the team deteriorated.

The first 40 minutes went at express speed and it was not long
before halftime, with the Pumas making a recovery to 13-9, that
JK yet again ripped through their defence on the blindside. It
was not that they ushered him through as much as a mixture of a
hazy understanding of blindside defence and a growing awe of
JK's power. I probably took a bit of a short-cut to get there because

World Cup, 1987, Commander Brian Lochore flanked by Lieutenants Grizz Wyllie and John Hart.

I anticipated his beating of the man. Having played with him for Marist and Auckland I had the firm belief there was nothing he couldn't do, no man he couldn't beat.

He broke away with only a metre to move in. He could have passed to Alan Whetton or Andy Earl but he flicked it to me for the try. Call it club affiliation.

I thought I had coped pretty adequately with the strangeness of the new position and, as a young player having his first test among the stars, I was excited to be part of the 46-15 win. It had been my big day. Maybe the greatest day of a young player's career, no matter what triumphs may follow, is his first test match, the first fern. Maybe that's why a newspaper column by a former All Black captain, Graham Mourie, cut so painfully.

He commented generously on my skills but reckoned I would never make it as an openside loosie, that my understanding of the position was, in a word, hopeless. I felt somehow let down by Mourie's comments which I thought were odd considering I was a novice to the position. And I remembered with satisfaction how, from the planet from which 17-or 18-year-olds make their judgements, I had once judged him to be too stiff a runner to be a top loosie. Another All Black captain, Andy Leslie, once said about himself, "I run as if I've got a stick up my bum." That's what I thought about Mourie.

His comments hurt because, essentially, that day I was playing openside flank by instinct. Three days before I hadn't known where to run, where to anticipate, where to hold, where to run-off. What I did was follow the ball, get there as quickly as possible, beat the other guy to it. The selectors were not stupid. They had a plan. I was there for a purpose and I knew that. They were looking for someone who could cover all three loose forward positions and it was important to give me a game in a position I had not previously played.

The whole World Cup campaign taught me what was required to be an All Black – not just any All Black, but a good one. I knew I was just a small cog in a team of incredible spirit and talent but I was never made to feel less a part of it than the big wheels. This was part of the greatness of All Black teams from that time through to 1990. It was the loss of this bonding spirit between men and the pride it compelled which was the beginning of the mental breakdown of 1991.

Even watching, as I did for all the games except that against Argentina, was an education, like a first year at rugby university, and when the team beat France in the final it was almost as if I had played in the game. At the presentation ceremony I looked across at Andy Dalton, the captain who never played. He was persuaded, much against his will, to get into a picture with David Kirk, reluctant to take any of the kudos from the man who replaced him as captain when he was injured.

Kirk had done a fine job both on and off the field but to me the man who underpinned the spirit of the All Black team was Dalton. Like Lochore, he was a quiet man with natural dignity. Like Lochore he was a man of the land. I hope that when rugby historians write about that era of the New Zealand game his part in it is recognised. It would be an injustice were his leadership of the Cavaliers' tour of South Africa to supplant recognition of him as a great player and captain. Andy Dalton stood for just about everything I have felt were ingredients for greatness as an All Black – immaculate fair play, courage, pride, leadership. I guess most of us at one time or another slip off those ideals but Dalton never did. His standards were naturally built into him and he never drifted off them.

60

5

The Brotherhood

I'll bet you could go to 50 people in the street and ask what the year 1987 meant in New Zealand history and 48 of them would say, "The sharemarket crash," one would say, "Booze and smokes went up" and the other, "Um. I dunno." The winning of the first World Cup was a big deal for a day or two. The players were on a magical high for a few hours, drank some good bubbles and threw some guys in the pool. Then we were told to pack up and go home. It was as if it had never happened. Yet it was the beginning of an era when New Zealanders basked in the success of the All Blacks. That year was one of the most significant in all of New Zealand rugby history for it launched on to the world scene an All Black team which had just about everything and the sum of those things was greatness.

Rugby the game should have been marketed like crazy on the back of the 1987 World Cup with national tours by the players, with visits to the country areas where an All Black was never seen let alone touched or talked with, with celebrations and personal appearances, showing the people – and especially the mums and kids – that these All Blacks were not some untouchable group of robots, just a bunch of ordinary blokes who played rugby well.

It should have been part of the World Cup plan that, in the event of the All Blacks winning, they should personally share the celebration with all of New Zealand. I have said that the heart of New Zealand rugby beats in places like Puhoi. Forget the political crises in the game and the shonky power-plays behind the scenes as top jobs go under the hammer and managers get tours because it's their turn and even captains fall foul of the movers and shakers. Don't relate those things to real rugby.

Real rugby starts in real rugby country with kids who can't afford boots and good people who make sure they have them. New Zealand rugby reading in recent years makes you wonder sometimes what part the players have in it. Books have been full of rationalisations, excuses, attacks, defences not of the playing of the game but of political horse-trading at administrative and, especially, coaching level. It is as if the players of the game are running second to its collars-and-ties.

A lot of the senior players felt let down by the off-hand finish to the 1987 World Cup campaign. At the time I didn't feel let down, just bewildered that what for me had been a magnificent event so quickly passed into casual and occasional pub-talk. Now, when I think back on it and compare it with the huge response and the official recognition the Wallabies received in 1991 I wonder whether we had not become so smug about the idea that rugby is our national game that, therefore, it was somehow below its status to push it, let alone let "the ordinary people" have a feel of its fabric.

I talked to Craig Green in Italy about his sudden disappearance from the New Zealand scene so soon after the World Cup. I had so much admiration for Greeno as a player. There have been few more astute wingers, if any. He was not blessed with blistering pace but he detected lines and angles so cleverly that he became one of the great finishers of all time.

Craig told me that after the World Cup and the convincing Bledisloe Cup win over the Wallabies which followed it he was on a colossal high. But, having returned to Christchurch on the Sunday night from Australia, he was up at 6 o'clock on a wintery Monday morning so he could hammer nails in someone else's house to make a living. He thought, "And just what the hell is all this about?" He said, "The highs were gone. The curtain was down and I was on someone's roof hammering nails with a southerly whipping around my ears. We had won the first World Cup and it was as if nothing had happened."

Two weeks later he packed his bags and took off to play in Italy where he has become a cult figure while playing wonderful rugby all these years.

When we toured Japan in the same year it was not as some exotic prize for winning the World Cup, although it could have

Craig Green...disenchanted after first World Cup.

been, and probably should have been, without any damage done. As it was, only 15 World Cup squad members were taken and if we'd had any bright ideas about it being a glorified holiday John Hart made sure rugby came first. There was an amicable arrangement that he would coach the team in Japan and Grizz would take the Colts on their internal tour at home. Grizz went as his assistant and I'm sure as he watched Harty in action he started to suspect he had opted for the wrong end of the stick.

This was just a passing notion based on a player's view of Grizz's body language. It was still 1987 and although the World Cup was under my belt I was still just a starry-eyed kid and, frankly, I didn't care much who coached the All Blacks as long as I was one of the coached. Grizz or Harty? Power-plays? I thought a power-play was the second shove in an attacking scrum.

And I can say, too, that when Grizz was elected All Black coach for 1988 I was surprised. Not angry or frustrated, just surprised. I had assumed, probably as Harty himself had, that having done the job so successfully in Japan he would have the inside running for 1988. But if Grizz was the coach that was OK by me, too, now let's get on and play some footy. That's just the way it was.

Japan was my first true tour. They sent us there to carry the banner but refused to call us All Blacks. That smacked of over-protection of the silver fern to me (and, what's more, I could have done with my four tries on the record!) As a flag-waving tour it was a huge success. Even though the Japanese players were distraught at the 74-0 and 106-4 margins in what the New Zealand Rugby Union was pleased to call non-tests, that tour set marks for the Japanese and excited interest in rugby. Had we gone there and held back the Japanese would have taken no pride from closer scoreboard results. They would have felt insulted.

The other major thing about the Japanese tour was that it was the beginning of the Buck Shelford era of captaincy. David Kirk had gone to Oxford University which was to be expected of someone who knew what "philistine" meant when he was three. I really related to Buck. Admiration was a large part of it but Buck naturally attracted fierce loyalty. I could not have known then what a huge influence Buck and his fortunes at the whim of selectors were to have on my own career. Trauma. Believe me. Trauma which will unfold before your very eyes, folks.

In the meantime, I'll bet if you were to ask a million people in the street what 1987 meant to them not one, unless it happened to be my mother or father, would say, "Hey! Wasn't that the year the three Brooke brothers played in the Auckland team in its historic Ranfurly Shield struggle against East Coast?" But that's the way it was, and probably memorable only for the Brooke family and for the boys from the East Coast and their supporters.

I remember watching television as the East Coast team trained at Eden Park. I could relate so closely to these guys. Every one of them was a Zinzan Brooke newly come to the city. And I know that about that time down there on the coast they had trouble selecting their team and being sure they'd all turn up for the game. It was adult Puhoi, shaking the tea-trees and playing whoever fell out.

At this training session they had tractor-tyre inner-tubes. The coach was yelling, "Hey! You fellas! We gotta tackle these Auckland fellas. We gotta tackle and tackle. You understand? OK? So when I bowl this tyre over there it's really a joker. OK? And

The cavalry, led by Robin, flanked by troopers Zinzan and Stevie McDowell, arrives to save JK from a North Harbour baddy.

I'm gonna call your name and you're gonna tackle this joker."
And he bowled out a tyre, called a name and yelled, "Hey! That
tyre! That's Zinzan Brooke! Now tackle the bugger!" And the
guy runs out and goes BOOM!, this huge crash-tackle on an inner-
tube named Zinzan Brooke. I tell you I was flattered. But these
players were going to go out there on match day and give their
guts and they were going to go back down to Tokomaru and
Tokararangi and Ruatoria and Uawa and Waiapu and Hikurangi
and tell their kids and then their grand-kids about the day they
tackled Zinzan Brooke, who looked just like a tractor-tyre inner-
tube.

Like me, what they didn't care about was which rugby power-
broker was pulling strings in Wellington or what underhand
influences were at work in the manipulation of national coaches
and administrators. What they did care about was that they had
their day at Eden Park in a Ranfurly Shield match and that their

great big prop Morgan Wirepa tackled Terry Wright and that their skipper Tuta Wilkie and coach Jury Harrison gave them the OK to run the ball at us, which they did.

So don't tell me the little unions shouldn't have their whack at the Ranfurly Shield or that big scores against them are an embarrassment and do the game harm. Tell that to the big band of East Coast supporters who came up to Eden Park, not expecting a win but accepting the occasion for what it was and making a big day of it. 70-0? So what? What about the Kururangi boys and Mani Waititi and Peter Davis…and all of them, having their lick at the Auckland defence and stretching it?

That day Marty locked the scrum with Gary Whetton, Robin played at the back of the scrum and I was on the blindside. In anticipation, we felt special things about the day and so did mum and dad. Here were three of the five boys they had given everything that was in their power to give, so little materially but so much of their own characters, and they were going out together to play in a Ranfurly Shield match.

Marty had come to play with me at Marist. Eric Kohlhase, the third grade coach, was saying one day what a hell of a disadvantage it was to be playing without a big lock and lineout jumper. I told him I kept a 6ft 6in brother at home in a cage. Eric couldn't believe his luck. He reckoned if we didn't win the championship now, we never would. So we did, for the first time in 33 years.

Marty had, and has, all the attributes for top rugby. When he was growing up he played with a dash of Maori flair and, like all of us, he had the kicking and dummying skills we had picked up naturally on our 30-acre playing field at the farm. He had played a lot of basketball and beyond most players, including backs, he had great skill with the ball in the air and his timing of the jump was just about perfection. As a working lock he bent his back to the donkeywork and just did his job.

Marty was a nice kid on the outside but with a hard core of aggression which made him a pretty scratchy opponent on the field. Marty could be very contrary. He could have done with a few more kilograms; he was rather in the mould of Ian Jones but physically stronger. He had "international" written all over him and I firmly believe he should have been in the All Blacks in 1989. Probably he would have been, too, had it not been for his loose boot. Well, a loose-cannon of a boot, actually. During a club match his boot and Peter Fatialofa's head, shall I say, collided?

Marty practises the Japanese-look.

It was after a later representative match, against Counties, that John Hart went to Marty and told him he would never play for the All Blacks because of that incident. Marty was devastated, completely thrown. At that time he was really driving toward an All Black jersey and he wanted it badly. Had Harty given him a thousand hard words about what he had done and warned him never to do it again if he wanted to be an All Black, Marty could have accepted it and absorbed it. I also say it was a subjective decision. Players have done things which were as bad, and have gone on doing them, been warned, punished and gone on to play for New Zealand again. I have always had the feeling that Marty was the victim of a very personalised sorting-out.

Marty and I played many games together for Auckland. He was a lock who could also play outstandingly well on the blindside or No 8. He was young enough to have played in the World Cup of 1991 and even of 1995. What Marty did warranted a severe reprimand. It did not warrant him being shuffled off into limbo and then lost to New Zealand rugby. Understanding there was nothing left here for him, he went off to France to play for Grenoble and then Japan for Mazda. It was in 1993 when we were searching for experienced locks that Laurie Mains rang Marty in Japan to sound him out about coming home. But Marty was locked into the system. He is a big deal in Japan but he is now at the stage where he has lost all aspirations.

Rob was not a naturally gifted player as a kid. He was a fine athlete but the hard knocks of rugby didn't interest him. He would play in whatever position we happened to be short but dad steered him toward the wing in the belief that of all places on a rugby field wing was the safest place for a ballet dancer to be. He could flit around out there without doing much damage to himself and in kids' rugby in those days the ball did not often get out there for anyone to run at him. Rob might or might not agree with this if anyone should find the guts to ask him about his ballet-dancing days.

He was a late-developer in rugby yet he had remarkable ability in other sports. But when he started to get the idea of the physical contest the game is and as he started to develop physically himself he found the challenge to his liking. It was not as if any of us had had ambitions to be All Blacks. I know there are players who say that from the time they had their first pair of boots they had this burning ambition. It doesn't really work like that for kids out in the country. Unconsciously we had ambition but it was never further ahead than the next game and it involved scoring a lot of tries.

As I have said, Rob, too, was strongly academic. He loved school. To me this was bewildering. It was also unforgiveable. I think now Rob looked at hard-nosed, rawboned farm kids like Naera, Marty and me, understood quickly this was not him and looked for satisfaction through something else and school was a convenient vehicle. And he found, too, that he had natural aptitude in other sports.

When he came to Auckland he was apprehensive about rugby. There was concern he might have broken his neck when he made a head-on tackle in a third-grade game. It put him in the spinal unit but he was lucky. The more we practised at the skills together the more interested he became in doing well and as he filled out into size and strength he started to appreciate that with his great natural athletic ability he had a wonderful mix for rugby. He got into weights and developed into a powerful man and, more than that, an extremely hard-minded player. Maybe that is some sort of over-compensation for his more timid ways as a kid.

He went to Livorno in Italy for the 1987-88 season and, really, that just expressed his attitude to the game at the time. He had no built-in conviction he was going anywhere in the game. He did not place himself anywhere near the international category even though he was having occasional games for Auckland. So he had rugby at home in the winter and rugby as a way of life in Italy in the summer – and turning over a buck while doing it. That appealed to him. The vita was very, very dolce.

It was while we were both playing in Italy in 1991-92 that it became clear the new All Black coach Laurie Mains was more than just casually interested in Rob. Laurie rang him several times on my telephone to encourage him to get back to New Zealand. It all added up to me that Rob was going to be an All Black but, for an academic, Rob didn't do those sums very well. He reckoned I was talking in fairy-tales. When he was named for New Zealand in 1992 he was stunned, couldn't believe it. I was in hospital with a badly infected leg and he was visiting me when the team was announced. I had to call for a bottle. Not for me. For him.

A few games for the All Blacks put a hard edge on his game and he is now very sure of himself and is understanding what he means to the All Blacks for his strength in the scrum and maul,

Contest of brothers…Robin (Brescia) and myself (Lazio) after a championship match in Italy.

his exceptional athleticism at the lineout and his mobility around the field. He developed a mental toughness he never knew was in him. Now he is a commanding figure, the player I see as being the cornerstone of the All Black forward performance.

The secret of his ability to beat much taller men for clean ball in the lineout is in his spring and impeccable timing. One-on-one, a 6ft 8in guy is not going to be cleaned out by a 6ft 5in with the same jumping capacity. Rob explodes onto the ball. He is a model for the lineout theorist who says the jumper has to "attack" the ball. He has the confidence to demand perfect velocity and trajectory in the throw-in from his hooker and if, in training, he doesn't get it he refuses to accept it. Andy Haden would not accept it, nor Gary Whetton. This insistence that everything is right at training rubbed off on Marty as it has on Rob. Even as the new boy on the block, if he didn't get what he wanted he let Fitzy know about it. And amid all the furore over whether Richard Loe should ever again play for New Zealand after the Greg Cooper eye-gouging Rob had his fingers crossed. Security, he says, is having Loey at three when you're jumping at two.

There is a bit of the nomad in all of us. These days young Simon's rugby is split between North Harbour and Ireland. He played for Auckland under-18s as a loose forward and has been in the North Harbour development squad. He's a rangy Brooke with such an easy disposition that while he might never make it to the top in rugby he's going to enjoy whatever he does wherever he does it.

Rugby was not the be-all and end-all of 1987 for me. The stockmarket crash was disaster, and maybe tragedy, for thousands of people with money invested but for me it meant opportunity because even then, though I knew zip about money and investment or profits and losses, I was cunning enough to scent a bargain.

Marty and I were working together as plumber and apprentice and when the crash came work dried up. But on the credit side for opportunists who had not lost everything there were crash sales in just about every industry and I homed in on the sales of building and plumbing materials. There was method in it. I had a long-term view, a lot of hope and a lot of determination. I went out and bought packets of timber at a fraction of their true worth. Some I bought at $1.32 a metre. Now it's more than $5.

I bought 200 or 300 lengths of copper because they were just about giving it away. Being an All Black helped. Many merchants were benevolent to All Blacks and I'd do odd bits and pieces of promotion for them. What I had achieved in the end was just about what I had aimed for – to have enough materials in storage to build a substantial house. And that is what the Brooke brothers, all five of us, set out to do. It was to prove more than a family enterprise to put a roof over our heads. For me, in a funny old way, it was the beginning of a business career.

I had come to Auckland with the skin on my back and little else in 1983 but I saved every nickel and dime. My first pay-cheque as an apprentice plumber was $82, a king's ransom. I saved $85 of it! I know there are cynics out there who look sideways at All Blacks who seem to be doing well with their lives…"Don't talk to me about amateur rugby players. Have you ever seen a poor All Black? Take a look at Zinzan and tell me he hasn't made a pile out of rugby." You've heard it.

Well, I could show the cynics a couple of All Blacks who were buried financially for their allegiance to a game which placed professional demands on their time. And I can point to what I have made of myself and say that I have worked my butt off to get my foot on the first rung toward a good life in material things.

The big house at Te Atatu was the beginning of it. What we had was know-how in plumbing and building. What we didn't have, in hindsight, was frightening. Between us we knew nothing about finance and had little of it, anyway. We didn't know how to go about taking out a mortgage, we couldn't keep our accounts balanced. We did know the colour of a dollar but those we had were through our hands and into someone else's pocket so quickly we soon forgot. Naera took out a loan, Rob and Marty weighed in, I sank my savings and borrowed $30,000 at about 18 per cent and Simon did his whack, and more, as understudy-chippie to Naera. Everyone dug in at one time or another. Ali broke a fingernail or two on the roof and Dad and Mum chipped in. It was family working for family.

The 18 per cent interest rate made sure we didn't live a life of seafood crepes and beef Wellington. Or even, very often, sausages and mashed spuds. We started on the house in 1989 and finished it late in 1990 in time for me to get away on the All Black tour of France. While we built we lived in a large sty or, if you had the imagination, a small apartment – four large men living on top of each other, banging elbows, heads and bums and eating garbage-

The beginning of "The Business" – roofing our Te Atatu house.

food. Only brothers could have done it.

Marty and I would start work on the house at 7am and get home at 5.30pm, stuffed. But then we had to launch ourselves out again for training Tuesday and Thursday and a match on Saturday. Often we were too tired to cook food. After training we'd go home and stuff ourselves with bread and butter and, if we felt like a banquet, we put jam on it. We were often sick as dogs from working out in all weathers, not eating healthy food, not able to sleep because of the clicking of the mouse-traps. But we slogged on at it, all of us, and in a contrary sort of way we loved it.

It was when we had the shell up, the roof on and the windows in that I borrowed the $30,000 to finish it. I didn't want any part of moving in before the house was finished. A week before the tour of France I'd slept on a hard floor once too often. I said, "Bugger this. We're moving into the mansion." And we did. It was something like Paradise after a trial period in Hell.

I have said the building of that house was some sort of beginning of a business career for me. So it was, for without the house and the sale of it a couple of years later, I would never have discovered the intriguing world of domestic property investment.

Property investment sounds all very grand. It makes you think of rich folk shovelling money into buildings and waiting for the market upturn to sell and make more fortunes. My sort of investment was not quite like that. It involved work. The upside was that it was work I loved doing. It was work with my hands, it was endlessly challenging and, without sounding too precious, it was creative.

I had this money from the sale of the Te Atatu house. I wanted to buy a house, strip it down and virtually rebuild it. The economy was still in the mire and there were houses lying empty all over the place. I was visiting John Kirwan in the suburb of Greenlane and I saw near his home a house that cried out for attention. You might have seen it as a broken-down old scunge-bucket of a house. It looked and smelled sweeter than that to me because under the scunge there were remnants of grace and old elegance. The carpets were threadbare, there were holes in the walls, there was grime, there was wallpaper hanging off mouldy scrim and the rats and mice laughed like hell when I reached for my chequebook.

It was on the market for $165,000. I bought it for $150,000. I paid out $38,000 and borrowed $112,000 so I would have money for materials. On that loan I was paying $750 a month so I had no time to waste. Zinny the plumber-turned-property-mogul hooked into it. I said to Ali, "Right, this is where we are going to live." She didn't even look doubtful.

I gutted it, ripped it to bits and all I had was a plan in my head. With Simon working part-time, I restored the walls, put up partitions, built a new kitchen and three bedrooms. The market was looking up, people were coming in off the street to see what I was up to and the further I went with it the more stimulating it became. There were half a dozen as-is offers but I wanted more of "me" in it so I expressed that in room-colours. When it was finished it was a graceful colonial house with double-doors on to the verandah.

A young woman came in, fell in love with it and bought it for $265,000. All up, I had cleared $67,000 in four months. A real estate agent gave Ali and me a book. It was just a thin thing with paper covers. It is my business bible. It is called *Making Money*

Patriotic young bro Simon declares his allegiance in South Africa, 1992.

in Residential Real Estate, $15.75, by Jan Somers and Dolf de Roos. On the title page it says, "Man's mind, once stretched by a new idea, never regains its original dimension". Neat, eh? And inside was a little story which carved itself into my mind. There were these two little kids. One said, "My dad is so poor he owes the bank $2000." The other said, "My dad is so rich he owes the bank $2 million." It taught me, Zinzan Brooke, standard 5 drop-out, the only way to make money is to borrow other people's.

And that's what I have done. I have bought houses, renovated them, sold them; I have bought houses, renovated them and rented them. Today we have six, plus our own. I went out before the World Cup this year and bought a section in St Heliers Bay. We will build our ultimate home on it. Part of its future valuation in dollar terms, which are not necessarily the most important, was that New Zealand might win the America's Cup. I thank the crew of Black Magic for their demolition of Dennis Conner. He deserved it and so did I.

At the heart of it all has been the challenge – and the enjoyment I have always taken from meeting a challenge head-on. But this is different. It has shown me there are challenges in life beyond 100 metres of footy paddock and that they can be just as stimulating. I feel the need to say to young people, "If I can do it you can, if you have the mind and stomach for a challenge."

Once, not so long ago, all I knew about figures was that Ali had a good one and that five plus two equalled a converted try. Now I owe the banks plenty and I sleep well at night.

6

Entertaining –
And Winning

I have played some of my greatest rugby from the reserves bench. You see and slice through gaps the players don't see. You make crunching tackles the players don't make. You pass for the halfback and you catch for the fullback. You find touch for the first five-eighths and you kick goals from anywhere. You grunt and butt heads for the props and you jump sky-high for the locks. You are magnificent. But you don't get too excited about it. Excitement is being out there and not seeing the gaps.

You may think the bench is an easy ride. To me the bench was tougher than being out there because it had none of the compensations. I became a bit of a reserve-bench champion in my early All Black career and while being on the bench was a good learning experience for me in 1987 I reached the stage when being happy just to be part of an All Black squad was not enough. Impatience and frustration are really the names of the splinters you get in your bum from sitting on the bench.

Even though you may be reserve to as great a captain as Buck Shelford or maybe even covering for a shooting-star like Michael Jones, being on the bench is drinking flat, warm beer while the boys out in the middle shower and shave in vintage bubbles.

That New Zealand team of the late '80s was such a top unit that test doors slammed shut on the fringers. Young men with hope in their hearts and fire in their bellies became dirt-trackers. I'm not sure who invented that term but what looms as almost permanent dirt-tracking can suffocate a million hopes and ambitions. The dirt-track the mid-weekers are consigned to may be all very comfortable for the seasoned sweats who have accepted long ago that if they ever get a Saturday game it will be by accident. But to young players with visions of fame it can become depressing – and especially if they are treated like kids by senior players.

One reason Buck Shelford was such a great captain was that to him all players were equal. He related to young players with ease and he had the respect of most experienced players. He gave loyalty and attracted it. Had he been a lesser player, leader and man I would have found my long stints watching him from the bench intolerable. As it was, I just found them deeply bloody frustrating. I needed to be out there playing, anywhere. Halfback would have been OK except I didn't much fancy being word-whacked to death by Foxy.

The teams of those years drove along, fired by the fuel which had been the thrust behind the 1987 World Cup campaign. The Wyllie-Shelford partnership was ebullient but soundly based. Grizz liked Buck's style as a player, forthright and uncompromising, which was much the same as his own rugby personality both as player and coach. Yet I found Grizz a difficult man to front-up to for a talk about my game, what he expected of me. He was uncomfortable and hesitant with this one-on-one scene, as if he could not find the words. In his bluff way, with a pint in his left hand and an amiable arm-punch (like a sledgehammer) in his right, he would compromise with hearty generalities and notice suddenly that his glass was empty.

Had David Kirk not gone to Oxford and had he retained the All Black captaincy there could have been serious personality clashes of a sort which would have disrupted the team. Grizz needed the company of uncomplicated men.

As captain of New Zealand at the World Cup, Kirk overcame the considerable obstacle of captaining a team of which he was not captain. He was a demanding skipper, a perfectionist. He sought excellence and could become decidedly miffed when he did not get it. His team-talk style was intense and his language sometimes a bit high-flown. But he knew what he wanted; he had a good head for the game and he was skilled and committed.

But for all his admirable qualities Kirky could never have played the piano for Grizz and produced a hit single. Intellectually, he would have sung along well with John Hart but it may have been

David Kirk…demanded excellence.

a happy coincidence for New Zealand rugby that when Grizz became coach Kirk had his head in his books at Oxford.

It is not a criticism of Wyllie to say that, given the head-start of that World Cup team, any able coach could have taken it through the next few seasons. A coach with no ability at all would have done quite well with it, too, because the players knew where they were going. The players were there who wanted to take the game to yet another level. What Grizz did was continue to push on with, and even enhance, the style which had made the team world champions, an expressive style played at pace but never remote from efficiency in the basic things.

The team had pride in itself, the players were enjoying their rugby and they played for each other. It was when all three of those qualities disintegrated three years later that the irresistible flow of a great era in New Zealand rugby came to a messy end.

The team destroyed Wales here with two 50-pointers in 1988, scoring 18 tries to one. For the Welsh it was a soul-destroying experience and for those who respected Wales for its great years and its history of fierce opposition to the All Blacks, it was a huge let-down. But the aftermath was more incredible for a nation with rugby in its blood.

The Welsh were too obstinate to learn from the experience, maybe too proud. By turning its back on its star player when he offered to organise clinics based on the lessons of the tour the Welsh Rugby Union contributed generously to the cause of rugby league. Jonathan Davies went north to kick goals and count gold and Wales has gone on paying and paying.

The same season the All Blacks scored 11 tries to four in three matches against Australia, winning the first and third easily and drawing the second 19-19. That draw was achieved out of a 16-6 halftime deficit and in character it was much like the 1994 match with the All Blacks playing zombie-rugby in the first spell and awakening to pull back the Wallabies in the second. It did not have the stampeding pulse of the 1994 second spell but the All Blacks played with cool purpose and it was a brilliant vision-switch of direction by Foxy and a huge chop of a sidestep by JK past Nick Farr-Jones which brought the try which drew the match.

In a new sense that game, though it was only drawn, demonstrated the immense character of those World Cup and Shelford years. The team so often cruised comfortably to victory that, in memory, it is often seen to have been a team from another galaxy compared with its opposition. That wasn't always so. There were hard games, games in which the All Blacks were forced to pull out reserves of commitment no other team might have found – and if we are talking greatness, that capacity to reach deep and find courage is as potent an ingredient in any team's greatness as the brilliant tries they score.

The French of 1989 scored five tries to our seven in two tests and Welsh clubs on the Wales-Ireland tour at the end of the same season put their bodies on the line, fought with the sort of doggedness and bloody-mindedness their country looked for in the national side but rarely found. It was as if when the players took off their club jerseys they peeled off their inspiration as well. When they became Wales at Cardiff Arms the best bits of their rugby character stayed behind in Llanelli, Neath and Swansea.

The Irish were what they always have been and will be for ever and ever amen. In the match-openers they were all elbows, knees, boots and flying bodies. If the Welsh clubs had fiery commitment the Irish came at you straight out of Hell. The opening of every game was like the first 15 minutes of the World Cup match this year. Frenzy. I had heard the expression "the madmen of Munster" but had discarded it as the sort of bullshit media people resort to when they run out of story-ideas. Well, they might not have been quite mad in the insane definition but they would have had to work hard to get past the psychiatric test. But when it was all over and you put your aching bumps, bruises and bollocks under the shower it was with a sort of admiration, not resentment.

It was on this tour that the Irish captain, Willie Anderson, went eyeball-to-eyeball and chest-to-chest with Buck during the haka. The Munster men might have been mad in their way but this was stupidity and ignorance and Anderson was not able to make good his bravado when the chips were down which made the whole show of arrogance even more pathetic. But for all that, I enjoyed – and enjoy – the Irish for their warmth and their love of simple, pleasurable things. Like rugby.

I had eight games of the 14 on the tour, felt involved and at the end of the tour on top of my game. I played against Ulster in the match following the Ireland test and then, when Buck retired at halftime, I had 40 minutes against the Barbarians. That half-game was a heady experience for me. It was my first game at Twickenham, which is some sort of milestone in every young player's career, but, more than that, there was a special meaning for me that it should be against the Barbarians.

Since I first saw it as a teenager I had always carried this film-image in my head of the Barbarians match against the 1972-73 All Blacks and especially of the little Welshman Phil Bennett weaving magic with his feet. There may have been greater players in the match, which the Barbarians won – I wouldn't know. Because as a kid I loved more than anything to beat players with footwork which just came naturally, I was mesmerised by Bennett's balance and ability to beat player after player late off either foot. He acted-out for me the beauty of the game when it is played with skill and imagination and I have always related it to the Barbarians.

This time it was the All Blacks who bamboozled the Barbarians with high skill set on a solid power-base. When I went on to the field my prime objective was to stop more than 18 stone of Phil

Phil Bennett...weaver of magic.

Davies who, given latitude, was playing merry hell in close encounters of the very physical kind. Seriously troubled by a neck injury he carried into the game, Buck had not been able to confront Davies with anything like his normal robustness.

It meant a one-on-one contest and that appealed to me as a great way to play my first game at Twickenham. Anyway, Davies became less effective and then, about 15 minutes into the spell, three of us young guys – Graeme Bachop, Walter Little and myself – clicked with a multiple-scissors which brought me a try. Even more than when I scored in my first test I felt that this was what it was all about. Elation. Exultation. But keep it bottled-up, Zinny, All Blacks don't kiss. Or even hug. Wallabies kiss and hug.

Buck's form and leadership on that tour are his lasting testimonial. It was beyond my imagination that within a few months his All Black career would be finished. Taken away from him. And in a few months where would Joe Stanley be? Gone, too. Two of a kind, Buck and Bullet. Bullet's contribution to the era was understated, often under-estimated. His capacity to pull in two defenders on one, to create space for his wings, to provide a base for loose-forward advances, to set up an aggressive midfield defence made him indispensable to the cause of the free-range rugby the All Blacks were committed to. And his almost intuitive understanding with John Gallagher and John Schuster made for some brilliant segments of rugby.

Rugby cost Joe Stanley dearly. For what he gave the game in New Zealand he deserved better than to find himself swamped by the costs of keeping his one-man business going while the game demanded more and more from him. In the two tests against Scotland in 1990 he was distressed by the chronic viral condition which was bringing him to his knees two or three times during a game and I could sense time was running out for him.

I had three overseas tours – beyond Australia, that is – with Buck. The first was the tour of Japan in 1987, the second the New Zealand Maori tour of just about everywhere in 1988 which generally registers in New Zealand as the tour when Buck led his team off the field at Rodez. It seemed not to matter back home what Buck said about it. The damage was done by the New Zealand Rugby Union chairman, Russ Thomas, who, without any knowledge of the circumstances, jumped in to condemn.

I was playing in that game against the Pyrenees Selection and I couldn't say the refereeing was straight out of Disneyland because

Buck on to Bullet...two of a kind.

even Donald Duck is three per cent intelligible. This referee had no English at all and it was too late for Buck to teach him. The result was total frustration and it was in that state that Buck took us to the touchline and called for the interpreter. Fix the scrums, he said, or we're off.

Just like that, the scrums were fixed. Magic. A wave of the big stick and Donald Duck understood everything. Buck did the only thing open to him and it worked. It was a means to an end but the speed of the official reaction at home seemed to us to be over-eager, opportunism. There had been hard words before the tour over the meagre daily allowance for the players and the Maoris sensed the New Zealand Rugby Union couldn't give two stuffs about the tour, even that it would prefer it would just go away.

France, Spain, Italy, Argentina...it was a great tour for many reasons but none as telling as the sheer enjoyment there was in that company of players. It was, you might say, very Maori. It had laid-back comedy and it had slapstick...We are in Seville where people park their cars in a lane outside regular parking spaces. They are very trusting. They leave them in gear with the handbrake off so that when the owners of the cars on the inside want to get out they just shunt the double-parkers out of the way. We have been socialising, which is a nice way of putting it.

We come out with our designated driver agreeably under the limit. We are boxed in and after a responsible discussion involving the use of several long words we reach what the Member for Northern Maori would call a consensus. We will do in Spain what the Spaniards do. We will shove the outside car forward. Normally, this would take one big person or two small ones. We are approximately six big ones. We heave with about the same velocity as an Argentine scrum, the car kick-starts and bolts with Frano Botica alone clinging to the towbar and gaining impressive speed for a first five-eighths over 30 metres.

The car and Frano part company. Frano returns. The car proceeds as far as it is mechanically able, which is as far as a wall which is not about to get out of the way. It is unlikely the owner will find the car in quite the same shape as he left it. Having picked ourselves up and dusted ourselves off we do the decent thing and leave a little note in fluent Maori with English sub-titles. We depart the scene shaking our heads over what we agree was an unfortunate accident. We hear nothing but when we are violently attacked by the crowd at Tucuman in Argentina two weeks later we assume the car-owner had South American mafia connections.

That Maori team often played rugby of a kind New Zealanders need to see more frequently. Maybe it would open up the little minds of the people who call Maori rugby racism, apartheid and other wildly emotive things. When you're in the clutches of the Latins there are going to be scraps on the field. There is no escape. Much was made of the few negatives of the tour, little of the many positives.

I know that going back a good few years Maori rugby was not always well served. There were allegations of tribally-influenced selections and the traditional character of the game as Maoris love to play it was at risk. New Zealand went through a period when coaching was rigidly conservative and Maori rugby was caught up in that and suffered because of it. Not now.

I do not feel I should have to justify the existence of Maori rugby as an entity. The Maori team did that by entertaining and exciting a big crowd when we ran the Lions to a standstill at Athletic Park in 1993. We lost narrowly but Maori rugby won that day because it shouted to the New Zealand Rugby Union that the game deserved us and we deserved the game.

Buck...a captain for every reason.

Maoris at play...a must for rugby.

Before that game there were articles which read like sermons about the place of Maori rugby in the New Zealand scene. We set out to show that if rugby is enjoyable for the players it is enjoyable for the spectators. I read a piece recently about Waka Nathan taking over the coaching of the Maoris in 1971. He said, "I see a way back to the top for Maori rugby and when it comes it will be more magnificent than ever…in my day I got tired of coming off the paddock after a Maori match and being told it was a fantastic game after we'd lost. I set out to produce fantastic games, but with the Maoris winning."

Buck Shelford said something of the same sort, offering Maoris the freedom to play the game as they naturally wished to play it but pointing to the need to sweat at the possession phases so we had the means to cut loose. That is what we did at Athletic Park that day in 1993 and had it not been for Damian Cronin, totally stuffed and tripping over a belly like a bagpipe bladder, we'd have won it. Damian, left miles behind the play, stumbled back into the middle of our backline just as I was making the pass which would have brought the try to win the match. He was still conscious enough to wave his hands in the air to convince the referee he was there by accident. There's no one more cunning than a stuffed Scotsman. Unless it's a stuffed Maori.

That sort of game gives rugby in New Zealand another dimension, the Maori dimension. Don't tell me it's not there, that it's just another game of rugby. Were it only by being in the middle of it, by listening to the crowd going nuts at Athletic Park, I'd know it was there. But it's more than that. I *feel* it. When my dad talked about a joker named Johnny Smith he spoke as if he was in church. Awesome. Spiritual. To me, Johnny Smith became a ghostly figure who glided around tackles, swayed through clutching fingers and was never, ever, put to ground by anyone. What Johnny Smith was, I know now, was a centre unlike any other. He was also a Maori and, dare I say it, he played like a Maori – on instinct and with love of the game.

Now that, hopefully, we have left the business of strait-laced, humourless rugby behind let's get on with it and entertain. If ever rugby union needed to entertain it is now and especially as we are coming to accept that you can entertain and win, too. The Maori element presents just one vehicle through which it can be done. It is why the itineraries of every major tour here should be designed to take in a match against New Zealand Maoris.

7

Buck, Me And Manly

The worst thing that ever happened to me was to be selected for the All Blacks at the expense of Buck Shelford after the Scottish tests in 1990.

What in other circumstances would have sent me over the moon became a nightmare. It was as if I personally had engineered some dirty underworld plot to prise Buck out of the team. The telephone and the radio were my worst enemies. There were abusive calls through the night from cowardly bastards who would run a mile rather than front-up. Talkback radio hosted hundreds of callers incensed by Buck's dismissal and most of them found a way to place the blame on me. They just could not see past me as an equal villain with the selectors.

In the early part of what became weeks, extending into months, of mad-headed controversy I agreed to do interviews. It always came back to one stupid question: "You have displaced the All Black captain. How do you feel about that?" It has to be carved into the interviewers' manual that when you cannot think of something intelligent to say you ask, "How do you feel?" They find someone in the middle of tragedy and ask, "How do you feel?" They find someone in the middle of triumph and ask, "How do you feel?" How do you feel about the death of your pet dog? How do you feel about losing the game 35-0? How do you feel about winning Lotto? How do you feel about shafting Buck Shelford?

I felt bloody awful and the more the talkback hosts jazzed it along the hotter my phone rang and the more I retreated. Often I wouldn't answer the phone. If I did I would say, "No, not home, not home." I would deny it was me. I felt humiliated, angry that there seemed nothing I could do to get these people off my case. It was as if I was the accused and the jury was laced with my enemies. Great for the pride. Great for the self-respect to have to deny your own name to some invisible wanker on the phone. What should have been an occasion for brief jubilation became a long, long funeral service. Bring back Buck? By all means. Go for it.

Public outrage was fuelled by Buck's great form on the 1989 tour of Wales and Ireland. I could understand that. Just as I could understand the huge affection the people had for him as a straight-shooter and an inspirational leader from the front. Old ladies who had never much liked this rough game tuned in just to watch Buck at the front of the haka. When Buck sorted out a couple of troublemakers on the paddock the talk was not that he should have been penalised but what a great left hook he had. By just being himself Buck had become a cult figure.

When I think back on events leading to The Dropping of Buck I have some uneasy memories, just the feeling that long before he was dropped there was influence in the selection panel to thrust me forward at Buck's expense. I remember the telephone call I had from John Hart at the time of the All Black trial at Hamilton in May 1989, when the bits-and-pieces team coached by Earle Kirton damn near beat the shadow test team to play the touring French.

I took the call in my room about 9.30 the morning of the trial. He asked if there was anyone else there. When I said there was he told me not to mention his (Harty's) name. He told me I needed a big game against Buck, that I needed to destroy him, outmuscle him, get wide, make sure I beat him at "everything". I was not to play Buck's game. I had to make him play mine.

My immediate reaction was that it was good of him to call. It was not unusual for him, as in 1987, to talk to me about my game. Later, I thought it was strange that as an All Black selector he should be ringing me to tell me to destroy the New Zealand captain in a trial. There was nothing sinister in the word "destroy". It's just a term. We all use it. But when I thought later about the call I wondered why Harty would want anyone to outplay his test captain. Maybe he wanted to see Buck placed under pressure; maybe he wanted me to understand I was in the running. Maybe.

Buck and I had quite different perspectives of the No 8 game

Buck 'n' me...friendly adversaries.

once the basic job was done. At scrum-time the No 8 is the link between forwards and backs. He must have acute judgement of the time to release or hold. He's the clean-up man, the support man, the cover man. He goes down on the ball, he picks up the ball, he drives the ball always with the determination to advance beyond the advantage line.

Beyond those things, for Buck it was involvement in the tight stuff, the heavy contact work. He was the hard-driving, hard-rucking, uncompromising, close-to-the-ruck, close-to-the-maul man. I was more the free-ranging No 8, covering wide, covering the fullback, comfortable with kicking recovered ball and happy to be part of the wider running game.

I had a natural tendency to throw a bit of risk into the game, to take a risk to make a profit. I was never worried about throwing long passes or kicking the ball. It has been said I kick the ball more than I should. I reject that. I have the confidence to kick because I can kick well; it was part of my rugby education. There is, too, great satisfaction in getting under the high ball, taking pressure off the fullback. And, of course, there was always Michael Jones. There was always profit to be made from following a loosie like Michael Jones. You knew if you followed him you would

89

The Incomparable...where he is, the ball is.

end up where the ball was.

Michael's instinct for the game became everyone else's bonus. Watch him still. See where he runs. Call it instinct. Call it vision. Where the ball is, Michael is. He smothers the options of the opposing first five-eighths, cutting out his space and time to think, offering him no room to extend options. The English critic John Reason has called Michael the greatest rugby player he ever saw. I am part of this universal acclaim for him. His rugby has helped my rugby. His rugby has been a significant part of my progress in the international game. He is my man.

In the event, I did have a good game against Buck that day in Hamilton and so did the whole of Mike Brewer's team against Buck's team before going down 31-25. It was, incidentally, my first concentrated session of training under Kirton and it was a stimulating experience. He was certainly different. He was refreshing, infectiously enthusiastic, bubbling over with tactics, strategies and theories. Yet his game-plan was sound as a bell. I have the feeling he is not fully appreciated because his Old School Tie demeanour doesn't sit comfortably with the judgmental New

Zealand rugby buff. Behind that scarf and the g-'n'-t anecdotes his head and his heart are in rugby.

After the Hamilton trial Buck captained New Zealand against the French for two hard-fought wins, against Argentina for two big wins and against Australia when, with Buck strong, the All Blacks controlled the last quarter of the match. Then we had the tour of Ireland and Wales from which the team and Buck as captain emerged to the general acclaim of the Brits and of New Zealand.

So after all that, how badly did Buck play in the two 1990 tests against Scotland that he would be dropped, never to wear an All Black jersey again? My view of those tests was that while he may have lacked a little of his usual command it was not so serious that it could not have been sorted out. It did not warrant the captain of New Zealand being dropped.

In the second test there was a lack of fluency in communication between scrum and halfback but those are mechanics of the game which can easily be put right. If selectors are going to drop someone he has to be playing too badly to be retained or the player they have in mind as a replacement has to be performing better. I do not accept that either was the case with Buck.

With the background of the Ireland-Wales tour it made no sense to me that the New Zealand captain should be dropped after two close tests against a team which was no pushover and which was a grand-slam winner of the Five Nations Championship. It is a telling factor, too, that the tests against Scotland were played without John Gallagher and John Schuster, who had gone to rugby league. It meant there was a rebuilding process in an area which had become one of the All Blacks' most potent attacking sources. The seriousness of the loss of Gallagher and everything his speed and timing could bring to attacking options was not fully understood.

It is hard for me to accept that the panel agreement that Buck should be dropped was reached without any forceful argument against it from at least one member of it. It seems the final decision was taken after John Hart and Lane Penn went to watch North Harbour play North Auckland while Grizz went off to watch the touring Wallabies and that Hart and Penn agreed Buck was only average.

It seems their advice was not what Wyllie wanted to hear but what he feared he might because he had been concerned, too, about Buck's form in the team performance against Scotland.

So Buck was dropped. But before the announcement I had another telephone call from Harty. He told me to be prepared because I was going to be named in the All Black team to play Australia. That was the first indication that Buck was going to be dumped. Harty's call left me flattened. There was no elation, no celebration. I would speak for any player in saying that among the greatest moments of your career are those when your name is announced in a test team. In my position, having been reserve to Buck for so many tests, the announcement would have been mind-blowing. Coming as it did, as some sort of advance warning, I was left wondering why the hell I should be in and Buck out, as if there had to be some sort of intrigue behind it.

To my mind it was like, "Hey, Zinny, you're in because we want Buck out." Then came the backlash. I was made to feel like some conniving plotter, currying favour with the selectors. All I ever wanted was to play rugby because I loved the game. Now I was in the middle of a bloody war, out in no-man's land with shot and shell from all sides whizzing around my head.

It was inevitable the rumours would fly and that they would be picked up and regurgitated over and over again on radio and in the papers. There was the one about the great Auckland players' conspiracy to get rid of Buck. If there were elements among the Auckland players who wanted Buck out they were very secretive about it because I never heard it discussed. A fight in the dressing room between Foxy and Buck? Show me the bloodstains. That was like suggesting Michael Jackson picked a stoush with Mike Tyson.

It is true that Gary Whetton was ambitious to captain the All Blacks. There's nothing wrong with ambition. Once he said to Bernie McCahill and me, "When I get to be captain things are going to change around here" but I saw nothing sinister in that. It is in hindsight, when you start to make one and one make two – or, you might say, three, four or five – that you wonder whether his ambition to be captain had powerful support from inside the selection panel and you come up with guesses. Mine is that Buck's "form-loss" was a convenience.

How far can you go with supposition? You think back on such things as some players sniggering at Buck's choice of words when he was making his speeches at dinners and after-match functions. When players start that sort of pettiness it is getting suspiciously close to trying to break down team unity by belittling

For Business and Leisure
Christchurch's most affordable Hotel
73 ROYDVALE AVENUE, CHRISTCHURCH: P.O. BOX 8108
TELEPHONE (03) 588—289, FACSIMILE (03) 583—953, TELEX 4464 RUSSHO

```
TO ZINZAN BROOKE


HAVE A BIG GAME.

LOOKING FORWARD TO WATCHING IT


WAYNE SHELFORD
                    21-7-1990
```

Message from a big man.

the captain. I will only say it made me feel uncomfortable, embarrassed, and that of all people Buck did not deserve that sort of sly bullshit.

I was never conscious of any out-and-out antagonism toward Buck from inside the team, just these little things which niggled away at his status. From the time Gary was appointed vice-captain for the tour of Ireland and Wales it was clear he was destined to become All Black captain when Buck finished. What was not clear was that Buck's demise was so imminent. Gary was very close, guarded almost, but I feel he knew his time was just around the corner. I think there was somewhere a desire to get Buck out and that it was all a matter of timing, waiting for the moment when dropping him might somehow be rationalised and accepted by the public. Obviously, that strategy didn't work.

I played against the Australians in the three tests here. Before the first I received a telegram: "Have a big game. Looking forward to watching it. Wayne Shelford." It said everything I had ever believed about the man and in the space of nine words it made trivial nonsense of all the abuse and all the humiliation of the previous weeks.

We won the first test comprehensively, scoring four tries to none, the second less convincingly and in the third the Wallabies beat us squarely, the first test loss for the All Blacks since the black day at Nantes four years before. We squandered chances and while we played with commitment in creating scoring position in the third quarter of the game we also played without efficiency when tries were there to be taken.

The Wallabies played with the same sort of intensity which had been built in to All Black performance through the great years but which now was giving way to the self-judgement that we were, indeed, invincible. One of the reasons behind the rolling success of the team of the '80s was that while being acclaimed it kept its feet on the ground. Now public expectation of the All Blacks, fuelled by the massive wins against Wales in 1988 and the high of the tour in 1989, was expressed not in hope but in certainty. Invincibility is dangerous praise. It encourages the infiltration of complacency and self-admiration.

What happened at Athletic Park on August 18, 1990, against the Wallabies was an expression of two things – the unmistakeable advance of Australian rugby both physically and mentally and the invasion of New Zealand rugby by an infection called habit. We had got into the habit of accepting our greatness. Great eras are just that. Eras. There is always going to be an end to them, whether a long-running provincial success like Auckland's or international ones like those of the All Blacks of the 1960s and the 1980s. Players retire. Rugby league reaches into rugby union's guts and plucks out some vital organs. The gap between nations closes. Buck Shelfords are dropped. You live. You die.

I played against Buck before touring with the All Blacks to France late in 1990. It was a North Harbour challenge for the Ranfurly Shield and a match which in any other circumstances I would not have played. Just by being there Buck forced me to play. I did not train the whole week before the game. I had damaged my ankle playing an Aussie Rules game and it was giving me big trouble. It was X-rayed but the break was not detected.

The morning of the game I could run only to the right but I bluffed my way through a test. Then in the warm-up I turned my other ankle. I went into the game with a jab in one ankle, both ankles strapped and a nagging guilt that I was there at all. But it was front up or be branded as chicken for dodging a confrontation with Buck. That was the way it still was with the Bring Back Buck campaign and the North Harbour fans in a rage. I played and was outplayed. It was Buck's day, he was named man of the match, the campaign was refuelled and I went off to France with a broken ankle.

Believing my injury to be no worse than a sprain I convinced myself it would come right with treatment very quickly. But it never improved. At the first run the pain was excruciating. This, I said to myself, is going to be a shit tour. I was right. I was unable to sustain any show of form and conceded my test place to Mike Brewer. We beat France comfortably in both tests but there had to be serious doubts about the direction of French rugby at that time. It was sketchy stuff, without a heart to it. Thin wine. The sort of stuff the French put in fancy bottles and export to places like New Zealand.

A Cat-scan when we came home exposed the break and that seemed to me to be a fitting end to a fractured year.

There were 30 players in that touring party but no place for Buck. I have no doubt at all that he was good enough to be in a party of that size. The only valid consideration for his absence had to be that the presence of the old captain could have inspired division. But that was a circumstance the selectors could blame on no one but themselves.

Buck gave himself one last shot at making the All Blacks for the 1991 World Cup. He came back to New Zealand from England and we were named in opposing teams for the final trial at Rotorua. The Bring Back Buck campaign was alive and well. Kids chanted from the embankment. Adults waved banners. To thousands it wasn't a trial for 30 players. It was Buck against me, me against Buck. My memory of the match is only that when it was over I knew I had been effective in the No 8 role I set out to play. I went to the World Cup to play. Buck became a World Cup columnist for an English newspaper.

And about that broken ankle in 1990...what, you may be asking, was I doing playing Aussie rules. I played for Rangers in Auckland on Sundays because it was just a great game to play. In a way it was escapism from the disciplines of top rugby while giving the opportunity to hone your handling and kicking skills. And the big bonus was getting to knock guys over from their blind spot. I was big on that.

The Rotorua trial, 1991. Buck brought back.

Even more than Aussie rules I loved to play Gaelic football. I started with Roskill Rangers in 1983 and played every summer for five or six years. Bernie McCahill and his mad Irish mates introduced me to Gaelic football and I unashamedly wallowed in the game, great for elevation skills, anticipation, kicking off either foot (a must), running, passing by hand or kick-passing. And the contact! The contact made the blood run whether you were taking it or giving it.

In the Australasian championships we played a team which had a giant named Jimmy Stynes they had caught and caged somewhere in the wilds. They unleashed him every Sunday and pointed him toward the opposition and this day they pointed him at me and said, "Kill, Jimmy, kill". My head came up to his armpit, which was an area I would not have chosen but there it was, all the time, just above my nose. Zinny, I said, you're not going to play much ball unless you get under this guy and take his legs out. So with impeccable timing I drove into his legs and on over the touchline and planted him into the Carlaw Park grandstand. He did not die. He got up, shook himself shaggily, grinned amiably, said, "Kill, Jimmy, kill" and came right back into the game. Jimmy is now a superstar of Australian Rules, playing with the Melbourne Club.

It was probably on the strength of that tackle on him that I made the Australasian team, an achievement no one seems especially interested in conveying to the Hall of Fame. Playing Gaelic and Aussie rules added up in a way to the sort of rugby player I am. In Gaelic, especially, the demands were for sharp hand-eye co-ordination, ambidextrous skills, kicking for the natural arc off left foot and right. Were I an Irishman I'd play Gaelic football till the day I dropped dead.

There was, of course, another stop-press scoop-exclusive which did the rounds when I was selected and Buck dropped. It was that the selectors were stricken with fear that I was about to become rich by playing league. Not that they minded me becoming rich but that if I went to league I would be gone for ever and that did not stack up with their planning for the 1991 World Cup. One reporter had given the same reason for my selection in the 1987 World Cup squad.

I signed for Manly at the same time as Matthew Ridge early in 1990. Very secret, but there was enough speculation around for Harty to call on me one day and ask me what my intentions were. It was a bit like an anxious dad checking out the morals of his daughter's boyfriend. The fact was I could not see a big future for myself in rugby at that time. I guess it was an accumulation of doubts but at the root of it was that I didn't want to become a permanent reserve and I could see no possibility of Buck giving the game away. Or being dropped.

I could see financial security in league. I was 26 and that was the age I had been told was the deadline for switch from union to league. Any older and you're not worth the risk. The approach was made through the financial adviser to the Manly Sea Eagles. He rang Ridgey and me often and we had several meetings at the Sheraton Hotel in Auckland.

Then Graham Lowe came to town and word spread that

Graham Lowe…a fistful of dollars.

something big was on. I was to meet Graham for breakfast at the Sheraton restaurant. We were not quite alone. There were two strangers there with their heads obviously buried in newspapers and so uninterested that I knew they were bloody interested. I said to Graham, "Hey. I'm sure those guys are reporters."

He glanced at them and said loudly, "So how much do you want, Zinny? A million? Two million? Three? Name your price." The newspapers rustled and the guys' heads came up.

Graham Lowe was great to deal with. He put no pressure on me because he wanted me to make the right decision for the right reasons…"Go because you want to play rugby league, not because the money is too much to turn down."

He wanted me to play in the second row and probably as the third or fourth runner up. He said, "Look, Zinny, I don't want to use you as a battering ram." I said, "Well, that sure suits me Lowey." I didn't want to be a gravity-feeder like Brent Todd, crunch up and go down.

The package was worth $A118,000 a year plus lurks and perks, accommodation found. I signed the contract at the Sheraton. Ridgey signed his at 11am and I signed mine at 1pm two weeks after the breakfast meeting. Ridgey and I were to tell only our families and then at an agreed time tell the Auckland team and make a public announcement. The chosen match was Auckland against Wanganui. After it, Ridgey stood up and said his piece. Then across a solid wall of stunned silence he looked meaningfully at me. I raised my eyebrows, yawned a bit and didn't get up and didn't say anything. Ridgey looked bewildered.

A couple of things had happened. Under Australian Rugby League rules there is at no time to be any exchange of contract details between players. Obviously some would be getting more than others. Ours was the classic case. I drove Ridgey home from Auckland training one night and he asked how much I was getting. I told him he knew the rules. He persisted and I threw up my hands and told him. He was shocked. He used very strong language. His contract was far less attractive than mine.

So he went back to Graham Lowe and renegotiated. When I asked him how he got on he said it was now OK. So how much, I said. Forget it, he said. And, unlike me, he clammed up. But he did say Lowey had emphasised he wanted me to go to league only if I wanted to play the game more than I wanted to play union. I agonised over it – did I really want to go on with this?

John Sturgeon gives fatherly advice to Matthew Ridge and me.

Hey, look…things are starting to happen in rugby; I can make a lot more dough through the game now. More dough? Chicken-feed compared with league, Zinny. But what about the environment I have here, great family, great relationship with Ali, great friends? Look, Zinny, you've bloodywell signed a contract. But what about having to learn a whole new ball game? With your skills, Zinny, you'll do it on your ear. Hey, what about those man-mountains with stiff arms and slack brains targeting this upstart All Black with the show-pony name? OK, Zinny, now you're making sense. And no more rugby? OK, Zinny, forget it.

So I did, with no regrets, no thinking back on it. Graham Lowe was very good about it. In no way would he jeopardise my rugby career. He made the contract disappear. A magician. There was, however, a sequel. After Matthew had been with Manly for a while Ric Salizzo went over there to film a feature on his lifestyle in Sydney as a league convert. Matthew was guiding the crew through the fine apartment we were to have been sharing for the first month or two. With the camera rolling he said, "And here we have the kitchen, and here is my bedroom and here is what was to have been Zinny's bedroom…"

It was a hot story had it ever hit the screen. Fortunately I saw it first and Ric's partner, JK, thoughtful chap, edited the it out.

When it came to JK's decision on league in 1994 there was a lot of cynical comment. But if he believed he had another two or three years of top football in him, why not? It was his life, his decision to make – and he has justified it.

8

The Gravediggers

I have said that eras are eras, a beginning and an end, and that usually there is no single cause when a great team drifts off its greatness and becomes just another rugby team, vulnerable to teams which even a year before it would have eaten for breakfast. There will always be cycles of success and failure but the deepest frustration of the downhill slide of the All Blacks from 1990 was the extent to which the players contributed to their own downfall.

First, however, was the increasingly aggressive assault on rugby by rugby league. In the space of a season that All Black team lost key players to league and then, later, one who had installed himself as an outstandingly gifted threequarter (Craig Innes) and another who had that invaluable quality of being a game-breaker (Inga Tuigamala).

I am not able to accept that the sole reason for the code-switch in all cases was the financial security league offered. Although he did not turn to league until after the World Cup, Innes, for one, had become disenchanted early in his brief career by what could fairly be seen as the callous indifference of some seniors to young players and by the gruff inflexibility of some of the training routines under Grizz. I have no doubt that these were factors, though perhaps not the major factor, in his decision to go.

When Ridge went he didn't know Gallagher was about to go and the loss of the pair of them was never adequately recovered. Gallagher had given the All Blacks brilliant attacking options. Ridge, without yet being a Gallagher, had a great range of skills and was tailor-made to fit into the All Black scheme of things. I have mentioned the Schuster-Gallagher connection and how the

Frano Botica...brilliant all-rounder.

pair worked with Joe Stanley. I am sure that had Gallagher not gone to league nor would Schuster. They were a pair, great buddies, and without Gallagher Schu was a bit like Butch Cassidy with no partner to Sundance with. To him, the kick of being an All Black was not enough if his mate wasn't there to share the laughs and make the tries.

And, of course, there was Frano Botica. Frano had been in much the same position as I had. On the bench. It was Frano's misfortune – and New Zealand's – that his career coincided with that of Grant Fox. He had qualities Foxy hadn't, and couldn't have. Foxy acknowledges that. Frano would be superb at first five-eighths the way the All Blacks are playing the game now. He

Foxy...the tactical organiser.

could kick goals with something approaching the precision of
Foxy and he could run and break. Foxy's advantage was in his
clinical approach to tactics and backline organisation, in his
pinpoint field kicking and his assessment of when to move the
line and when to turn the opposition around. He was the man for
the time, when the All Blacks were very formulated – urgent, but
formulated.

My sort of player would be Frano, maybe because he was a
lot like me in attitude. He could duck and sidestep, jolt into a
gap. He could create uncertainty in the opposition and that is
always a huge plus in a five-eighths. It must have been touch-
and-go between the two of them. Had the All Blacks beaten

103

Australia in the 1986 series following the Baby Blacks' defeat of France Frano would probably have been the long-term All Black.

None of this detracts from Foxy's stupendous contribution to New Zealand rugby, something a lot of New Zealanders did not come to understand until we no longer had him.

I can see another Frano-Foxy case looming, though not with all the same ingredients. With Andrew Mehrtens grasping opportunity and showing much the same sort of vision as Foxy, but with the advantage of running well, another outstanding talent in Carlos Spencer may be forced into long-term second place. You look at this sort of situation and say it's healthy to have such talent in depth. Tell that to Carlos. Mention it sometime to Frano.

Recently, looking down on New Zealand rugby from a great height, the secretary of The Rugby Union of England, Dudley Wood, had a sneer at what he called our "paranoia over rugby league". He was referring to the early stages of movement here to introduce a professional payer-paid base to the game at the top level. But what would he know? I might refer to Mr Wood's paranoia over calling shamateurism amateurism for the sake of appearances.

"So they lose a player or two? So what? There are others." That is the rigid mind-set that blocks understanding of the cold truths the players have had to front-up to and which England's players were no happier about than New Zealand's or Australia's. And, if I might say so, Mr Wood, England's players do very nicely indeed under the elastic "ethic" of amateurism.

Lightweight criticism of his sort betrays an administrative attitude which makes puppets of the players. What we lose here when league strikes are not just rugby players. We are losing people. To the players who are left there is a deep sense of loss. It is a sadness when stimulating, funny, exhilarating people are suddenly gone. It is taking a piece of the heart out of a team and for too long we have let these players go too easily. The players we have lost in the last five years are irreplaceable because while you may find adequate replacement players you cannot pick replacement people.

When we speak of Gallagher and Schuster, Ridge and Botica and of Tuigamala and Innes we are speaking of players who created character in teams not just by the act of playing well on the field but by their personalities off it. Frano and Schu were comedians and Ridge the cheekiest, most irreverent of all. There he was, a year out of school and in the Auckland team, a cranky little Armenian doing his own thing surrounded by a team full of All Blacks. Rules and regulations? Yeah-yeah.

I took Ridgey under my wing on the 1989 tour and, without actually baby-sitting him, kept an eye out for him. It wasn't easy. You get a band of crusty All Blacks, tensed-up for a team talk, sombre and edgy. Except Ridgey. He's chewing gum, twirling a ball on the end of his index finger, giving it a nudge with his head. Team talk? Yeah-yeah. Hey, man. This is me. Ridgey. Guys from out of Auckland stir uneasily and glare at him from under their scar tissue. Richard Loe and Andy Earl grumble and shake their heads. Who *is* this little shit? Get him outta here.

But they got to know him and they also got to know him as a gutsy, very skilled player, a champion goalkicker. When we lost him we lost both the player and the wonderful little screwball stirrer he was.

Craig Innes would have become one of the greatest All Blacks. His loss was much more serious in the playing sense than that of Inga. He was calm under pressure, a power-tackler and a brilliant playmaker. When he was a kid at school there was informed talk of him going to Japan for the tour after the 1987 World Cup. He had giant boots to fill when Joe Stanley was finally gone and he was a good enough player, in Joe's presence, to find a test position on the wing on the Ireland-Wales tour. Now, he would have been a test player for seven years and only in his mid-20s.

So don't preach to us, Mr Wood. Ignorance is a fragile pulpit and a total lack of concern for any problems outside your own smug little parish makes for sermons of bigotry and hypocrisy.

There is no point in All Blacks being uncomfortable with the way rugby and rugby people are in New Zealand. The people of New Zealand own the All Blacks. We are their property. They have the right to demand the All Blacks win. If you like, the people of New Zealand *are* the All Blacks. That's the way it is because we are three and a half million people tucked away down here in the South Pacific with 60 million sheep and ten million rugby balls.

The All Blacks are the little guy who goes to the corner of the bar, drinks a quiet half-pint and wishes he could get a ticket for Saturday's test. The All Blacks are the big brash guy with his seventh pint in his hand who tells the whole bar he knows Pinetree, BJ, Beegee, Foxy, Grizz, Harty, Laurie, Jonah, Fitzy and Loey intimately – but not so intimately that he, too, isn't wishing he could get a ticket for Saturday's test. The All Blacks are housewives and barristers, househusbands and stock-brokers, chief executives and dole-collectors, parliamentarians and protesters…

When the All Blacks win well people go to their offices and their construction sites and their shearing sheds on Monday and they work with a bit of extra zing. The boss shouts morning tea. The stock exchange is buoyant. When the All Blacks lose getting up to go to work is a pain in the arse and when you get there the boss bawls you out for no reason at all and the morning-tea milk is sour.

Because all this is true, the people of New Zealand need to know *why* things happen with the All Blacks, not just that they happen. They need to know why the transition from one era of rugby to another should get caught up in a sort of barbed wire entanglement of negative rumours while the truth gets swept under the carpet because it may not be attractive to expose it.

When Buck Shelford was displaced and the mood of the New Zealand rugby public was one of suspicion over the reasons for it plus a conviction he had not been given a fair crack of the whip, new responsibilities were thrust upon the players and the new captain and team management. The team-strings had to be pulled tightly together by captaincy which embraced the qualities of the great All Black captains and by management which, while firm, had to be enlightened in such things as public relations – the presentation of the public face of the All Blacks.

From what I have read of the eras of Wilson Whineray and Brian Lochore they were role models for All Black captaincy. From what I experienced, however briefly, with Andy Dalton he had much the same qualities. They carried themselves with dignity and they had a natural sense of courtesy to others no matter their status. They were captains for all seasons and all occasions.

Gary Whetton had qualities as captain of Auckland which made him a fair bet to lead New Zealand successfully. By "successfully" I do not mean just as a successful match captain although as a player there were elements of greatness in him. When he was on top of his game, which often he was for Auckland, he was truly impressive, remarkably athletic for a big man, mobile and assertive. If there was one quality his mentor Andy Haden had which he lacked it was the capacity to totally dominate a match. Andy taught Gary many things from the time the raw young lock joined him against the Springboks in the final test of

Gary Whetton...bewildered young players.

1981 and among them, later in his career, was to time his highest lineout jumps and cleanest two-handed "takes" in front of the grandstand, the selectors and the cameras. In the public memory two or three of those spectacular takes becomes a dozen. I do not say that critically. I say it with admiration for the concept.

Gary captained the All Blacks to that 2-1 series win against Australia in New Zealand and the 2-0 win against France in France in 1990. But it was on the magical mystery tour of Argentina in 1991 that the nuts-and-bolts of the All Black chassis showed signs of wear-and-tear. It was a sort of warning that if something serious was not done to put internal team matters right the wheels would fall off – which, a few months later, at the worst possible time, they did.

I have to say that ambition to be an All Black captain and the achievement of it did not bring out in Gary a Lochore, a Dalton or a Shelford. He was, of course, his own man and his perception of what captaincy at this level involved was a matter of his own personal judgement. There were times when that perception caused disharmony among the players – and deeply-felt resentment in some cases. It is no secret now that players tried in Argentina in 1991 to elastoplast rifts but it had no apparent effect.

The surprising thing was that off-field problems were not urgently addressed. The signs were clear but the drift persisted with no apparent concern for it from those who should have been doing the welding job. Young players were first perplexed by and then resentful of what they took to be their second-class status. They found Gary's treatment of them off-hand at worst and inconsistent at best.

I know Gary well and I have seen his mood-switches in action, affable one day and unapproachable the next. I am sure he worked on the basis that the captain of the All Blacks has to be with the team but apart from it. That is neither unusual nor undesirable but the difficulty is getting the balance right. That was a problem he never resolved satisfactorily and because of it he was not able to inspire allegiance throughout the team. It was sad but true and it troubled those of us who were his long-time team-mates.

I was part of a discussion which developed from a casual get-together of a group of players in a bar in Argentina. What emerged was so disturbing that I went to JK and told him things were seriously amiss, that team morale was cracking up and that young or new players like John Timu, Shayne Philpott, Craig Innes, Walter Little and Inga were at a loss to understand where they stood in the team. Considering that Craig and Walter were the test midfield and John a test wing it was quite a revelation. JK and Colt Crowley took the problem to Gary and Grizz but there seemed little acceptance of it. Nothing seemed to change.

Young players becoming All Blacks move in with senior players who have been their schoolboy idols. They expect the experience to be an inspiration. They look for acceptance and they need to be made to feel they are part of the team in every way. But here we had new players, having achieved their schoolboy dream by playing in the same All Black team as the men they idolised, discovering that in reality even idols can be disappointments. It was a shattering experience.

My own tour of Argentina might indicate that players who had been around for a few years had problems, too. I went to Argentina as the first-string No 8 and could honestly judge my form there to be pretty good. But when the first test team was announced I was dropped, Michael Jones was at No 8 and Paul Henderson on the open flank. I did not know why and Grizz certainly was not about to tell me. It was a communication vacuum, bizarre in an All Black team which was supposed to be bonding for the big thrust to the World Cup.

A player must have the confidence of knowing he is there if he is playing well enough. If he is not there he not only needs to know the reason why, he deserves to know. It was not that Grizz was dishonest. It was that somewhere in there was a vein of insecurity. Those who know him well may agree with that. Those who do not know him will find it ludicrous for they see him only as the cult-Grizz who could beetle-brow his way through any situation.

The general uncertainty led to divisiveness. My position was only one of the signs that what at that time had to be an all-for-one and one-for-all team was unravelling fast and stuff-all was being done about it. It is why I have to say that in a crucial area of captaincy, the restoration of team unity, Gary was not able to take the step up from provincial captaincy to national statesmanship. When he tried, it was far too late.

There followed the unsatisfactory home-and-away against a Wallaby team which already had the demeanour of a side which was going to make a killing at the World Cup. Their 21-12 win at Sydney was clearly a more comprehensive job than our 6-3 win at Auckland. The Australians will take no consolation at this late stage when I tell them they were denied another three points in that second match when the touch judges ruled that a Michael Lynagh penalty attempt from about 48 metres dropped under the bar. I was there, right at the spot, and I know the kick dropped just over the bar at the angle with the upright. Sorry, you jokers. What a mistake. It broke my heart at the time, I can tell you.

There seems little point in yet again mauling through the backstage politics which led to Harty joining Grizz in that unholy alliance of coaching at the World Cup. The players understood clearly the two did not get on and for what was already a team almost compulsively losing focus, anyway, it was just another shove down the slope. I could understand Harty's dilemma when he was placed under pressure to go and I could understand Grizz's belief that he was under siege from the top and, not least, from Harty himself. Grizz "knew" Harty was after his job and as the campaign went on that conviction became set in concrete. Neither trusted the other to do the job, the pretence of mutual regard became transparent and then disappeared.

Harty had to back himself to go to the World Cup and win it. It would place him in line to be the All Black coach. Had he not gone he would have been judged by some to be letting the show down. Should Grizz win the Cup on his own he would have the kudos and the job for just about as long as he wanted it.

So, sensing all this and the contest that was involved, did the players pull together to try to make it work? Hell no. The players were so far up themselves that they thought winning the Cup was no more than they deserved and that it would happen as a matter of right. It was a team awash with arrogance. It was not the healthy arrogance I would relate to the Auckland team of the time, built on justified confidence and self-knowledge. This was a false, brash arrogance which led to self-destructive behaviour.

The players became bigger than the game. Now here was a runaway train headed for the big crash. Inflated ideas of our own worth became embedded. As playing-through world champions we were a highly marketable commodity and we sold ourselves dearly. Spoiled brats with our hands out for bucks – but, even better, pounds sterling. Some players were more tuned-in to the ching of the cash register than the codes of the lineout calls. Gain became bigger than game and pride in the black jersey was one of the victims. It is long past time this was acknowledged from within the team. It may be long past time, too, that the New Zealand Rugby Union acknowledged player-contracts may have anticipated this sort of problem.

An endorsement of a product here, a bit of a promotion there? Yes. How much? What's in it for me? And there was indifference and sometimes plain rudeness to All Black supporters who only wanted a wave or a word or an autograph. No wonder those incredibly loyal people who followed us around the World Cup trail were first hurt, then angry, then bitter. I cringe now when I think back on the supporters we wouldn't give the time of day. It's time we said we're sorry rather than pretending it didn't happen. In a way we tried to do that by going to the New Zealand supporters' area after the 1992 test against South Africa at Ellis Park.

Had we been playing our rugby against Canada or Zimbabwe we might have got away with it. But we were in against the big boys, and they were big boys who had learned a thing or two

John Hart...at his best, penetrating, focused.

since the 1987 World Cup. The difference between the good and the great is minimal and given the day and the circumstance the good can beat the great. The trouble was that the greatness we wrapped ourselves in was past its use-by date. Where there should have been hunger there was complacency.

We still trained hard and well but we were so immersed in "business matters" that our match-focus became hopelessly blurred. If we searched for an excuse now it might be that through the years players had become so frustrated by professional demands without professional returns that they saw what may have been the last opportunity to make a killing. But there was no excuse for allowing that to take over from what should have been our life's aim.

The obvious question, then, is that if what was happening was so blatant why wasn't there a big move to pull the show around?.

The answer has to be that Hart and Wyllie were too involved in their own mind-war to grasp what was happening and Sturgeon, a players' man through and through but with no assistance from such people as a campaign manager or a media liaison officer, identified his place primarily to be defender of the All Blacks from the pressures of the media and the supporters. It was, of course, a public relations disaster made more so by the genial Wallabies who took media and supporters in their stride.

It was during our last training run before the semi-final against the Wallabies at Lansdowne Road that I knew we were in trouble. It wasn't that I personally submitted to the Wallabies in advance. It was that if this training was supposed to be the basis for a winning performance against a top team then we were lost. I doubt that I was the only player who left that training concerned for what had not been achieved.

As a coach and a man Harty had such great things about him. His feeling for the game was backed by an analytical mind. He was a brilliant planner. He was also a showman and that last training run became his stage. His audience was a huge turnout of New Zealand supporters, probably a couple of thousand. It was as if the presence of all those people inspired him to perform. He took over the training and ran it like a circus. It was not Harty the penetrating, focused rugby coach. It was no sort of convincing training event for the players a day out from the virtual final of the World Cup. It was as if we were grasping at straws with no sharp consciousness of what needed to be done. It was the culmination of all that had been wrong from Argentina on.

Initially both he and Grizz had a hand in the session. But when Harty took over Grizz stormed off the paddock. I was told by a long-time pressman who was on the sideline that Grizz was in a high fury and snapped, "If I go down that **** goes with me." That day brought the most depressing evidence of all that it was sheer folly to throw Harty and Grizz together and tell them to win the World Cup. The first act cancelled out any possibility of the second – and more especially so considering the splintered state of the team they were supposed to coach.

It was an interesting commentary on the public face of the All Blacks that a British journalist, Stephen Jones, wrote a story pinpointing the deterioration of the quality and spirit of the team and, much as I felt after that training run, he predicted that no team in this mental condition and with this sort of preparation

Buck Shelford retiring injured at halftime against the Barbarians at Twickenham in 1989 allowed me to join the action and pretty soon Graeme Bachop, Craig Innes and myself had worked a triple scissors move that produced this try.

Showing off a winner's medal after Marist's victory in the Gallaher Shield club final in 1991.Andrew Cornaga, Photosport

No, we're not trying to waltz a little. Otago winger Paul Cooke and I are actually disputing the ball in the 1992 Ranfurly Shield game at Eden Park. Cookie scored a try but we won 21-16.
Andrew Cornaga, Photosport

One of the rare occasions when Buck Shelford and I opposed each other in an All Black trial – at Rotorua in 1991.
Andrew Cornaga, Photosport

Probing the blindside on a freezing afternoon during the 1991 World Cup quarter-final against Canada at Lille.

This Scottish defender's been having a ripping time. Graeme Bachop and Steve McDowell await developments during the play-off for third at the second World Cup.

Provincial teams aren't supposed to put 60 points on international sides, but Auckland managed it against Ireland at Eden Park in 1992. We whipped them 62-7, then nearly lost the first test a week later! Troy Restieaux, Photosport

Picking up the pace in the second half against the British Lions team of 1993. Auckland trailed by seven points at halftime but came through to win 23-18. Michael Jones, as always, is in support of the ball carrier. Troy Restieaux, Photosport

Call me Luigi! Fresh home from Italy in May, 1993, and looking like someone who's had too much pasta.

Andrew Cornaga, Photosport

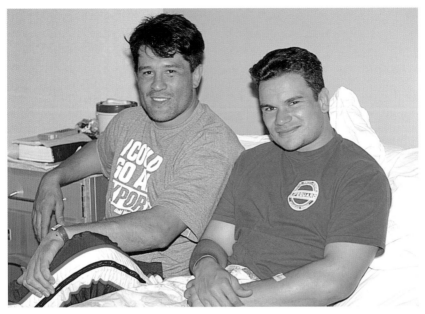

How unlucky can you be? Michael Jones broke his jaw in training late in 1993 and had to pull out of the All Black tour of England and Scotland. I visited him in hospital. Andrew Cornaga, Photosport

Relaxing with Stu Forster on the tour of Scotland (and England) in 1993.

Andrew Cornaga, Photosport

How's that for support play. Fellow forwards Blair Larsen, Steve Gordon and Graham Purvis are right with me as I surge for the tryline against South of Scotland at Galashiels in 1993.

Clive Brunskill

Tryscoring became infectious for the All Blacks at Galashiels in '93. I picked up four, as captain, and the team 12 as we hit 84 against South of Scotland.

Clive Brunskill

Relaxing after training during the '93 tour of the UK with brother Robin – whose calf muscle injury didn't allow him to play – and Jamie Joseph. Andrew Cornaga, Photosport

A bit of a rough-up for Midlands' test lock Martin Johnson at Leicester in 1993. It was a game we struggled to win 12-6. Andrew Cornaga, Photosport

Auckland lost the Ranfurly Shield in 1993 but there was consolation three weeks later when we defeated Otago in the NPC grand final at Eden Park. I find Sean Fitzpatrick ready for the pass as Arran Pene halts my progress.

Andrew Cornaga, Photosport

Arran Pene and I give our halfback Stu Forster a lift prior to the New Zealand Maori team's early season visit to South Africa in 1994. Andrew Cornaga, Photosport

We had to work overtime to take out the first test of the 1994 series against the Springboks at Carisbrook. Adriaan Richter and Brendan Venter are determined to stop this All Black assault. We won the game 22-14.

Andrew Cornaga, Photosport

Our good victory against the Springboks at Athletic Park in '94 was unfortunately overshadowed by the Johan le Roux ear-biting incident. Above: It's pure rugby here, though, as Graeme Bachop and I probe the blindside watched by Bok halfback Johan Roux and Irish referee Brian Stirling. Below: The war wounds are forgotten as the final whistle sounds, the All Blacks two-nil ahead in the three test series.

Andrew Cornaga, Photosport

The third test of the '94 series produced a rather colourless draw at Eden Park. Unlike the World Cup a year later, there would be no extra time played, however. Involved in the action here are Springboks Hennie le Roux, Fritz van Heerden and Francois Pienaar.

The 1994 NPC final between Auckland and North Harbour got a bit out of hand at times, resulting in suspensions for some of players. But it didn't diminish the thrill of winning the title. Inset: A hug from Auckland's assistant coach John Graham. Below: In possession of the handsome new NPC trophy presented by Air New Zealand.

Andrew Cornaga, Photosport

Auckland paced itself well during 1994, producing its best rugby late in the season in the play-offs. While this victory over Otago at Eden Park was encouraging, there was greater satisfaction in beating David Latta's men in the semi-final at Carisbrook.

Andrew Cornaga, Photosport

I may not have a reputation as a demonstrative character on the rugby field, but I deliver the message when it's needed.

Andrew Cornaga

John Timu...needed at fullback.

would beat the Wallabies. And that was even after the Aussies had had to call up a miracle to beat Ireland. The irony of it was that had Ireland held the Wallabies out in the last seconds we, who were working so effectively against ourselves, would almost certainly have played England in the final and most likely beaten them as we had done in the opening match.

Apart from all the other reasons I do not think that in the selection of the team to play Australia we helped ourselves. The approach was conservative where, if even only because of the Australians' familiarity with us, we should have gone for something much more liberal.

With Terry Wright injured we had given John Timu a run at fullback against Canada and there was excitement in his game, the second of his two tries being a great one. Now when we needed all the attacking strength we could muster it was decided Timu was a risk at fullback against skilled kickers like Michael Lynagh and Nick Farr-Jones so he was returned to the wing. This meant that a potential game-breaker in Tuigamala was left out and that a replacement player, Kieran Crowley, obviously short of match fitness, was at fullback. None of this made much sense to me, and especially the judgement on Timu.

Walter Little or Bernie McCahill at second five-eighths...They settled for Bernie, a very organised player. But it had to be a close call. Bernie was a great distributor off either hand, one of the best anywhere. Walter had brilliance and unpredictability. Both were good vision-players.

Being in the top grade as a distributor, as Bernie was, is going only part of the way. It means the opposition can just keep pushing its defences wide, whereas a player like Walter will unsettle because he cannot be predicted.

Inga had multiple advantages – the requirement he placed on the defence to concentrate two or three tacklers on him, the prospect that he would burst through anything but the most resolute defence, his ability to stand and feed from the tackle.

One of the justifiable criticisms of our rugby at that time was our predictability but it seemed we were prepared to absorb that, say "so what?" and get on with being predictable. In the state of mind we were in – closed-book complacency – I don't think we accepted our predictability. If there was risk in selecting a team for attack and variation, especially against the Wallabies, it was risk worth taking.

The Australians went into the game knowing they were winners. They had come off that mad game against the Irish unfazed; in fact, perhaps this knowledge that they could pull a lost game from the fire just added to their confidence that they could do anything. Their philosophy was positive. They studied where they might shut us down. They understood us.

When David Campese scudded across our defence to score the first try in the corner I didn't see it. I had made the first tackle and from the bottom of the ruck had looked at the ball, lying there within my reach, wondering whether it was worth risking a penalty by giving it a bit of assistance in the right direction, which would have been the wrong direction for Campo. Don't do it, Zinny, this voice said. So I didn't and when I got up the try had been scored and I wished I had.

What our grand plan was for that game I do not recall. The memory of bad feeling in our camp overwhelms all else except the crushing disappointment of the day and the humbling knowledge that, other than most (but certainly not all) New Zealanders, everyone seemed bloody happy we were beaten.

The British media wrote about our defeat with unbridled delight. And why not? While knowing the nature of that particular beast we had, by our jumped-up attitudes and our indifference to All Black tradition and pride, not only dug our own graves, we had bought the bullets for the ratpack, loaded their guns and pulled the triggers for them.

9

Lasagne, Lira And Laurie

I'm glad I finally got to know Laurie Mains. For a long time it looked a fair bet I wouldn't. And that would have meant this book would have been called *Goodbye Silver Fern, Hello Rising Sun*. It would also have meant I would have had no part in the making of what, fired by New Zealand's approach at the 1995 World Cup, should be a revolution in world rugby and the way it is played.

And just as regrettable, I would have been trying to fit 6ft 3in into a 5ft 5in bed in a mini-apartment out of Tokyo.

It is hard to get to know someone who's not talking to you and after the World Cup of 1991 Laurie, the new All Black coach, gave a great imitation of someone who had me filed under A for Auckland and for Avoid (at all costs) or D for Dismiss or Don't touch with a bargepole.

It made for an uneasy relationship even on long-distance telephone when the calls specifically excluded me. After the World Cup and the spirit-restorer which was the wedding in Italy of JK and Fiorella, Robin and I went to our Italian clubs for another exotic season of lasagne, lambrusco, lira and rugby.

You do not play in Italy to improve your rugby. At club level rugby there is without much discipline or plan. But it is a great place to meet old friends who also appreciate the good life laced with some light-hearted and often frustrating rugby.

Soccer is the grand passion of Italians. Because the Italians become so deeply and emotionally involved their passion for soccer is hotter by far than ours for rugby. But the devoted little segment who turn to rugby do it with fervour. A hundred people at a game sound like 50,000. Their boss-idol in rugby is Romero. Hey, Romero! They chant for Romero and Romero puffs out his chest and struts up and down the touchline pleading with the crowd for more and more adulation. The hair-mousse glistens in the sun. The oil on the thigh-muscles sends them wild. Hey! Romero! He is an average rugby player.

Italians are very relaxed about their rugby. Rugby, compared with soccer, just doesn't matter enough to your average Italian. In the minor clubs like mine it is brilliant OE for stressed Kiwis. Here, the Italian players wake and go to work at 9am. They stretch and dream through a three-hour siesta from noon, dress to go out for dinner at 11pm Training? Ahh, si, training. Well, OK. But just a little bit. Dinner is better than training.

Yet there is money behind it and the championship is fiercely fought. And the crowds are so loyal, so fervent, they make you want to do well for them. Why is it that New Zealanders are so reluctant to let their emotions hang loose? New Zealanders need a few, or a lot of, beers in and then they're either incoherent or cantankerous. All the Italians need is the event, the opportunity, and they're away.

I loved my time in Italy. Italy educated me in ways I could never have dreamed of. I saturated myself in antiquity. At home, I'd look at an old farmstead as we drove past and say, "Hey. Gee whizz. Look at that. It must be 100 years old. There, I lost myself in buildings and art works so many centuries old I couldn't count them. I was a kid again. Who walked right here in this little back street 2000 years ago? Who put his foot right here where mine is? I'll bet I'm the only person since some bloody-handed Roman senator in AD100 to put my hand on this exact piece of stone in the Colosseum. I was Puhoi in Rome.

Rob was staying with me in my flat in Rome when the first call came through. "Gidday," I said. "This is Zinzan." The guy at the other end wasn't impressed. "Mmm," he said. "I'd like to talk to Robin Brooke." "That's cool," I said. He talked with Rob and Rob looked disbelieving. He came off the phone and told me it was the new All Black coach, Laurie Mains.

Well, I thought, he didn't even give me the time of day. And nor did he when he rang again and again. Rob was flavour of the month. Zinny didn't exist. He wanted Rob to break his contract with Brescia and get back to New Zealand in time for the trials for the All Blacks to play the World XV and Ireland as part of the

The Sweet Way Kid kicks again. Inset: On the run Italian-style.

New Zealand Rugby Union's centennial celebrations.

Next time I answered the phone I was tempted to say, "Yes, this is Zinzan. You must remember me. You know, beaut old Zinny, the staggeringly brilliant All Black No 8. How are you Laurie? I've been wanting to meet you for a long time. Gee, you coached some great Otago teams, Laurie. I'm keeping pretty fit over here. Looking forward to getting home, though, Laurie. Big season, eh, Laurie?" But I didn't and he asked for Rob and they talked again. Big deal.

I really didn't know him although Auckland had played his Otago teams often enough. The first time I saw him I thought, in my childlike way, "Yes! Thunderbirds! Parker!" He was a dead ringer for Lady Penelope's unsmiling minder. That image stayed with me. When the phone rang I was talking to Parker and when he didn't invite me back for the trials it was Parker being difficult and soon the Laurie inside him would emerge and say he needed me.

Laurie never did come out of Parker. Rob cut his contract short by a couple of weeks and I thought, "Bugger this. I'm going home, too." We went home together, arriving the morning of the first test against the World XV. Laurie, Peter Thorburn and Earle Kirton seemed to have their priorities well and truly sorted out. It seemed to me that Laurie had settled for Arran Pene, his Otago No 8, and Peter for Richard Turner, his North Harbour No 8, which was very neat and tidy but which left very little room at all for Zinzan Brooke, the Auckland No 8.

I smouldered a bit, then tried to look at it realistically. Arran was a driving, straightforward sort of No 8, a close-to-the-ruck-and-maul player of the same breed as Buck, if without Buck's dynamism. Richard Turner was very strong, more mobile than Arran and a hell of a man to stop close to the line. And I came to terms with my situation. It would have been hard to get back in even if Parker had shown any interest in me. Or even if Laurie had.

It meant that I had just two games to try to restore myself at least as a challenger. I had good games for Auckland against Wellington when I scored two tries and then against Ireland when they called me player of the day. But when the numbers went up for the first test against Ireland neither Rob nor I was there. Arran, who had displaced Richard Turner for the second and third matches against the World XV, was the preferred No 8 and the

Arran Pene...the obstacle.

scrum was locked by Blair Larsen and Ian Jones.

What had happened, of course, was that in the clean-out after the World Cup debacle the selectors had not invited Gary Whetton to the trials. It became clear he was filed away under N for Never again, Not wanted at any price. What the selectors were implying publicly was that Gary was not a good enough player to be among eight locks in the trials. Taken at face value that was ridiculous. So what they were really saying was that they did not want Gary Whetton, captain of the World Cup All Blacks, to have any part in the rebuilding process for reasons other than playing ability. If he alone was being made to carry the can for what happened in 1990-91 it was unfair; that could never be leeched home to any individual.

119

Gary was part of the problem and he needed a bollocking just as some of the rest of us did, but to eliminate him without trial was over the top, an insult to someone who had played for New Zealand since 1981. Players deserve to be judged for what they are against the competition of the day, not for what they were at the peak of their powers. The truth was that there was not an adequate replacement lock. Larsen and Mark Cooksley were promising, no more than that, which rams home how inflexibly the selectors had turned against Gary.

Gary did not play outstandingly at the World Cup. He did not play close to what he would consider to be his capacity. But the evidence is that even had he been a substantial figure on the field he would not have been required in 1992. Laurie should have lined Gary up and reminded him what was required. It might have been all that was needed. He would have been left, at least, with the dignity of trial selection and the chance to prove himself again.

I do know that what happened to Gary and what seemed to be happening to me was a sobering experience. I learned later that had Sean Fitzpatrick not persuaded Laurie that there should be a place for me in the team to tour Australia and South Africa my chances of making a full touring team – of ever being an All Black again – were slender. Laurie was not easy to convince.

Fitzy told him I had never been given the freedom to play the same sort of game for the All Blacks that I played for Auckland. I made the touring party, but under sufferance, and was made to believe Laurie didn't really want me in his team – just as Thorburn didn't want Foxy.

Auckland players sensed, rightly or wrongly, that between Mains and Thorburn there wasn't a great deal of respect, let alone admiration, for them. It was as if, because of its record of national championships, South Pacific titles, Ranfurly Shield records and huge representation in New Zealand teams, the province was judged to be a bit above itself. In its way it was some sort of tall-poppy complex.

Yet I concede, too, that Laurie inherited a can of crap from 1991 and, in the best way he could, had to turn it into a bed of roses. In the process there were bound to be casualties. It was the most difficult assignment for any coach in my time in the All Blacks but he received little recognition of that and often was held up to ridicule by people with axes to grind. Only a few days before the 1995 World Cup semi-finals Andy Haden was still subjecting him to judgements which were both sarcastic and subjective. He used the line, "Laurie Mains couldn't lead a silent prayer" when it was becoming clear to most, including international critics, that Mains-coached rugby was creating a sensation.

Laurie changed during the transition period, too, and his vision for New Zealand rugby broadened until we were producing what could be called the total game in the World Cup, the final notwithstanding. He had personality glitches along the way and I know he took aboard some criticism of his public demeanour which was seen to be too grim, too intractable, without humour. He even came to accept that Aucklanders are blokes, too. Maybe he took some time to accept that, in spite of the divisions and rifts of 1990-91, in an All Black team there are no Aucklanders, Wellingtonians, Cantabrians, Otagoites or whatever. Just New Zealanders.

The two Irish tests were won but the tourists were within an ace of pulling off a gigantic upset in the first before going down 24-21. The New Zealand performance was without conviction, ragged, formless.

There were changes for the second which brought Rob into the team for his first cap, locking with Ian Jones. Rob took great satisfaction out of a game won 59-6 and in which the tight five clamped total control on the Irish.

Then Laurie relented to the extent that I was named one of seven loose forwards for the Australia-South Africa tour. I had the feeling I had been pulled in as an extra more as a gesture to Fitzy than to me. When we assembled at the Poenamo Hotel I felt like a stranger among strangers. Laurie did nothing to ease my way. I had been in the All Blacks since 1987 but this was like being in the side for the first time with the added burden of a coach who didn't want to know me.

The squad had been together for five matches and the players were obviously at ease with each other. I wondered why I should feel like surplus baggage. It was back to square one and if Laurie felt I needed the experience of humiliation he could not have done it better. He ignored me. I wasn't expecting to be treated like anything special. Just to be one of the boys would have been great. But, it seemed, Laurie had invented the cone of silence just for me. It was unnerving.

I had just come out of hospital where I had surgery on a leg which had become deeply infected from a minor scratch. I was

Laurie Mains...the silent treatment.

conscious I had lost fitness and needed to do a lot of work. Laurie was a specialist in that, too. I was new to his excruciating 150s, the end-to-end sprints which can be unrefined torture until you learn the tricks of the trade. But my dedication to training didn't open any doors to Laurie's acceptance let alone his heart.

If we met in the corridor he passed me by without a word or a glance. I came to dread meeting him and being ignored yet again as if I didn't exist. It got to the stage where I'd avoid being in the same room. I had to think, "What the hell am I doing here?" Then one day when the players had a bit of a get-together I felt all the old player camaraderie and I told myself, "To hell with this, I'm not going to be made to feel like some inferior dick." And from that time I isolated myself from the negative vibes Laurie was throwing out.

It was as well I did because nothing changed after we started the Australian tour. The atmosphere was just as frigid and I was slotted into the mid-weekers which was about what I expected but which didn't help my temperament much. I knew the dangers of being relegated to the dirt-trackers. Once you're tarred with the mid-week brush it is very hard to get rid of it. Many players never do. I set my mind on breaking the mid-week shackles before they became a habit in Laurie's mind. My competition was not with Arran Pene. It was with Laurie. I did not have to be playing a bit better than Arran. I had to be playing miles better before Laurie would acknowledge it.

Maybe it was a matter of style...what Laurie wanted from a No 8 rather than what Harty or Grizz had wanted. Harty would encourage you to get the basics right then cut loose on the wide-ranging style. It seemed to me that the new panel was more intent on picking up on the Buck style, that it was just another expression of what in those days was Laurie's conservative approach. Maybe he was insecure enough to limit himself deliberately to more restrictive options. Yet even then I think his vision for New Zealand rugby was probably formed, just waiting for its time.

I will always remember Manly, the seaside haven across the harbour from Sydney. Laurie spoke to me for the first time at Manly. Not what you would call an animated conversation. We were preparing for our next game, a night mid-weeker against a Victorian Selection in Melbourne. The players were walking from the hotel to training when Laurie caught up with us and, as he passed, said, "Zinzan, you'll be captain on Wednesday night."

That was it. I didn't say, "No thanks, Laurie, all I want to be is a shearer" or "Thunderbirds are go, Parker". I thought, "Breakthrough, Zinny. Make it stick." So I told the guys what I wanted from them within the scope of Laurie's patterns, called a few moves around myself, we won by about 50, I was into the Saturday team to play Queensland and then took over from Arran for the second and third tests.

Rugby players are boys enough to think back on certain performances and cherish them as being special, whether because they played outstandingly or for any number of reasons which lifted the games out of the ordinary. That second test against Australia was my special challenge. It was my chance to answer Laurie's indifference and it was a doorway back into regular test rugby.

If there was a disappointment it was that while starting at No 8 I moved to the openside of the scrum after seven minutes when Kevin Schuler was injured and Arran came on. I had set myself to play No 8 on that tour, wanted to re-establish that as my position and this was the chance to show Laurie my way of playing No 8 was the way we should be going. Players know when they have played well and they certainly know better than anyone when they have played badly. This was a good game for me, a big-tackling game and at the end of it I felt satisfyingly stuffed. We had lost 19-17 but as a team performance it was a great encouragement.

That was a magnificent series, three great contests with the winning margins one, two and three points, the tries evenly shared 6-6, the first two tests to the Wallabies and the third to the All Blacks. The making of a great series is not necessarily, as many New Zealanders would have it, the All Blacks winning by plenty. Players may be elated coming off the paddock knowing they have won easily by scoring brilliant tries in an open match. Equally, they take deep satisfaction from a contest which is truly a contest, team-on-team, one-on-one – a comprehensive match-up with bruises, scrapes and bloodbins. There is in exhaustion a different sort of elation. It was an old-fashioned test series, hard and uncompromising and for us a sign that all was not lost after 1991.

For a team under reconstruction, emerging from the mire of 1991, the All Blacks were starting to look like a team on the move. Yet at home there was a negativity which was bone-deep. It was apparent to the players that little they did was acceptable unless they were winning – even against a team which a few months before had won the world championship. There was little understanding of how far the Australians had come on, and none that we had been overtaken and now were fighting back.

Much of the resentment at home had little to do with the players. There was an ongoing hate campaign, or ridicule campaign, against Laurie Mains. When I think about that I regret that I, too, made some pretty shallow judgements. It was too easy to slot Laurie as he was then, uncommunicative, into a category below John Hart or Grizz. No account was taken of the massive job he had on his hands following the failure of those two, as a pair, to pull the All Blacks into line and steer them through the 1991 campaign.

The other factor, of course, was the Wallabies. It was not only that they had learned from us in such things as the need for control before cutting loose; they had come to understand that at the roots of our game was physical conditioning. They took from our game what they wanted and they took conditioning to a level

Jason Little and Tim Horan...class act.

even beyond ours until where athletically we were much the same, on a power-weight ratio they were stronger than us. They had become our hardest opponents bearing in mind the absence of South Africa. They had class acts like Tim Horan and Jason Little in midfield, twin generals in Nick Farr-Jones and Michael Lynagh, and they had size, technique and mobility in the forwards. And, of course, mercurial Campo, Forest Gump's box of chocolates – you just don't know what you're gonna get.

The strength of top players like Farr-Jones, Horan and Little was their excellence in all facets of the game, defending, attacking, tactically. And they were able to show they didn't need each other to be great players.

With involuntary help from us the Australians pulled themselves up to the standard where we now have ding-dongs instead of walkovers. That is great for the game. Rugby exists on shaky ground if the biggest satisfaction you take from it is predictable defeats of your opposition. I come back again to "the contest", the sort of tightly-matched series of 1992. It is not just that it is good for the spectators. It is good for the players because it means that mentally as well as physically we are being tested to

125

come up with something to turn games in our favour.

There is a huge sense of achievement now in beating the Wallabies where for old All Blacks it was so often just another day if not another dollar. We are no longer feared by the Wallabies and their win over us at the 1991 World Cup was the expression of that. You could take those Australians position by position and find that in every one there was a very healthy confidence.

Where once the Aussies might have folded, now they don't. We could be confident once that in the last ten or 15 minutes the battle would be ours. Not now. Their attitude of mind changed and they replaced the Springboks as the team we had to beat to be the best. Once their rugby was hubbed on club football with home-and-away interstate and internationals. The difference between club, and even provincial, rugby and internationals is immeasurable. Only the players really understand it.

Queensland this year played Auckland, Tonga, Canterbury, Orange Free State and Transvaal in the Super-10 and that was about it for them. Rugby is there all the time for us, whether Super-10, national championships, Ranfurly Shield, tour matches, trials, tests. It is too much. There has to be space to revitalise, to give you the edge to go back in there with hunger. The Australians have that space. We do not.

We start in February (as this year), go right through the year to the World Cup, Bledisloe Cup and, after completing that intense season of provincial championships, we have a tour of France and Italy. The public expectation is for constant performance at the top level no matter the programme but the mind won't accept that and it will not allow the body to accept it.

Before I ever played against Australia their game was accepted as being more open than ours, brilliant individuals having a freer game and that it had to be to attract support in the face of the massive competition from rugby league. Our game was very structured. Very test match. We played chess on a paddock and traditionally we kept our moves very close to our chest. The players felt they could not afford to lose. Fear of losing can be highly motivating but it can also be dangerously restrictive.

Of all the Australian players, and even considering the great class of the Horans, Littles, Farr-Joneses and Campeses, I always come back to a forward named Simon Poidevin as typifying the breed who brought the country forward so dramatically. He was the last word in commitment, the finished example of the

Simon Poidevin...ultimate Aussie.

requirement not to concede an inch to anyone without leaving your blood on the grass – and that went double for bloody Kiwis.

Laurie and I were still at a distance even at the end of the Australian tour and the beginning of the short tour of South Africa which followed it. South Africa was a personal challenge to Laurie. He had toured as a player in 1976 and had become one of many All Blacks who had suffered defeat there while wondering what the hell had happened to the rule book we played to in New Zealand. To kids back here it seemed we were always getting robbed over there by blind referees all the Springbok players called "uncle".

That might have been over-simplifying it but I know we all felt pretty good about justifying All Black defeats by saying, "Yeah, but they cheated." They were all dirty players (except Morne du Plessis who, as a kid, I reckoned must have been the best footy player ever invented) and they broke Pinetree Meads' arm and they tore off Peter Whiting's ear and they kicked Kevin Eveleigh nearly to death – and he was only a little joker, but he had their big jokers so shit-scared they took him out. Just childish images of relentless giants with blades in their boots, but they stay with you.

They were also all as big as your normal everyday kitchen dresser. And that's about all I knew about the South Africans when we arrived there in 1992. They said our arrival was "the return of the prime foe", or was that "primeval foe"? Whatever, they meant it in the nicest possible way and they turned out in their thousands at 2am to welcome us.

What did we know? We knew about Naas Botha and Danie Gerber and the Cavaliers had talked to me with awe of a "giant" loose forward named Wahl Bartmann. And when we got there Wahl was still king. Wait till you play Wahl Bartmann, Zinny. He will sit on you and you will disappear. Wahl Bartmann is bigger than Table Mountain. Wahl Bartmann is the biggest and the best in the world, man. Wahl Bartmann's UBS…Wahl Bartmann's chest measurement…Wahl Bartmann's virility…Wahl Bartmann's nose-hairs. UBS? Upper body strength, man. I looked at a picture of Wahl. The caption said he was 1.90 metres and 116 kilograms. The same height as me. But 116 kilograms! The man has to be a tanker.

And the rest of the 'Bok forwards. Giants. Everyone said they were giants…"We grow them like barns here, man, bloody barns. Shoulders like barns, chests like barns, arms like barns, hands like barns, legs like barns." We reckoned that made about 80 farm buildings in one pack not counting the feet and I looked at our guys and I thought this had to be the biggest mismatch since the renowned Foxy-Buck bloodfest.

It did not matter to South Africans that a few months previously the Wallabies had won the World Cup. That was a matter of no relevance at all. They saw the All Blacks as the ultimate foe and we were made to feel it everywhere we went. For the All Blacks the fever was catching and we knew that whatever new levels the Wallabies had achieved they had not displaced the Springboks in the New Zealand rugby psyche.

Rugby to South Africans is what soccer is to Italians but somehow more formidable. It is built rock-solid into their souls, immovable. When we played the first game against Natal at King's Park the atmosphere, not the prospect of the opposition, was daunting. It pressed down around our ears and squatted heavily on our shoulders. The hair stood out on the back of my neck. Then the Natal players sprinted out of the dark snorting like bulls and the place erupted. So this was South Africa. No locking this out.

I looked at the Natal players and my eyes were dragged to a mountain. Rudi Visagie. The look of granite. His head was as big as Richard Loe's bum and as he worked his shoulders I swear the wind swirled. So where's Wahl? I found him at lineout time, found myself looking across and down to meet his eyes. Wahl? Can this really be you, Wahl? What are you on? Magic shrinking pills?

At first contact we dominated the Natal forwards, these massive men desperate to do the right thing for their province and for their country. The frenzy of the crowd worked for us, too, and we resolved to take it to them. They kicked a bit deep, we took it in and marched them back. And about Wahl's UBS…in one of the first mauls he was on the move, ball in hand. I ripped it away and we turned them around. Me! A little kid from Ahuroa. When I ran from the scrum he didn't come for me. I felt let down, sort of unfulfilled. The expectation of the massive collision came to nothing.

While we took confidence from that game into the test at Ellis Park there were in Johannesburg other factors to uplift the South Africans but which also encouraged a new sort of inspiration in the All Blacks…I am one of 15 players these 70,000 people and millions who are not here want to see hammered by the pride of South Africa, a Springbok team representing the past, present and future of a game which is the religion of the white nation.

The whole scene made the blood pump. The unbelievable babble, the rigid belief of the South Africans in their superiority made us bristle for the contest, too. And you absorb the truth that you are one of the lucky guys who happens to be around to play in this test match in a country which has been so long in isolation. There had been nothing more exciting in my career and even momentous rugby events which were to come would never replace it.

In the event, the Springboks' hearts and guts were in the right place but they had only the sketchiest ideas of effective defence around rucks and mauls. The problem was with their heads. There was still the old South African belief that size conquers all, whereas we know size only helps if everything else, like technique and mobility, is right. With memories of the freedom I was given to move in close-quarter play at Natal I was able to run the open from inside our 22 and punt deep to turn them around. That indicated the loose grip they had on the modern forward game technically and tactically. That we allowed them back into the game toward the end was more that we had come to the end of our tether in the rarefied air than that they had sussed us.

I know the try I scored in that test is seen to be some sort of quick-thinking masterpiece. But I can't see it that way because I don't know why I did it. We were all aware that while we had the game comfortably in hand we were only 3-0 up with a few minutes to go till halftime. We needed points on the board, not in our heads.

What happened when we were awarded the penalty close to the line was some sort of instinctive throw-back to life on the park at Puhoi. It was a blur. Maybe it was even irresponsible. That didn't occur to me. The Springboks walked back waiting for Foxy to kick the goal, I ran up, grabbed the ball, tapped it and dived over. Real flashy. Had it not come off I'd have been a turkey, Laurie would never have talked to me again and Foxy would have given me a bloody good hiding.

It had happened during the Auckland Shield era that I would back myself against the opposition and against the odds. Against Counties once we were given a Foxy benefit-kick and I ran up, tapped it and dived head-on into a prop's knee. It was a painful experience but I also put the ball across the line. Unlike the match against Hawke's Bay when I tried the same cute little trick and dropped the ball. This voice rocketed out of the grandstand, "You're not in bloody South Africa now, Brooke" and I had to admit he was right.

You have to back yourself, have to take the chances whether it's rugby or life. You can't go through life wishing you'd done something else. That destroys any chance you have of turning it around.

It was after the Ellis Park test that Laurie broke the ice. He made a point of crossing my path in the dressing room and he said, "Thank you, Zinny. That was great. You've proved me wrong and Sean right." It had been a long winter.

Two years later in New Zealand the Springboks had advanced beyond anything I would have expected in selection, athleticism, commitment to the grafting work of the pack, overview of 80 minutes of rugby. They were still not a great side in 1994, not as good as the 1981 team. They lacked polish and the hunger to destroy teams but they were on the way under a fine captain in Francois Pienaar.

And a year after that, having steadily prepared themselves on a feast of international rugby, they went into the World Cup and, match by match, playing with efficiency and economy, they marched into the final, set up by an indomitable defence mentality, and beat us at Ellis Park.

10

Curing The Killers

The All Black build-up to the 1995 World Cup started the day Laurie Mains was first appointed coach. Though there were some pretty rough goat-tracks toward the goal, selection experiments and inconsistencies which frustrated the public and the critics – and sometimes the players – he believed what he was doing would result in a player-pool from which he could select two teams to play the sort of sublime rugby he had dancing around in his head.

He said once that during his tenure as selector and coach he wanted to develop 30 or 40 players who could play test match rugby. There were times when that intent backfired to the extent that there were so many players, so many changes unforced by injury, so many switches of judgement that combinations became sketchy and what should have become an instinctive understanding between players could not develop.

But in the face of savage criticism following the 1994 series loss to France and the drawn third test against the Springboks he persisted with experiment. Even in 1995 Laurie pursued his own course when I, among others, thought we were dicing with time when only three or four weeks before we left for the World Cup we had apparently not settled on key positions and combinations.

With such a short time to go before the main event we had players thinking, "My god, how did Lee Stensness miss out on another trial? Who's the first-five going to be? What about the crowd of loosies? Who am I going to play alongside? The first-five doesn't know who the second-five's going to be. Who's the third prop – Craig Dowd or Richard Loe?" Doubt creeps into the minds of the players.

Do you pick Michael Jones when he won't play in critical games? Well, we've got Josh Kronfeld but he's new to this level of rugby, Mike Brewer, who has had a bad run with injuries over recent seasons, Paul Henderson back in the fold when it seemed he was gone forever, Arran Pene's around and what about Jamie Joseph and Blair Larsen…and me? All this army of guys fighting for places three weeks before the World Cup.

And the backs. Jon Preston is out. No he's not, he's in. Are you sure? I was, but now he's out again. I think. Walter Little's injured and Stensness doesn't quite know where he stands. And Jeff Wilson's on one wing. What about the other? Marc Ellis, Waisake Sotutu, Eric Rush; hey, what about that awesome kid Jonah? Fullback? Shane Howarth? Glen Osborne?

Are we the only ones who haven't got it all settled? What about the French, the unpredictables? They know. The Poms know and the Aussies know. Yet on the evidence of the Cup campaign who could now say Laurie was wrong? Critics looked for bolt-holes as the All Blacks hit the world headlines with the style of rugby Laurie had sketched then hardened in his mind long ago.

When we speak of "the campaign" I'm sure that to Laurie the campaign was not just half a dozen games in South Africa. The campaign was alive and working when he picked his first team to play the World XV in 1992. And it was still alive and working when, having re-established myself as the All Black No 8, I let myself down – and maybe Laurie, too – when I hid an injury going into the British Isles tests of 1993.

I was a bloody fool, and a selfish fool, too. I placed my career at risk and played sub-standard rugby in the first two tests against the Lions before being dropped for the third. At the time I believed I could not afford to let go. There was a fear that if I gave up my position I might never see it again and I had been through that sort of trauma once already. What happened, of course, was that by playing I opened up the way for Arran Pene to return and put myself into some sort of limbo.

The trouble with sciatic nerve damage is that it knocks you about both physically and mentally. It was excruciating first thing in the mornings. I lay there not knowing which leg to move or which way to turn to ease my way out of bed. Throughout the day it nagged and nagged and at night it kept booting me awake. I would go to training and try to hide it. But I couldn't bend properly to hit rucks and mauls or tackle-bags. I couldn't keep up in the 150s because I was favouring the leg. But no one picked me up on it. In a way, it would have been a relief if they had, yet I couldn't bring myself to confess the injury and stand down. I cut my own throat.

If rats played rugby the first two tests against the Lions could fairly be called ratshit. Likewise bulls. It wasn't much fun being part of them, knowing that in the first you wanted to do Fitzy's 50th test proud but being unable to play with the sharpness the occasion demanded, and then losing the second deservedly for reasons which were not unlike the bad, but winning, performance in the first. I couldn't jump and I couldn't push in the scrum off my left leg. We planned for what we knew would be inspired negativity from the Lions but we actually exaggerated the effectiveness of their strategy by committing unforced errors and the Lions, in fact, were much more inclined to run the ball at us than we had anticipated. We were so uptight about those games. We played like a team on a knife-edge instead of one with the confidence the performances against Australia and South Africa the previous season should have brought.

We won the first 20-18 and lost the second 20-7. As steps along the way toward 1995 they were more a stumble. Our approach to the first two tests was basic and simple: to confront the Lions' forwards and by superior technique and commitment outmuscle them for possession. In the event we did not have the firepower to do it.

The Lions complained long that they were harshly dealt with by the referee in the first test. It was as if they had taken a crash-course in advanced whingeing from the experts, their media. They might have considered that had they won the game it would have been on the back of a melodramatic Gavin Hastings dive which, from an unobservant referee, brought a penalty for a late charge. The Brits will talk forever about Andy Haden's notorious dive from the lineout in the match against Wales in 1978 but Gavin's was just as comical, just as cynical, and escaped media attention, not even a tut-tut let alone a bellow of outrage that the game was being taken over by twisters and cheats.

I was driving across the Auckland Harbour Bridge on my way to have treatment for the sciatic problem when the car radio told me I was out of the third test. I had anticipated it to some extent but even while you accept there is cause, you harbour hopes and make up reasons why it may not happen. Maybe you weren't too bad in that second test. You know, Laurie, weigh up the good against the bad and maybe, just by a whisker, I did enough? No? So it's Arran again? It is? This could be a long, cold winter. And next winter, too?

Watching from the reserves bench at Eden Park while the All Blacks comprehensively beat the Lions 30-13, with Arran a great force driving for advantage, I knew my future might be in house renovation. The All Blacks had yet to play the Wallabies at Carisbrook and the Western Samoans at Eden Park before touring Scotland and England.

The No 8 jersey was Arran's for the next five tests and although I was to wear Michael Jones' number against Scotland and England I put down my future prospects as uncertain. So much so that, while not actually learning Japanese, I did quite conscientiously try to accept sushi as a viable alternative to medium-rare porterhouse and seaweed as a puha substitute. It was in 1993, while playing golf with Joe Stanley, who was by then well settled in the Japanese rugby scene, that the yen-option to the All Black substitute's bench seemed to make a lot of sense.

Had New Zealand lost the series to the Lions it would have been as devastating a blow to rugby as to the players and to Laurie. The All Blacks were in the process of restoring the game as a spectacle of movement based on all-round 15-man skill. It was a one-way street. The Lions seemed intent on screwing the game, suffocating the broad attacking opportunities which had made Lions teams of old the most scintillating in world rugby. It had become popular and convenient for the Brits to pin labels on the All Blacks, designating them as the grim reapers of rugby, the win-at-all-costs merchants. Now, with the boot so obviously on the other foot, the Lions' approach was hailed by their media.

It was not until the World Cup when, moved by the impact of the New Zealand game, the British pressgang hoed in to the stodge the English called rugby and held up the All Blacks as the example of the way the game had to go. In a way that was as great a victory for New Zealand rugby as any we achieved on the field because very often in the past the foe who fought dirtiest was the press. After the World Cup Stephen Jones wrote in the *Sunday Times* of London that the All Blacks had reached heights no other team had achieved. Terry O'Connor, the realist who now writes for the *Sunday Express,* wrote of "an All Black team who have

134

produced some magical rugby" and asked, "When will England learn?" And, perhaps most astonishingly of all considering the time he had to inject some beauty into English rugby, the former England coach Geoff Cooke said England could learn from the All Blacks' style.

It will take a lot more of the same to make the All Blacks who toured Scotland and England in 1993 forget or forgive the cynical hate-campaign the English journalists waged on them as a team. It was contrived. It was over the top. It was, in the tabloids, a competition as to which could paint the most lurid picture of Evil versus Good.

I am convinced that part of it was a hangover from 1991 rather than the realities of 1993. The arrogant image we projected in 1991 came back to haunt us. Maybe part of our problem with the media was that we had beaten the Lions. I am told that during the third test at Eden Park one English journalist, with a record of erratic behaviour, leaped to his feet screaming "Kiwi bastards!" It was the same guy who before the tour had written a story designed without conscience to inflame British opinion against New Zealand and New Zealanders. A screwball piece of journalism.

Whatever the cause, the media set out to have a feast and when the pickings were lean they concocted their own dog-tucker. And when the South-West Division centre Philip de Glanville emerged from under a ruck with a severe eye injury it was banquet time. The journalists went crazy for blood. De Glanville's face had certainly been opened up by sprigs, but deliberately? Television did not show that and you could play the video a million times and it would not show it. But who needs evidence when you have the opportunity to indulge your spleen and your imagination all in one go?

The *Sunday Observer* dug deep and called in Colin Welland, who wrote the script for *Chariots of Fire*, and he churned out an hysterical tirade of such exaggeration, such haughty bigotry that it became high melodrama, very funny – and very badly written.

Those of us whose memories were less selective could still see Frank Bunce's ear hanging by a shred after he had been dealt to by Dean Richards' boots at the bottom of a ruck when the British Isles played North Harbour. No question here of intent or accident. No doubt about a culprit. No remorse or apology from the British management. They celebrated the occasion by

Dean Richards…searching boots.

appointing Richards captain for the next game. And the British media found it so distasteful they could hardly bring themselves to mention it. And was it not the English who, with the boot, started the violence which infected their match against France in the 1991 World Cup? And didn't Ben Clarke jump on a South African with God knows what intent? On none of these occasions did the *Sunday Observer* hire Colin Welland for a handsome fee to ham it up with condemnation of "dark and uncivilised behaviour".

Welland's bizarre piece about us appeared the week after we were beaten by England and two after we had demolished Scotland 51-15 in a match in which rucking was a superb vehicle for clean possession by both sides. It let fresh air into the game after rugby had suffered so much from the English compulsion at all levels to kill the ball – and if that meant killing the game then to hell with the game.

For all that, England beat us squarely, 15-9. They kicked their goals and we did not, but that was not the whole story. We could not, or maybe it was just *did* not, play the match with vitality a week after the Scottish test. Touring rugby is hard enough but when in a tour of 13 matches the two tests are laced into the agenda on successive Saturdays someone has been at work who either doesn't understand or doesn't care about the demands on the players. Had we played all our Scottish matches and then the Scotland test as a segment and then the English matches and the test as another it would have made sense. Quite apart from those things, in the couple of days before the game we were not test-focused in the deliberate hard-minded way we needed to be for Twickenham and which we should have been almost as of habit.

Our golden boy, Jeff Wilson, left Twickenham hurting. He had had a dream debut against Scotland, a smashing game for three tries and a touch line conversion. Against England he was weighed down with what would have been a difficult job for a much more experienced goalkicker. You always play your first international on adrenalin, get caught up in it emotionally. There is nothing you cannot do. The ones that follow are the hard ones and this one was especially so because where the Scottish defence had been fluid England's was rock-solid. Different patterns, new adjustments, new pressures. After the loss you pick yourself up, absorb the lesson and get on with it. Just as Jeff did.

Where Jeff scored a hat-trick against Scotland Marc Ellis, playing at first five-eighths, scored two. Marc's versatility could be his worst enemy. He has played test matches from first-five to wing. He thrives on rugby and is such a gifted player but is he to have the utility label slapped on him and have an erratic career as a spare-parts man? When he went to Otago from Wellington it was as an outstanding schoolboy first five-eighths. I begin to wonder whether his is not a great talent wasted.

Having scored seven tries against Scotland, against England we could score none. Tactically, we were astray and we should have changed the approach during the match. We used runners off the rucks and they had three or four lazy buggers standing off to shut down the ball. They played a screen defence to shut us down. The heart of the England game was in their determined tackling and we gave them every opportunity to do that.

Our image, already tarnished by over-eager and uninformed criticism, was done no good when Jamie Joseph stamped on the ankle of the England halfback, Kyran Bracken. It spilled fuel on the dying embers of the de Glanville affair, the media were all lit up again and Will Carling had the opportunity to brand us a dirty team, which he took without hesitation.

Jeff Wilson...left Twickenham hurting.

We had our own internal problems, too, when Mike Brewer was called into the reserves for the England test. Mike was not in the touring party and had played only three first-class games for Canterbury that season. He was in England on a business trip. His call-up meant that tour players like Liam Barry and John Mitchell were put aside and for Barry especially it was a terrible blow. In his position I would have been out of my skull with anger and disappointment. It was said that Liam had been taken on the tour for the experience and that Mike offered reserve options Liam could not. That should never have been a consideration. Liam was on tour as an All Black, just as Mitchell was. He had worked his butt off, slogging away at training all tour and he deserved better.

I have the greatest admiration for Mike as a player and a man. But this was wrong. He should not have been placed in a position of acceptance or rejection. Had he turned it down the knowledge that he had even been approached would have created dissidence in the team and would certainly have alienated Liam Barry. Laurie reacted tersely to criticism of his decision but he was wrong and I doubt whether, given the same circumstances, he would make the same decision again.

The designated No 8s for the tour were Pene and Mitchell which meant that I had travelled the road very quickly between first-choice and no-choice but I understood and accepted the reason. Having taken over after my sub-par performances against the Lions and having seen through the successful Bledisloe Cup match Arran was a natural and John was the ideal selection to bring maturity to mid-week leadership. He had great respect among the players and his rugby for Waikato had been consistently effective.

As it was, my form against both Scotland and England from the open flank was my best by far for the whole year and I felt on top of my rugby for the first time since the 1992 Australia series and the Johannesburg test.

Then we were torched again for playing the traditional Barbarians match as if it were a test rather than a celebration. We played the game to win because we needed that after Twickenham. The Barbarians played it the same way but that was seen to be acceptable.

It would be a liar who denied that give-and-take exists in most test matches, though it has become fashionable for England to

Brian Moore…compulsive mouth.

claim purity, probably because it plays in white. The players know
the score and when a mouth like Brian Moore claims after matches
that this happened and that happened and that Fitzy taunted
Victor Ubogu racially it is incredibly funny to the players because
Moore is known to a whole world of players as a compulsive
troublemaker on the field. Moore might even remember the
formal reception after the England test. All the players were in
their number ones, wives and girlfriends present and everyone
being very civil. Everyone except Ubogu. He had annoyed us
with a newspaper article he'd written earlier in the tour claiming
the All Blacks had deliberately taken down a five metre scrum
against England South West. Ubogu called us chickens in his

column, saying the local side – of which he was a part – would certainly have dealt to the All Black scrum and scored a pushover try. Anyway, he was right in his element that night, telling all who would listen that his chicken remark had indeed come home to roost.

There have been episodes of mindless violence in rugby since the game began and they are not dictated by nationality. We have to answer for Richard Loe's elbow on Paul Carozza's nose and the gouging of Greg Cooper's eyes. We do not have to answer for the slicing of Phil de Glanville's eye though in the event we apologised that it had happened. The teams of all countries are responsible for incidents they have to live with, incidents which may be bitterly regretted.

All its self-righteous bullshit aside, England has much to answer for. Its adherence to practices which turn the game into a turgid indulgence for a handful of players and a bloody bore for the rest has created a mind-set which may take years to loosen up. It was a revelation to hear Rob Andrew say during the World Cup that there were some top players in England who would welcome the acceptance there of hard rucking to discourage the deliberate killing of the ball which is the killing of the game as a spectacle.

It is that very practice which is at the root of much of the condemnation of All Black rucking in England. It is based on ignorance of rucking techniques and on blind acceptance that the killing of the ball is an acceptable technique to deny quick possession. We were simply not allowed to ruck for the ball in 1993. British – and especially English – teams have no real interest in presenting rugby as a game to excite. For all the lip-service paid to the traditions of the free-flowing game, rugby there is being systematically suffocated as other countries are reawakening to all the game's wonderful possibilities.

One of the most amusing pieces to come out of the English press was that which, during the 1991 World Cup, argued that the All Blacks had no care for the game, that we set out by any means to smother it as a spectacle. Assuming the writer knew something about rugby – a fragile assumption – this had to be a dangerous pretence aimed at bending the minds of his audience. What Rob Andrew said in South Africa exposes it as ludicrously biased nonsense. When the press sets itself up in this way as some sort of home-team propagandist to ram home a fiction it destroys itself.

Jeremy Guscott...wasted brilliance.

It is important to place the self-serving English "abhorrence" of rucking into the context of the way the English have been playing the game and continued to play it in the World Cup – by shovelling it into a wet sack with a bunch of big forwards and a kicking stand-off while players of high skill like Jeremy Guscott and Carling and the Underwoods idly break the icicles off their fingers and toes and try to stay interested in the unlikely event that someone will pass the ball to them.

Their rugby has searched back to the New Zealand rugby of the '50s to find the best possible way of winning without scoring tries, when the touch line was king and you kicked the ball out as a habit because backlines stood up so flat that death by halitosis was an ever-present threat. You won by 9-6 and it was a magnificent game not because 30 players had had a hand in it but because you had won a test match. If you lost 6-9 in the same circumstances it was a shit of a game.

So English rugby has delved back 40 years to find its character not from the great Lions team of the time but from their more conservative opponents. Without being too precious about it I would say that in the same time New Zealand rugby has advanced with the times and the times demand a spectacle as well as a win.

The laws have allowed the positive side, hard on attack, to be deprived of possession and the negative side to gain the put-in so it can kick the ball anywhere as long as it lands deep. Ball is killed because it is safe to kill it. As an occasional captain during a tour my attitude has been to encourage hard, legitimate rucking on the grounds that, once rucked, a player deliberately killing the ball will be bloody reluctant to kill it again. I think of the England loose forward Neil Back, a hell of a player in that tearaway mould, but a designated ball-killer.

The trouble with northern hemisphere referees is that they kow-tow to the culprits and penalise the player who puts the sole of his boot on the body to separate man and ball. So the ball and the game are killed by bludgers who know they are safe to do it. That is exactly what Rob Andrew was saying. It may seem to be support from an unlikely source but I embrace it because it could be the beginning of some sort of revolution in English thinking.

Our second-phase ball from the ruck was the greatest ball you could have but there has been an orchestrated campaign to outlaw it while, in effect, condoning ball-killing. New Zealanders have killed ball, too. Of course they have, but not as robots programmed to kill everything and turn the game into a showpiece for zombies.

It does not stop with killing the ball. It takes only half the forwards to hold up the maul advance. The off-shoot is to have the other half hanging around as part of the defensive screen so that when the referee calls "free it" and the ball is released the game is smothered by the defensive scavengers.

There is no incentive to drive it up the middle for the release to the backs and the classical one-on-one attack and defence, the cut and thrust the British, so I have read, used to be so good at. When you have a couple of flankers, a lock and a prop seeded through the defensive backline, cluttering up the space, the game is reduced to an irritating stop-start procession. If it takes a law to commit the game's spoilers to a limited work space then let's have one.

The detection of violence (not to be confused with aggression) with its attendant video-judgements, allocation of blame and disciplinary hearings has bounded ahead in New Zealand. There has been a significant move to eliminate violence or, at least, to identify and punish elements in rugby which damage the game's image and throw out the wrong message to parents and kids. Most players understand the need to present the game as a good and safe one for young people to play. There are habitual trouble-makers who make the game suffer and there are a few rare players, the loose cannons, who should not be in the game.

I know it is overdone to say that in a game of such constant physical contact there will be incidents of confrontation and retaliation – and even of getting the retaliation in before the confrontation. Yet, for all that, it is true.

Many of the players in the national championship final between Auckland and North Harbour last year were taken aback by the general uproar which followed it. Television viewers watched what was described as an outrage, a blot on the game. The spectacle was condemned from one end of the country to the other and when you get that universal feedback you need to accept that what people saw dismayed them. For the players there were a number of flare-ups in a game in which there was more animosity than in most and in which two were ordered off. But they were unprepared for the flood of criticism which followed it.

It was a game pre-ordained to be "difficult". I need to take some responsibility for its fiery opening. The North Harbour publicity for the game was all-out gung-ho. Auckland was lambasted on radio and through banner displays. One huge banner on the Auckland side of the Harbour Bridge proclaimed something like, "Nike…these boots were made for walking and this week they're going to walk all over Auckland…" The Harbour captain, Richard Turner, pumped it up on radio. We were shown a menu for the celebration that was to follow. It was headed North Harbour, 1994 National Championship Winners. To that extent the North Harbour boys were the architects of Auckland's motivation.

The Auckland players were pretty edgy about it. There's a healthy rivalry there at any time but here it was high tension stuff, Harbour having beaten us for the first time in 10 bridge battles in a thrilling 35-31 match not long before. As Auckland captain I used Harbour's self-praise mercilessly. Before the game I played on the Auckland boys emotionally and in language they understood. I told them we had suffered all the North Harbour pre-match bullshit without retaliation. We would take our retaliation where it meant something. I called Harbour a bunch of imposters and something very much worse, too… "Now get out there and kill them…"

"Getting out there" meant Onewa Domain, a nondescript little ground with a 13,000 capacity – and this was the national championship final! Across the bridge 15 minutes away was Eden Park where North Harbour had already beaten us. Some administrators have this vision for rugby which begins at the eyes and ends at the nose. In this case the decision-makers thought long and hard and scored a fat zero for logic and a minus-10 for imagination.

When I told the guys to get out there and kill them I didn't really have in mind the act of personal extermination. I have to say if some of the players took my suggestion literally I don't know that I blame them. I blame myself. It was bristling stuff and, really, not our style at all but they were so wound up it couldn't be contained. Up to the eyeballs with fired-up patriotism brother Rob got to an early maul in a hell of a rush and mowed down our old mate Eric Rush in the process. Rushy, it seemed, was unlucky because Frank Bunce ducked.

I was involved, too. In the first few moments of the game Blair Larsen came around a maul and shoved into it from the side. I pushed my elbow at him without evil intent. But Blair was well stoked up, too, and took offence. Then Ian Jones was having a bit of a go at one of our guys on the ground and I gave him a nudge with my knee and said something like, "Come on, Jonesy, piss off." Video charged me with grievous assault. The really big whack of the day came from Rushy on the back of my head. It was a beauty and after I'd had a good cry and wiped my eyes with the ref's handkerchief, I thought, "That's not the Rushy I know and love" and watched him disappearing for an early shower. I reckon he was still in orbit from Rob's first charge.

Rob and Rushy didn't exactly shower together but Rob got the best of the hot water, too, sent off for what we said was rucking and what they said was stomping. They won.

I had the feeling at the judicial hearing into my case that it was just a shade pompous. The three "judges" were down one end of the table and I felt like a criminal in the dock at the other. Maybe that's the system working to make you conscious that "this sort of behaviour will not be tolerated". So, fair enough, I guess. They gave me a week in the cold for both incidents which was about

Eric Rush…needed for the sevens.

what I expected. But I couldn't believe that for the king-hit of the day and a sending-off Rushy got only two weeks. With no malice toward him, I couldn't accept that measure of leniency compared with my own sentence. And I was incredulous when a member of the panel said that, while I might think my sentence was harsh compared with Eric's, they had taken into account that New Zealand needed Eric for the Hong Kong Sevens. Oh, I said, is *that* the way the system works?

Rob got four weeks and, with his lawyer, flew down to Wellington to appeal the severity of it. Before there were any submissions he was told he should understand that by the nature of the appeal system everything would be reconsidered and at the end of it he could find his punishment increased and that was the risk he took. Rob was shaken because he had not been advised of that possibility and he let the panel know fairly strongly that it had wasted his time, his lawyer's time and its own time by not explaining that element of the appeal system before he went to Wellington. He withdrew the appeal.

We both felt there was a need for less courtroom formality in the hearings and that this could be done without lessening the dignity of the court while making "the accused" feel more at ease.

11

Instinct And Cunning Bastardry

I don't take easily to losing. I don't actually fly into a tantrum and I can give the crowd a glad-hand and I can shake hands with the opposition. But if you look closely you will notice I am not actually smiling. I take loss very personally. I hated losing to the French in 1994, though I was on the reserves bench for the first test. I was actually off the paddock when they scored that impossible, exhilarating, brilliant, terrible try to win the second, though I couldn't have done anything about it had I been on. I didn't like drawing the final test with the Springboks and I hated like hell losing to the Wallabies in Sydney after we gifted them the first spell then swamped them with movement at high pace and with intense support-running in the second.

The most urgent emotion has nothing to do with whether a loss was deserved or undeserved, whether we blew it or whether they did us like a dinner. It is the fact of loss which kicks me in the guts. A loss is a blow to the pride. A loss is marked down in black type beside your name in the family Bible. A loss is a hell of a waste of time and effort. And a loss means I personally haven't paid my dues to New Zealand rugby.

When I say I hate losing it doesn't mean I have taken no enjoyment from the game. Losing may be the consequence of a badly-played game or a well-played game. It does not detract from the enjoyment in the effort of striving to win. An international player once said he had taken no enjoyment from playing test matches during a long international career. Had that been said by an English threequarter I could accept it. But this player said test rugby was an agonising grind without reward, the performance of a duty without promotion. He said matches were exhausting, painful experiences at the end of exhausting, painful training and that if anyone could honestly say he enjoyed battering away at another maul or watching the descending soles of someone else's boots at the bottom of a ruck he had to be some sort of masochist. So that's what I am. I take a lot of pleasure from playing tests. I take no enjoyment from the training until the day I find it coming easily and then there is deep satisfaction in knowing I'm fit.

The result, the win…that's paydirt. That's getting the big bucks after a week's shearing. That's having the family buy a new car with the cash you earned by the sweat of your brow. The guy who said there was no enjoyment in playing test rugby still played. He's the masochist. It's the nature of rugby that if you give everything you're going to hurt and the hurt can go on and on. I couldn't imagine anything more exhausting and painful than the triathlon. Run 42 kilometres, cycle 200, swim five. But triathlon competitors keep on competing. If there is no satisfaction in hurting so you can achieve, the goal is worth nothing. The 80 minutes of every test, the passes given and received, the tackles made, every giant mental heave you give yourself as exhaustion creeps up on adrenalin-rush and threatens to overtake it …all are part of it. I may hate losing at the end of it but that's irrelevant. Winning is a bonus.

Having said all that I have to add that had we won the World Cup I would have looked back on the losses of 1994, and the loss to England in 1993, too, as being just about worthwhile. I could have rationalised those games as being steps along the way to the big one, part of the development curve to the World Cup when all would be revealed and justified at Ellis Park in June 1995.

The World Cup has become all-important. One closes, the next opens with the first touch of the ball in the new season. The target is four years away, players will be four years older but the campaign plan is planted and at its roots is the style to be perfected and polished over four years. Losses along the way, infuriating or humiliating at the time, are expunged from the public mind if you emerge at the other end of the tunnel with a gold cup in your hands.

Taken to the extreme that is a shaky platform for rugby in a country as mad about it as ours. Youngsters need role models who win with style, not lose with the excuse that it was an experiment along the way to the World Cup in three years. But there was not a player in the World Cup squad who even now would say that if losing those matches enhanced our chances of winning the cup the price was cheap. The birth of the tri-series with Australia and South Africa next year will settle that sort of hash, anyway. The stakes in national prestige will be too high to approach any of the matches as anything less than a World Cup final.

The All Blacks and their coach learned a lot about themselves in the process of wins and losses between 1992 and 1995 and it was through those lessons that they took to South Africa the style – and the confidence to play it – which became the talk of the tournament. We played some good rugby, at times some great rugby, during the losses to France and Australia but I'm glad I didn't have to convince even a bunch of kindergarten kids that the first test against France in Christchurch was a constructive step in the World Cup build-up.

The guys let themselves down. There was no purpose to it, no commitment to placing the French under pressure. It was playing by numbers and the French thought all their Bastille Days had come at once. They were unimpeded by any New Zealand desire, or even the spark of an idea, to turn the game around as they plundered on to a 22-3 win. When we speak of humiliation in a loss that is what we mean, a round stuffing with never the hint of mounting a challenge to prevent it. I'm not into the business of criticising an All Black performance unless I happen to be part of it, but watching this one I was disbelieving.

It is the international perception of French rugby that it is unpredictable and undisciplined. That is the first trap. French rugby is very soundly based on their understanding of what a forward pack is there for and on where the most effective running from set play should be directed – the wider the better. The unpredictability is put down as both their strength and their weakness. I suggest that their unpredictability coming off a beating by Canada to a massive performance against the All Blacks was thoroughly predictable. Anyone who thought the French gave more than a passing "c'est la vie" to the match in Canada doesn't know the French. The French target was New Zealand. If, by

149

Philippe Benetton and Laurent Cabannes, part of the great back row, celebrate after France's first test victory, Lancaster Park, 1994.

happily contributing to a "shock loss" to Canada en route they could prepare the way to take the All Blacks, they would do it laughing.

For all that, no team is so likely to go from a sublime performance on a Saturday to an almost comically inept game on a Wednesday than the French. That is not unpredictability. That is their special sort of madness. And it does tend to set up the next Saturday opponent. The French at home are different from the French on tour. The so-called "regional selections" they turn loose on touring teams are sky-high on passion and patriotism, numbingly physical and often harder to contain than the test team. They are in there to die if need be and if on the way to dying they can decapitate a few of us that is very patriotic.

So how do you plan to beat the French? Getting them pissed the night before is an appealing way to start. But short of that, to beat them you have to play with precision. You must cut back their space, shrivel their option-time. You must achieve better than parity immediately in the close exchanges, not give them the germ of an idea that they have superiority anywhere because they thrive on that. But, above all, cutting back their space is crucial.

Grappling with Abdelatif Benazzi, a magnificent player, second test, Eden Park, 1994.

In the second test at Eden Park the All Blacks were transformed from the ghosts of the first. We had 70 per cent of possession, 70 per cent of territory but we lost the game in the last seconds and no team other than the French could have done that. No other team except, and only perhaps, one from Heaven coached by God could have produced the try which won the game. Our failure was that for a split second, by an error of judgement, we gave them space. The idea was right, the direction was right but from the time Stephen Bachop took that ounce of weight off his kick the French sniffed the opportunity. But for an error by the All Blacks the world would never have seen one of the greatest of all rugby tries. Shouldn't we have been given a few points for that?

We had talked about this scenario, about bringing the defensive lines up and shutting the gate if we gave the French that feeling of space with the ball in defence. When the kick goes long and the French get back in numbers both our defensive lines come up…a bit like rugby league. There is no way they should get through. So, you can look for the kick back in return. It is the strategy whoever we're playing, but especially for the French.

So, Bach under-weights his kick, the loosies come up, the backs

151

come up and the tighties come in behind. Impregnable. Impregnable to the English, to the Scots, to the South Africans, to the Aussies. But to the French? No way. Just as they have the fatalism to lose to any team in the world so they have the instinct to beat any team in the world and here instinct took over. Saint-Andre gathered inside the 22, scooted, linked with Gonzalez who was held up but freed the ball...Deylaud, Benazzi, N'Tamack, a brilliant direction-switch by Cabannes, Delaigue, Accoceberry, Sadourny, try. I watched it all from the injury bench and when they got beyond halfway I thought, my god, they're going to score here. Then I put my head in my hands as the crowd went raving mad.

The great players in every sport are those with the instinct for the game, for the opportunity, for where to be. Great rugby players are not great just because they are trained to be good. They are players without rigid mind-sets, who instinctively see beyond the obvious. There are effective pattern-players but the players who take the extra yard by instinct are the great ones. Where more French players than most seem to have the instinct they tend also to let themselves down by a casual acceptance that, ho-hum, they don't really feel up to playing today. There is pattern to this, too, for too often they fail through inefficiency at the tight-five or through a flyhalf who thinks today is not a good day for thinking.

When I look at a loose forward trio of the sort they had at Eden Park I see a beautifully balanced three, Philippe Benetton, Laurent Cabannes, Abdelatif Benazzi – Buck, AJ Whetton and Jonesy a la France. Given a tight-five who decide today is a work day no three in the Five Nations championship could match them. Those three can roam wide, get their hands to the ball, run with it, sidestep. Cabannes has the skill and the instinct, the killer instinct.

The French are so contrary. No other country so graphically illustrates that rugby is a game for all men. They have these wispy, floating backs who can tackle like men twice their size. They specialise in merciless front rows with noses all over their faces, scar tissue hanging off their scar tissue and ears like cheese scones. So hard, but not so hard that they should ever have tried to dirty-trick Stevie McDowell in 1990. I am surprised that after Steve dealt so effectively and openly with France's most decorated troublemaker, Laurent Seigne, the French didn't give him a nonexistent but very high-salaried job, put a false moustache and a beret on him, call him Pierre and slide him into their test team. Steve would have been a starter for that.

The great days of the French are memorable. I will always come back to the France-Australia semi-final of the 1987 World Cup in Sydney as the greatest test I have seen. It had everything: fluent movement, crunching tackling, brilliant advances and desperate retreats. And the result hinged on a last-minute movement of exactly the same brilliance as that which won the game for the French at Eden Park in 1994. At 24-24 and from deep inside their territory, France latched on to an Australian error...Sella, Blanco, Lagisquet, Lorieux, Champ, Ondarts, Rodriguez, Charvet, Berbizier, a mad ballooning pass which by sheer chance found Lagisquet, Rodriguez, Blanco, try.

The Australians made their tackles but the French constantly freed the pass. Sheer magic, which could never in a million years be matched in any other sport. It was a magnificent demonstration of what rugby can be when two teams take advantage of all the opportunities the game gives to the brave and the bold. Watching it, I wanted to be playing in that game. I wanted to have some part in what was the most compelling expression of the sort of game rugby can be.

I have seen, and played in, tight games of rugby which can be enthralling for the nature of the contest but for the sort of entertainment the game must now give the crowds and the television viewers if it is to stand up to the developing challenge of rugby league and justify its own massive sponsorship, there has to be an awareness of total rugby, the game as it was devised for the full exploitation of 15 players.

New Zealanders were so overwhelmed by the French try at Eden Park in 1994 that it buffered the awful impact of another test loss. All over town, and in every town, talk was not of sacking anyone – an incredible event following a losing test – but of the unworldly brilliance of the French try. There seemed to be as much elation as if the All Blacks had won and that says a lot for the New Zealand rugby public which can become extremely miserable and very vindictive after a test loss.

It had been a match which, until I left the field only a minute or two before The Try, had brought me a lot of personal satisfaction. It was a big-tackling, hard-driving game for me, something I had to have to justify my selection and to consolidate

153

my drive for the No 8 jersey. One of the critics wrote after it that there was no way the New Zealand Rugby Union could allow me to "defect" to Japan before the 1995 World Cup. Word was out, of course, that I was counting yen in my sleep.

At its rugby administrative level Japan, through Shiggy Kono, is a vigorous and rigorous defender of amateurism. So it is some quaint anomaly that the same country, through its major corporations, has become more and more a feared raider of our players. I have been told the corporations feel bound to pay their imports for work, work-education and increasing corporate input as well as attracting them to play rugby.

After the final New Zealand trial at Napier, less than three weeks before that second test against France, Ali and Japan Air Lines spirited me out of New Zealand for a meeting with Nippon Steel. Graeme Bachop and I had been rooming together at the trial. We had talked the Japan option through and its attractions were obvious. It was at a trial dinner that Laurie pulled me aside and said, "Zinny, you're not thinking of going to Japan are you?" Japan! Me? Hell no, Laurie. I couldn't look him in the eye. I was uncomfortable, embarrassed and lying through my teeth. I didn't want to do that but secrecy seemed paramount. While I had a stronger regard for him then I still had to wonder whether I had a future as an All Black. I was unsettled and, even after the tour of South Africa, had felt constricted, as if I was playing strait-jacket rugby.

The next morning Ali and I were at Auckland airport. I had my collar up and my cap pulled down over my eyes and I felt like a dork. Ali checked the luggage through while I shrank back in the car like someone in a bad Maxwell Smart episode. First-class flight and a glass of champagne settled my stomach till we landed at Fiji where there was a telephone call for me. I didn't take it. Unbridled fear.

Negotiations with Nippon were cordial. I had been in the All Blacks for quite a while and I had been made very aware that to the Japanese experienced All Blacks were a very attractive commodity. They were relaxed about my bargaining power and seemed more comfortable with me pushing the price up than I was. I couldn't speak the language so I sat there writing down figures and raising my eyebrows. The original contract was worth $US75,000 for the first year. We agreed finally on $US90,000 rising to $US110,000 for the second and third years plus accommodation, car and business-class flights home twice a year.

Accommodation would be an apartment about the size of a decent hotel suite. They would renovate it to my requirements up to $US20,000 and this would cater for my acute dislike of banging my head on the top of the doorframes. I would be working in international corporate relations, a field in which I, as a Mahurangi College dropout, was vastly experienced.

We lived for a week in a replica apartment. For me it was claustrophobic and, speaking no Japanese, I felt cut off. It meant doubt was intruding, but not so seriously that I felt compelled to call the whole thing off. To an extent I felt caught up in how far the arrangement had gone on. Not trapped in it, but obligated to it. They were so enthusiastic, so excited about having their own All Black. Ali and I had a dinner with the Nippon Steel team. They treated us like royalty. As we left they formed an archway and chanted my name and that seemed to be the ball-game. I rang Marty from the airport and told him we were coming to live.

It never happened, of course. By the time I had played the second test against the Springboks, playing maybe the first test in which I felt uninhibited by what I had felt were constraints and restrictions, the movement to keep me in New Zealand was growing. But it was in the belief I would be going to Japan that I played that Athletic Park test as I had wanted always to play my rugby. I was the Puhoi kid all over again, drop-kicking for goal – once when it was really on and once when I was marginally optimistic – kicking for territory, kicking to space, tackling, driving, running. I was my sort of No. 8, a free spirit but eager to do the work as well.

About those drop-kicks: I took the first because time was running out in the first spell and we were only five in front. That could have been eight with a penalty but because we had exposed the Springbok scrum for a pushover try earlier, Fitzy opted for another and Olo Brown was penalised for boring. It was a dumb ruling, as many scrum penalties are. The scrum didn't go down because Olo was boring. It went down because Guy Kebble, big but soft as butter, couldn't hold it up. Then the referee said next time out was halftime. I was out on the touchline and decided that if it came to me I'd have a droppy. It didn't miss by much. The second was hardly a flash of genius. I was about 40 metres out and should have run it up.

This was also one of the best of test matches. It had the

155

Horizontal Guy Kebble...couldn't hold the scrum up.

Johan le Roux...otic starvation.

character of classic All Black-South Africa tests, different by far from the flowing magic that was the France-Australia match of 1987. This was a stirring contest between one side desperate to establish itself as an All Black team of the best quality and another desperate to rediscover the steel of the old Springboks and take it onward to the World Cup in their own land. The 13-9 scoreline showed that test rugby does not need to be a ten tries to seven tries spectacular to be a standout. Of course, flavour was added to it by Johan le Roux's unusual appetite for ears; one writer put it down to a rare disorder called "otic starvation" and Fitzy was a handy source of food without which Johan would have succumbed.

It was after that match that the All Black Club and Sky came up with the package deal I signed and which led to an apology to Nippon Steel who were, understandably, not amused. The warmth of their welcome to Ali and me and their willingness to talk turkey on salary and conditions made us very uncomfortable about not going. There was a threat of court action. Ali and I wrote a letter trying to explain the position but I did feel I had let them down. I sweet-talked about repaying the air fares and the whole thing simmered down. While deeply regretting the circumstances of the time neither Ali nor I have regrets that we stayed in New Zealand.

The strongest pull for me to stay was Laurie Mains' broadening vision, his willingness to let not only me, but others, use the reserves of initiative and, to some extent, the adventure we had in us, his pushing of the pace at which we had to play the game and which became a great strength of the All Blacks. I felt that through these things I had more to offer the All Blacks.

If there was a trigger-point which rammed home to all of us the pace we needed to be playing at it was the 1994 Bledisloe Cup match at Sydney. At halftime we looked at a scoreline of 17-6 to the Aussies. It was the reflection of two segments of rugby which betrayed misjudgement or ineptitude – or a bit of both – by us and not helped by a couple of bits of misjudgement by the referee, Ed Morrison of England. But it also was a reflection of an Australian team confident of its world champion status and boosted into a playing superiority for most of the first spell by a fundamental error by us which led to a try 17 seconds after kick-off.

Most writers said we lost the game in that 17th second when Jason Little scored his try. I say we lost the game in the first three seconds when we dropped the Australian kick-off. It was a bad kick, too deep for the Australian forwards to place pressure on it and ours for the taking, to pull in and control. We had practised under kick-offs all week but Mark Cooksley went up in the air, the ball wasn't where he aimed himself and he scored a clean miss; lack of confidence on the big occasion. You may think it an over-simplification to say that had Robin Brooke been playing, with the authority and precision he brings to that area of play, we would have won the match. But I say it, anyway.

The result was Australian possession and a David Knox hoist to our goal-line. Deja vu. Black, black deja vu...the Pat Howard hoist to our line at Carisbrook the previous year, John Timu earthbound under it, Tim Horan soaring into the stratosphere without a jet-pack and falling to earth with the ball and the try. Now it was Shane Howarth earthbound, John Timu standing off with God knows what awful memories sprinting through his head, Jason Little climbing up all over Shane for the clean take and the try. The Aussies were laughing. In the grandstand Bob Dwyer was laughing. Hitting the Kiwis with the same bomb twice in succession? Yair. Worth a go. Give it a burl. Kiwis can't fly. So they did – and, incidentally, just as they had done it to the Springboks in 1992. Creatures of habit? No. Cunning bastards.

Then they scored again from a scrum which should have been ours after Campo knocked-on when pressuring another Knox bomb. From it, the Aussie loosies set up Phil Kearns who was awarded a try when he nearly got to the line. But did we complain? We sure did. The fact is that at halftime the Wallabies were up 17-6 and deserved to be. It wasn't that we were soft in the first spell. We didn't get ourselves into the game positionally. Having conceded those early points we should have punched the corners and set ourselves up. Where was Foxy when we needed him? Playing the game in his head, every move, every kick, giving the halfback the message, jabbering behind his hand at the second-five, as involved from an armchair as he would have been out there in the heat of the kitchen.

At halftime there was no debate. Who's tired here? Who's buggered? No one. Should we go back and outmuscle them? No way. Let's get out there and out-run them. And that's what we did. We ran them off their feet, forced uncertainty, forced holes. Michael Jones was clear for a try – if my pass hadn't been forward. Shane Howarth scored a cracker after sustained pressure and a Bunce switch from left to right.

George Gregan's tackle on Jeff Wilson over the tryline a couple of minutes from time has been recorded as the game's match-saving sensation. So it was, but Gregan made other tackles which, in the morale-raising sense, were a huge influence on the Australian performance. His tackles on Richard Loe and Mark Cooksley, the little guy crunching the big guys, were the stuff which lifts tired forwards, inspires renewed effort. Loey is a terrible man to run upright. He must be the easiest man in New Zealand rugby to tackle, soft as a cream-sponge, because he just won't put his body into the low-slung, behind-the-shoulder

George Gregan...took scalps of Loe, Cooksley, Wilson. Inset: Grim Bob
Dwyer...but laughing in the stand.

driving position. There he is, a huge scrummager, a monster mauler, but with the ball in hand he runs straight at you at his full height and falls down like a short totara.

After that match we knew, all of us, that the pace we had played in that second spell was the pace we had to make our own and the intensity of the support-running had to be the pitch we hit all the time. It was not that we had any immediate understanding of how fast the game had gone in that 40 minutes. But when we listened to people talking about it and watched it on replay we realised how frantic it had been. Yet after it all we were ready to go another 40 and that was a tribute to Laurie's single-minded concentration on a fitness regimen beyond anything we had ever experienced.

In one televised review of the game, one of those talking-heads programmes when the mouths do all the talking and all the thinking, too, one of those inactive experts for whom nothing is ever good enough discarded the second-half performance as skittery stuff, lacking direction and control, just mad-headed desperation. It was the sort of closed-mind comment we had come to expect from those more concerned with giving the knife a twist into Mains than with giving him and the team just a modicum of credit.

I have one especially bitter personal memory of 1994. After the National Championship match against Canterbury at Eden Park David Kirk, who was then an advisor to the Prime Minister, came to me shaking his head. He said, "Zinny, Zinny, you're doing a very stupid thing." What the hell was he on about? He told me the strong word was around at Parliament that I was making frequent visits to Wellington to use cocaine. I was staggered and doubly angry because Kirky seemed to believe it. I said to him, "Take me now and give me a blood test. Take me down there and let me front up to whoever is saying this. Let's get this bloody thing sorted out."

I went to Rob Fisher, the Auckland Rugby Union chairman and a lawyer. He couldn't believe it. And I left it in his hands. Three All Blacks, including myself, were given drug tests on the Tuesday before the second Springbok test in Wellington. Really, it was a pre-arranged cover for me. The tests were clear.

To this day I have not got to the bottom of it. I have never used drugs. It is just outside my philosophy of life. It's just not the way of the Brooke family.

12

Tests And Tortures

What the people see from the grandstands is not always what they get. They see two teams of international players running out on to the ground. They open their mouths and they roar. They are roaring in anticipation of a great All Black win and preferably in a great test match – unless they happen to be crowds in Australia, South Africa, France or Britain when they roar for all the wrong reasons. They see the players who should give them these things because they are international players and that's what they are there for. When they get neither an All Black win nor a great test they become very disgruntled.

When New Zealanders saw the All Blacks lose the World Cup final at Ellis Park they reacted against the flow. They were sad rather than disgruntled and they gave us a magnificent welcome home and told us they were proud of what we had achieved playing rugby with style. More than a week after we came home I was in a hotel dining room in Wellington and a man came over with his daughter, a table napkin and a pen. They wanted my autograph. I apologised we hadn't won the cup for them. He said, "Do you know, it didn't seem to matter that much because by then you were winners in every armchair theatre in New Zealand for the way you played the game."

In their own disappointment, the players have been surprised that this is the general reaction here. I have this uncomfortable feeling of being flattered, that I don't deserve this, yet the sincerity of the people who have come up to me is overwhelming as was the warmth of the welcome in Auckland and at the parliamentary reception in Wellington.

It has been a revelation to the players. They know now there is a swell of support for them because, while losing in the final, they brought New Zealanders weeks of rugby which entertained them and they are conscious that the people in "the armchair theatres" cared more about their winning style than the loss of the final. The players will never accept that the first outweighs the second but the support has certainly softened the blow.

Traditionally in New Zealand the players have always known that the crowds who demand victory from them have no feeling for what has to be done to prepare for the moment when we run out on to the ground. Crowds acknowledge the day. They have no knowledge, nor do they want it, of the week before the day nor the months before that when players have gone through the stresses and strains of getting themselves right for the big day so the crowd can praise them for a two-point win or condemn them for a two-point loss. What they look like when they run out is what they are: fit and, hopefully, invincible. How they got that way is no concern of the people who watch.

In fact, the players have been thinking of nothing else but this game all week. From the moment I am named I start thinking about the opposition. What's this guy all about? What does he do as an individual? My opposite number is going to be Tim Gavin so I pull out the mental file marked Gavin T. So he's a rangy, raw-boned farmer from out in the sticks. He gets a tick for that. He's quite slow off the deck at the base of the scrum. He doesn't take it up too much. He likes setting it up, bringing his other loosies in to run off him. He's a good lineout jumper near the back and he jumps better off his right than his left. He can't kick. He can't drop goals. I thought all No 8s could do that. He's an elbows-and-knees Todd Blackadder type who needs to get wound up a bit. He's a very committed, consistent sort of player, a top international.

If it's Troy Coker I know he's a bit vulnerable at the back of the lineout. He doesn't like going backward on the long throws. I reckon he's better suited to jumping at two. He likes his ball thrown up to him at the peak of his jump, coming forward, and if you get him at the moment of contact with the ball he can be taken back. One good hit on him and he'll think before taking you on again. Built like Gavin but not as hard-nosed.

So it's to be Dean Richards. Oh hell. He's going to get in the bloody way and he's going to muck up good ball. He doesn't

Troy Coker and I embrace affectionately.

care about his body and it shows. He'll take everything that's coming and some more. He's an openside loosie's nightmare because when he's not mooching around in front of them with his elbows out and his body in the way, he's rolling at them with everything working and there's a lot of him to work. He's a strong bugger, hard to take to ground. He's the model of the loosie who prays every Friday night for a heavy ground to bring the pace of the game down to one he's comfortable with. He's a loiterer with intent, getting in the way of the halfback, blocking vision to the first-five. For complete and utter nuisance value I don't know a better one.

Dean-o, Dean-o, Dean-o…they chant his name like a religious rite. They love his image. So un-rugger. The shapeless kid from the wrong side of the tracks, with his socks around his boots and his white legs indecently exposed and his jersey out, beetle-browed and angry-looking with his lot in life. Deano is great at what he does.

But who will I give more thought to than most? Abdelatif Benazzi, whether they play him on the blind or at No 8. A hard, hard man and big. As an all-round loosie he is magnificent because to match his size he has the skills and the working heart. He runs powerfully and he likes making big hits. Number one priority for me is to get in with the cruncher first because if he gets the feeling of physical dominance he can run a game.

So having sorted out my mind I go through the chores. Assuming the test is at Eden Park I have to get to the Poenamo Hotel on the North Shore. I have to pack my bags. I hate this. I hate it because I'm so disorganised about it and I always leave it till the last minute. But I can sleep-in anyway because it's a home test. I can stretch and think about breakfast and I know that while I'm crunching toast and marmalade the Christchurch and Dunedin guys are in a mad panic because the alarm didn't go off and it's a long drive to the airport.

While I'm brilliantly catching my third slice of toast from the pop-up, down on the farm Richard Loe is checking his hair parting, choosing the lapel-flower for the day and fretting because he's left time short to pat his Massey Ferguson and promise he'll be home Sunday.

Late morning, having showered slowly, I pack. Packing is shovelling everything I own into a soft bag…shorts, socks, jersey, toilet bag, number ones, underwear, jeans, boots, mouthguard, strapping, extra after-match cologne for Loey…and off to the Poe for lunch. Who am I rooming with? All I know is that it won't be Fitzy because, being skipper, he gets a room of his own, his only visible badge of office. Loey's arrived and I make the mistake I always make. I ask him how the sheep are and he tells me sheep-by-sheep, name by name, with not a few tears for the ones that have gone to someone's Sunday oven, the story about his heroic rescue of the one that fell down a bottomless abyss, the one that answers the phone when he's out in the blizzards and by the way did I tell you about the cows? No? Well, there's Molly, Daisy, Mandy and…

Richard Loe…getting focused.

Over lunch we rarely talk about footy and when we do it's wildly parochial about our clubs and provinces. You're just settling on which of the smells coming out of the kitchen you're going to eat, rare and with chips and eggs, when you forget it and have a banana and an apple because you're told it's running shoes only for training. That means today isn't actually training, it's torture and torture is better on a banana and an apple that on steak, eggs and chips.

Laurie is a torture specialist. Down-and-ups are not the pleasurable down-and-ups fit

Graham Purvis…the abominable slowman.

young men might delight in. They are torture down-and-ups. There are also 150s, which have become the Mains trademark-torture. You run dead-ball to dead-ball, sprinting one way, jogging back, not once but 24 times – say 24 150s three times a week. I have mentioned my introduction to 150s when I was recovering from a poisoned leg. It was all bad. I had lost weight, vitality and now my lunch. That day, after we had done 50 down-and-ups, I thought training was over. Then we did 20 150s. I clearly remember that renowned speedster and prop Graham Purvis beating me in four or five of them. It was all bad. Purvy! Purvy was always last. All Purvy did was one pace; jog and sprint were the same. Everyone knew when Purvy was behind them because he had this raspy air-ejection system. I heard it getting closer and I thought, "Please God, don't let Purvy pass me. Not Purvy. Please!" And when he passed me I started thinking very seriously about my relationship with God and my future as an All Black.

After that, we split into forwards and backs, go through our drills and come together as a team. At night there is probably a function where you mix and mingle for a couple of hours before going back to the pub to worry about Purvy beating you in the 150s tomorrow.

There's a team meeting in the morning then a bit of a walk to get the blood moving before breakfast, training, lunch, on to the table for a slap and some scientifically-applied pain. There may be some school visits or rugby on video, dinner.

Forty-eight hours to go. Now you get the feeling in your belly. I ask myself, "Zinny, are you ready? Ready for a game right now? Is your body right? Is your mind right?" I search myself and all the answers are "no". The test match is won before the game. That's what I keep telling myself. And I roll over in my mind the means of coping with their loosies. I always imagine myself making big tackles. Thursday is a private training day, maybe at Whenuapai air base. It's getting tenser and maybe today there's a tendency to make mistakes.

Tension has been known to flow over at training, like in the Whenuapai run before the Scottish test of 1990. We pull in players from outside to fill up a scrum against the test pack. Here we had Ron Williams, Gavin Walsh, the New Zealand Colts captain and a hard man who should have gone places, Warren Gatland, Sam Poching, Andy Earl, Peter Fatialofa, the Brooke bros. And what did we do? We screwed the test pack and this was not accepted with any humour at all. The more we had them going the scratchier it got. It was old bull v young bull stuff, test bull v dirt-tracker bull. Andy Earl said something like, "Come on you guys. Pull your fingers out and hook in" and it became explosive. We had a rare old punch-up and a few beers afterward over a few wary looks.

There was the training at Cardiff in 1989 before the Wales test. The scrum went down with Ron Williams binding on to the side Andy Earl was policing. Ron's arm came round to grip and whacked Andy on the way. That was a good scrap for a minute or two.

Andy Earl..."pull your fingers out and hook in."

Friday is butterfly day. I look at Loey and his eyebrows are down, a straight bar across his nose. I know he's getting focused. We go to Eden Park and go through the calls. I want to keep my own company. I lie on my back on the grass and think about tomorrow. I listen to the quiet. This time tomorrow there will be 12,000 people chattering and three hours later 45,000 roaring. On another part of the ground some of the boys are chatting and I hear it as a murmur. The grass is bruised and smells sharply. I can hear the birds in the trees over on the back

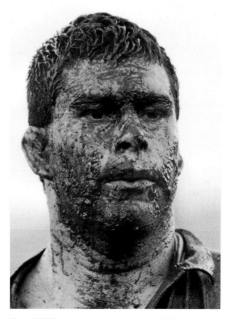

Ron Williams...loose arm trouble.

167

Kieran Crowley...bought his dairy herd with my money.

ground. It's a drowsy, absent sort of sensation. I think how lucky I am. And I'm a kid at Puhoi and I'm thinking the All Blacks turn up, put their boots on and play a game of footy just like me. Oh yeah, kid. The groundsman starts up the tractor and it smashes through the quiet. Dreaming over.

Back at the Poe we just browse. Fitzy calls the skipper's meeting. He talks quietly from the heart, Fitzy. It's not how much you say or how much you dwell on past glories and what the country expects. It's what is pertinent to this game and to these players. It's pushing the right button on each individual. We get our 300 bucks and play euchre till 10. What a bloody shark John Timu was. And Joe Stanley. And Kieran Crowley bought his dairy herd with what he won from us. When he takes visitors around the farm he points them out. "That's Gary Whetton's cow, that's Bruiser's cow, that pretty one is Loey's cow, these are Zinny's ten cows…" I was never much good at it, 3-card loo, show poker, guts, euchre. All blind optimism and loud regrets.

Lights out. I sleep well. I like to be up and about early on match day. The hardest time of the week is the period between waking and match-time. Time drags. I wish the match was at 10am like it used to be at Puhoi. When I first played big football I never ate before a game. I thought the more I ate the more I had to carry around. Before some of those early games for Auckland I wouldn't eat breakfast or lunch and I was dog-tired with 20 minutes to go. I thought there was something wrong with me. It wasn't till the dietitians got through to me that I understood I had to eat to keep the body fuelled up for 80 hard minutes.

That's in the past. Match morning now is a big breakfast morning, a few lineouts on the ground over the road, watch the kids playing their age-group games. You keep walking because you know if you stop parents will ask you to talk to the kids for a while and they won't understand when you say, "Any other day but today." The main thing is the kids know you're there.

Back to the room, check boots, laces, mouthguard. Pack up. Laurie's team meeting. The last words. Something to get the blood pumping. He might pin some to the wall with a look and a few well-chosen words. He might twist the knife to focus Buncey's mind on the requirement to make every tackle stick and hurt. He might cajole some, appeal to others, hammer the props with the message that if they don't function the scrum won't function. Loey's eyes are marbles.

In the bus what is there to do but doze along the way? Closer to the ground people clamour to see. Little kids wave and look for a flicker of response. I never got to big games as a kid. I knew about the All Blacks but their next match couldn't hold a candle to our own. Anyway, there was too much else to do. Country kids were happy doing what they were doing. I knew about Sid Going and Bryan Williams but the big clamorous rugby world out there beyond Ahuroa and Puhoi might as well have been on the moon.

At the ground I am still locked up into myself. I don't much like going out on to the ground to put my thumb into the pitch or throw grass into the air. I get into my gear quickly and strap my ankles. That takes 10 or 15 minutes. I got into the habit of strapping my own when we were in Italy and the physios were pretty rough. In the dressing room I might kick or pass a ball with Fitzy then hop out on to the number two ground and try to find my second wind because it's bloody frustrating looking for it after the game has started.

I drink a lot of water; jog around the dressing room in

169

sandshoes. Some guys will go through a fitness thing to raise a bead or two of sweat – a bit of mauling, running through grid pieces. Ten minutes before start time I put my boots and makeup on, make sure the eyeliner and lipstick are a fair match and then, it's showtime. Now I am absolutely focused. The mind is an arrow. There is no room for random tumbling thoughts about the game. Too late. The plot is three-dimensional: preparation physical, preparation mental and play knowing the other two have been covered.

The ref blows his whistle out in the corridor. Time for another pee. Another pee! That's six. Where does it all come from? How can the referee pull a trigger and make me go again? And if he blew his whistle twice I'd go twice. Refs have a lot to answer for.

I'm on the move. The adrenalin's rushing. I hear that hollow scraping sound of sprigs on concrete and I'm bristling. There's a massive roar as Fitzy hits the sunlight. Then I'm out there with grass under my feet. It's the time I was dreaming about as I lay on my back smelling grass right here 27 hours ago. All I see is arms. A million arms waving, some with flags on the end. All I hear is the one-voice buzz of 45,000 people. I shut everything else out. I don't want to hear some moron calling me a wanker for kicking the ball. I'm so highly strung out here that I'm likely to run off the paddock and do an Eric Cantona. I can't make those mindless idiots out. Vegetables with voices. I'm here, they're out there. I came in free, they paid. There's got to be a good reason for that.

I'm restless during the national anthem. Why don't they make up their minds what sort of song it is, anyway, and sing it like that. Haka time. I look at the opposition. Who's it going to be? You or me? I sort out my opposite number and do the haka at him. This is not a commercial, brother. This is the real thing. It's ritual and I believe in it. It's too often done. When we're on tour it should be reserved for tests only. But I believe in it. And then the test's on and you do what you have to do and you kick in a few bits of your own.

And here's a try for the All Blacks. Who is it? My god, it's Loey, over at the bottom of a heaving, sweating tonnage of hairy flesh. Loey looks funny when he smiles. It doesn't look right under iron-bar brows. He shrugs off someone who wants to hug him. Fitzy smiles! That's not on. Rob just about smiles. Loey looks slightly embarrassed when Kamo smacks him admiringly on the bum. Come on, we're all blokes here, aren't we? I mean real blokes. Leave the kissin' and huggin' to the league boys, the Poms and the Aussies.

So we're pretty laid-back about tries. But it doesn't mean we don't take great satisfaction from them and especially when they are the result of a planned move. I think of Olo Brown's try against Canada this year, perfectly planned, perfectly executed, his first try in 18 tests, and with a bit of a hip-swerve to show props are more than just pretty faces. Thousands of people look down from the stands, watch a try being scored and think no further than the fact of the ball being pressed behind the line. What has gone into creating the try escapes them. If they did appreciate its beginning and its middle, its end would be much more exciting for them.

More planning goes into the construction of tryscoring opportunities than people on the fringes of the game can envisage. They do not realise that for all the set pieces there's a call. How many, for instance, understood that the World Cup try Josh Kronfeld scored against England – that magnificent try which started in our 22 – came from a called move? We backed ourselves to run the ball from a position in which any other team, with the possible exception of France, would have booted it to hell. From the time Rob delivered the ball and Bachop missed Mehrtens most people believed the purpose was to clear with the kick. We were never going to do that. Little donkey-licked Guscott, Osborne pulled smoothly clear to Catt and gave it back to Little and he found Osborne again before Kronfeld drove on for the try. The origin of it was the firm decision to run the ball out from inside the 22 as a segment of the game plan.

Moves are called to manipulate the defence, to create uncertainty so that holes appear where they would not normally be. When a planned move comes off perfectly it is a leaping excitement for the players whether they show it or not. It is what they have practised for, what they have "walked through" to perfect. It is high-speed, dynamic chess on legs. It used to be said that no team needed more than a couple of moves. Not these days. It is not just that the game has changed. Teams are now playing each other much more often and with the familiarity that brings move-variations are many and more complicated.

The "Varsity" move which brought me a try against Canada in the 1991 World Cup is a fair illustration. Graeme Bachop picks up the ball from a scrum on the left side of the field, runs from the base straight across the field, cuts with Bernie McCahill, the

171

second five-eighths, who drags in the opposing first-five which creates a hole just inside their second-five. With the ball Bernie has popped up to me I can prop off the right foot and take that gap. There is a real cute variation on that...Bachop on the cut with Little, Little pulling the first-five into the tackle, me cutting deeper, pulling the second-five to make the tackle and popping the ball to Bunce who started wide out. Bunce, of course, scores. Is that simple or am I going too fast?

One of the positive things which may come from our 1995 World Cup rugby and the continuation of it as the New Zealand style is that it could restore spectator-excitement in the test match. Tests have become commonplace and that has created a ho-hum spectator, especially in Auckland where spectators became so used to years of Ranfurly Shield tenure that familiarity with top rugby bred contempt and winning or losing was never sufficiently in doubt to create excitement. The habit of not getting too excited about anything is still there.

It is not till you get down to Carisbrook among Earle Kirton's scarfie mates that you get the feeling of, and for, old-fashioned test match excitement. They've been on the turps all Friday night and Saturday morning, get along to the footy and yahoo their way through the game as if they're actually enjoying it and want the All Blacks to win because we're their jokers. Shouldn't they be brought into line and told a rugby test is far too serious for enjoyment?

And the scarfies are experts, too. They let the ref know what bad habit he has that makes him blind. The scarfies know more about refereeing than Dave Bishop knows about med school, that's for sure. Who is the ref, anyway, and what do the players want from him? Perfection? Just about; at least someone who can control the game while understanding the players. Pedantry has wrecked more rugby tests than knock-ons and professional fouls. Is he going to let us ruck a bit? We don't want free licence to maim, just the freedom to use a legitimate technique to free the ball from the compulsive cheats who will be less compulsive next time. Aw, come on ref, give us a fair go. What about advantage? What about some consistency here?

And we don't like referees who whistle on guesswork. There's the obvious one about penalising an attacking scrum for boring and collapsing. If he's looking for an early moment to stamp his authority on the game let him do it somewhere else, like where he has every excuse in the world, at the first lineout on halfway. And what about reffing on guesswork…remember Athletic Park, second test against the Springboks, 1994? It wasn't actually reffing, it was touch-judging on guesswork. Clearly from inside the 22 Stephen Bachop finds a good touch to relieve our line. Running touch is the Australian ref Wayne Erickson and from away up the line he guesses that Bachop was outside the 22. Bad, bad guesswork, Wayne. The sort of guesswork that can cost a team a test match.

The players want referees who use the laws to enhance the game. Roulette-wheel refereeing denies the players and the crowds a fair deal.

Come to think of it, though, I feel sorry for refs. They've been handed a bucket of the same stuff Laurie Mains was handed in 1992. How can they possibly referee the lineout? Someone has called the lineout a minefield of restrictive laws. Of all the criticisms which may be made of rugby the one that sticks is of the amount of time the lineouts take out of a game, the way they call an abrupt halt to a flowing game. The ball is kicked out. The forwards get up for the lineout. The ref tells them to take the metre between lines. The forwards shuffle aside reluctantly. Fitzy wants the call. He gets it relayed by Bruiser from the back of the lineout through Grimm Bachop, the halfback. Fitzy tries to do the sums but is distracted by the crowd so asks for the call again. Then he walks over to Grimm to make sure he's got it right. The designated jumper is Jonesy. How does he want it? He signals Grimm with his fingers and Grimm signals Fitzy with his fingers. Oops, Fitzy's forgotten the call. It's that bloody crowd. By now the forwards are shoulder-to-shoulder and glaring at each other. The ref calls for the metre, doesn't get it and walks down the middle of the lineout looking very pissed-off…

I don't go along with those who want the lineout deleted. It is a distinctive part of rugby and, at its best, a wonderful athletic spectacle. But something has to be done to simplify it, to quicken up the process. Former All Black and All Black coach Ivan Vodanovich says sensible protection or wedging should be allowed inside the centre-line, encouraging clean two-handed takes and eliminating slapped-back ball. John Hart says just get the ball in and as long as it's straight and there's no foul play get on with it.

I say, whatever you do, do it quickly. But fix it.

13

Shield Loss, Rugby Gain

Auckland lost the Ranfurly Shield under my captaincy in 1993 and it was a good thing for rugby. During 61 successful defences since its first in 1985 Auckland had dominated provincial rugby in New Zealand, and dominated it to the extent that by 1993 not only the rest of New Zealand but Auckland was getting bored by the long procession. If Auckland still held the Ranfurly Shield the trophy would be a dead duck. Two more seasons would have killed it. By now we would have been up to 70 or 80 defences and the motivation would have been compelling to make that 100. It would have been a deadly century for New Zealand rugby.

When Waikato lifted the Shield from us it was as if a great weight had been lifted from the shoulders of rugby. Waikato went wild, Canterbury and Otago cheered, North Harbour shouted "Yes!" and in every other union in the country there was a sense of relief, as if at long, long last there was a chance for everyone. When it changed hands again, from Waikato to Canterbury, it was final: the gap between Auckland and the rest had closed, inter-provincial rugby had become a whole new ball game with any one of the top half-dozen capable of beating any other. In a bizarre twist, by losing the Shield Auckland had won back credibility for provincial rugby.

Not least of those expressing relief was the public of Auckland, to whom the trophy had ceased to matter. It was as if the same star was collecting the Oscar and making the same speech year after year – the sort of inevitability which kills anticipation of the event.

Anticipation of great rugby occasions is often more rewarding than the actual occasion. It is the building-up of excitement which creates the atmosphere on the day. But Aucklanders had lost that long since. The vibes to the players from those who religiously, if not passionately, attended Eden Park were that habit had a hell of a lot to do with it. I have said earlier that it is because Auckland is the widely-flung province it is that, as a patriotic entity, it falls far below Otago and Canterbury, Waikato or, now, North Harbour.

Auckland seems to have no identity, no collective pride. Boot-parties in the car park is Auckland's way of doing things, not getting painted-up or so excited in anticipation as to make a Ranfurly Shield match a ripper of a party. During Canterbury's great Ranfurly Shield era their crowds never went stale on it. Every Saturday Lancaster Park was a heaving, restless, screaming arena. The magic was always there. It has something to do with provincial bonding. In a place like Canterbury it didn't matter whether they were office-workers, carpenters, plumbers, burglars, bankrupts, lawyers or the sons of the sons of the sons of wealthy squatters. Cavalry twill and tweeds went in there yelling with jeans and jerseys. As a people they were Cantabrians through and through. They were Grizz nutters, Craig Creen nutters, Jock Hobbs nutters, Dale Atkins nutters, Vic Simpson, Robbie Deans, Wayne Smith…and red-and-black to the core. The further the Shield tenure went the stronger the belief in the team. One-eyed but wonderful.

We had our nucleus of loyal supporters, sun or rain, but when, for the umpteenth time, Auckland went in to defend the Shield against Waikato it was to the deafening clamour of cowbells. All of Waikato came to Auckland with all of their cows and a few they rustled-up on the way. We were on our ground but their supporters made it sound like Rugby Park, Hamilton. Aucklanders became so used to winning, even so used to seeing what was probably the greatest provincial team of all time, that they became spoiled by it. As the wheel turned and some of the players packed it in there was bound to come a reckoning. In the end we sensed plenty of Auckland people came along hoping to see Auckland lose. That would never have happened in Canterbury had they held the Shield till the year 2020.

Aucklanders were watching their team, laden with All Blacks, every week and when that happens the wonderment of All Blacks becomes much less. Our parents had it good, really. To them a

175

rugby test was a huge event in their lives because it was a rarity; watching All Blacks was a privilege. You have only to read what the tests against the 1956 Springboks and the 1959 Lions meant to New Zealanders to understand that now one of the magical ingredients of rugby, the test's rare and special place, has gone…"I was on the bank at Eden Park the day Peter Jones scored that try against the Boks." For as long as I can remember old jokers have been saying that to me at after-match functions. When the old jokers have gone will the next generation be saying, "I was watching when Zinzan Brooke scored that try against South Africa at Ellis Park in 1992"? They won't. They'll be saying, "Of the 110 test matches I have watched on television which one was it when that Maori joker scored that try against the Springboks?" The test has become commonplace. Switch on the telly, put your feet up, pour a single malt and compare it unfavourably with all the tests you saw last year or the year before. Exactly the same thing happened to Aucklanders and the Ranfurly Shield. All Blacks? They saw a whole bundle of them every week. Familiarity bred boredom.

The importance of the Shield has not diminished for me. Having captained the team that lost it, I wanted to captain the team that won it back.

Auckland has been the linchpin of my rugby career. It gave me the base, the encouragement and, without going over the top about it, the inspiration to play rugby as I wanted to play it. Team plans and patterns were in place but there was always the space for a player to express his individuality. As Fitzy told Laurie Mains, he would get my best rugby from me by giving me the rein Auckland gave me. It may be some sort of proof of this that in 46 Ranfurly Shield matches I scored 43 tries and up till the end of the 1994 season had scored 83 tries in 115 matches for Auckland. It is the opportunity, the confidence to take the chance and the colossal factor of having a team like Auckland's around me that results in that sort of statistic.

There was criticism of Auckland toward the end of its run that it was playing not as well as it could but as well as it had to. My view is that there was a gradual loss of the professionalism which had carried us through the '80s as a team which took error-free rugby to a new level. Then we got to a stage where error in training was, if not acceptable, just something which would happen from time to time. That attitude became built-in. It must have been a huge bonus for the rugby writers when we were seen to be vulnerable because for years they had been searching for something new to say about a team which was playing reprint rugby week after week. Later, as measures were taken to ensure player-freshness in big seasons, players were rotated to bring match experience to the full squad and performances were less consistent, but still sufficient for the purpose.

It was a persistent criticism that in the two or three years before they handed over to Graham Henry, Maurice Trapp and Bryan Williams were taken

Maurice Trapp...astute fine-tuner.

over as coaches by the senior players. It was a matter of philosophy. Here they had a team trucking along and they needed only to pull us over from time to time and talk patterns for different opponents. They were fine-tuners, not barking loudmouths. Maurice was a very astute coach, very awake to any drift in attitude.

In 1989 we were to play Wellington at Athletic Park and a Wellington reporter set out to pinpoint what he saw as developing chinks in the Auckland armour – Inga's static defence, a tendency for tight forwards to desert the hard work in favour of the wide open spaces, Fitzy drifting off the pack too often, Gary Whetton falling off his peak. That sort of stuff. The boys were very fired up about it and even more so when Maurice took the story item by item and suggested the players should just look very closely at themselves because maybe there was something in this. We went out and annihilated Wellington. It was one of the three occasions that I scored four tries for Auckland.

After the match Maurice publicly thanked the writer for his "perceptive piece" and the writer sent a fax to him and Gary offering his services, at a huge fee plus perks, as a full-time professional motivator.

Lindsay Harris...superb and under-rated.

What made Auckland great through the Ranfurly Shield era was the balance in the team, the confidence the experienced players gave the younger that they were part of a special team which could do special things and the vision of coaches who encouraged young players of skill to spread their wings. I think back on a player like Lindsay Harris who had such sublime qualities but never made the All Blacks, and on what must have seemed to other provinces as a bottomless well of quality players and I understand what I was part of.

We had towering confidence in ourselves and, yes, it was an arrogance, but a healthy arrogance because it was the result of performance. When you can base your pattern on a tight five like

John Drake or Peter Fatialofa, Fitzy, Stevie McDowell, Gary Whetton and Marty or Robin Brooke; when you turn to loosies like Michael Jones and Alan Whetton, one a genius and the other a truly great player; and to backs like Foxy, JK, Joe Stanley, Terry Wright, Bernie McCahill, Craig Innes, David Kirk, Brett Iti...there has to be an almost demoralising sense of inevitability in opposing teams.

I guess because of its very success Auckland set itself up for criticism. One was that in defence of our line we became a team of professional foulers rather than concede tries. The temptation to do it is almost overpowering and it has become a universal tactic. Certainly it applies to most teams playing at the top level of provincial and international rugby. The agitation for penalty-try awards for the cynically contrived penalty has become quite fierce and referees are now much readier to dish them out. But what is cynical and what is not? Another burden for the referees. Mind-reading the mindless?

Even in those days people used to say I kicked too much. My attitude was that if I could kick equally well off either foot and if I practised kicking as I did, I was better kicking the ball than giving it to some back who couldn't kick as well. I could not understand that in first-class rugby there were so many backs who couldn't kick the ball well and with either foot. It became accepted that Foxy could kick the ball, the fullback could kick the ball and the halfback could shunt them over the top and that was good enough, thanks Zinny. But it's not good enough and never will be. That's like bowlers who reach test cricket status but are hopeless batsmen. That doesn't make any sense at all to me. After all those years of playing cricket, they can't bat! Not only can't they bat, they don't know how to hold a bat, where to put their feet or where to put their head when an unaccommodating West Indian bowls a bouncer at them. Talk about specialisation taken to screwball lengths.

I have to say that were I a cricketer I would need to bat, bowl and field better than anyone else. And if I couldn't bat well I'd practise until I could. Or is that being unrealistic?

Through the great years Auckland played such rounded rugby with so many brilliant passages that plucking out the ultimate expression of its powers is difficult and will always be a matter of opinion. The first to come to my mind would be the 40 minutes of the first spell against Otago in 1990. It was a Ranfurly Shield challenge and Maurice and Beegee had targeted it as a key game.

In the lead-up Shield match against Southland we scored 14 tries in a 78-7 win but that was not necessarily the preparation we needed and we were conscious of that. It was also clear Otago had come to do the business after having given us a hell of a fright two years before. But in that first spell everything we did clicked. Mike Brewer took a gamble on holding us in check with the wind but the Auckland wheels spun freely from the beginning, the scrum took control and we were up 39-0 at halftime. Terry Wright scored two brilliant tries from fullback, hitting the line at full throttle with that deceptive, smooth action of his. At his peak as a fullback I rate Terry a better attacking player than John Gallagher. He had great extensions to what were sound basic skills and, like Glen Osborne, had the speed to motor out of trouble. For a player who looked so fragile he made tackles that stuck.

Foxy was devastating. He converted all six tries, dropped two goals, one with his left and one with his right, and his kicking for position and high to embarrass Greg Cooper was sheer precision.

From the back of a dominant scrum I picked up two pushover tries and another from broken play. I have a bit of a thing about pushover tries. They came frequently for Auckland, so frequently that they somehow achieved ho-hum status. The pushover try is the result of an efficient scrummaging effort, high on technique. The pick-up and launch from No 8 is a matter of timing and skill after controlling the dribble. I get the halfback to call the distance from the line and I prefer to go a little earlier than most. People do become blase about forward-controlled tries, though the South Africans were not too blase about the one I scored in the second test of 1994. The referee turned his head to check on offside backs at the precise moment the ball sneaked out the back of the scrum and he didn't see me hook it back in with my foot. His timing was perfect. So was mine. He turned back to see the try.

Great memories are not just of overwhelming wins. As a match, as a great Shield contest, I would go back to that Otago match of 1988. They played with such character. It is the way of Otago rugby. They have such spirit and pride. I can see Noel Pilcher still, motoring away like a vintage Bentley for the intercept try which took Otago to 17-12 15 minutes into the second spell then having the bloody cheek to take off again in a cloud of blue smoke through two or three tackles and, with his momentum just about exhausted, getting monstered by Frank Bunce just short of the goalposts. The conversion would have taken Otago out to 23-12 and in this sort of match that is usually one bridge too far.

Our fightback was through powerful scrummaging, desperate pressure and through the tactical mastery of Foxy, who also kicked 19 points but in a scoreline which showed two tries apiece the 10-point margin at the end did little justice to Otago. What a game it was, and a sharp reminder to Auckland that the big day out on the paddock is everyone's chance for glory.

Graham Henry made me captain of Auckland in 1993. It was a surprise call. I thought that after Gary Whetton the call would be for Fitzy who was, after all, captain of New Zealand. From Graham it was a gesture in deference to Fitzy, to give him the space to play his rugby for a good period of the season without the responsibilities of captaincy. Captaining the All Blacks is burden enough given the extent of international commitments these days. Fitzy and I have talked the thing through and he is able to accept the situation comfortably. At pre-match talks I make a point of giving him the opportunity to contribute because I am conscious that he has much to offer.

The transition from the great years has been hard. Schoolteachers seem to follow me around. That makes me uneasy somehow. It is as if they are trying to track me down. Headmaster Graham Henry called in headmaster John Graham as his assistant coach. That's a lot of headmasters. They were an exacting pair, too. Graham Henry, having felt his way for the first year or two, became a wonderfully easy man to communicate with. He has given young players the taste of what it is all about and I am sure Auckland will feel the benefit of this as he seeds them through the team. For the first year of captaincy I was spoiled. I had Foxy to run the show and that invited laziness from the captain. I stopped thinking games through because with Foxy calling the shots I had this sense that what he called would be spot-on. From time to time we would consult but from the point of view of directing play I could hardly claim to be a hands-on captain.

I have missed the sort of input, both on and off the field and for both Auckland and the All Blacks, of a player like Alan Whetton. He gave more than any spectator could ever know to every game he played. It was not just that he was as near to the ultimate blindside flanker as there could be, but that he kept the forwards thinking, intensely focused. He was always talking, calling up support, demanding intelligence reports from the No

Alan Whetton...the great communicator.

8 in scrums, demanding alertness at lineouts, rucks and mauls..."Come on, Zinny! Talk to me, talk to me. What's happening back there." He kept everyone's mind ticking over. He brought a sharp edge to my perception of a game.

In the rebuilding phase I had a team largely of strong, silent men. Last year, following Foxy's retirement...Junior Tonu'u, a dynamic little yapper in the way halfbacks are; Carlos Spencer, an exciting young gun maturing quickly but at that stage of being still a little in awe of his surroundings; Lee Stensness, a quiet man; John Ngauamo, quieter; Waisake Sotutu, speechless; Shane Howarth, too far-out to say much; Eroni Clarke, singing hymns out on the wing; Michael Jones, just gets out there, does the job; Mark Carter, hardly garrulous; Robin Brooke, noisy but not talkative; Richard Fromont, talks because he has this compulsion to talk; a front row which, though it has a renowned talker in Fitzy, keeps its collective head down.

I am not the sort of captain who, in leading by example, will restrict the way I play the game. Where Buck Shelford was a very straightforward, driving, essentially physical leader, I do not place limitations on myself, do not reel myself in from the broad way which has always been my preferred way. I will still rush in to take the quick tap; I might even let fly with a left-foot drop-kick. My style is to encourage players that, while conforming to team patterns and plans, there is always room in the game to cut loose and use their flair. I am concerned that young players should feel relaxed and as much a part of the team as any All Black.

For instance, I recognise in Carlos Spencer a great talent. He has such deft skills and a good understanding of the disciplines the first five-eighth role demands. He also has a feel for the time to run I would never want to see suffocated. I trust players of his sort to switch on at the sniff of an opportunity and go for it, for this is the lifeblood of rugby.

I try to convey that a player is not fit for a game unless he is as mentally fit as he is physically fit. You can't wake up on a Saturday morning, stretch, yawn, fart and say to yourself, "Ho-hum, another game of footy today." You may feel fit enough to play another 40 minutes at the end of 80 but if you have not prepared yourself for a contest of minds as well as of bodies, you are not fit. As much as any other sport or recreation rugby is a thinking game. From fullback to the front row it is a thinking game and if you find, at the front row end of it, that this is too great an exaggeration, you do not know rugby.

Fitness does not come through training sessions. Training sessions are for practising moves, for establishing familiarity. Fitness comes with the groundwork individual players do for themselves. What I do during the season is maintenance work. What I do before the season sets the baseplate for my fitness. I read somewhere that "modern" players do not do enough slogging work on the roads. I hate road running. I love running through paddocks, across country, up the hills through slush and mud. Getting on to pavements and mixing it with vrooming cars and exhaust fumes is my idea of hell. Run around the bays? God. Plod, plod, plod. Not another 10 kilometres of this; people staring at you through car windows, tripping over dogs peeing on lampposts and doing worse just around the corner where you don't see it till you've trodden in it. This is training for enjoyment?

I want to smell the grass and feel the "give" of it under my feet. I start by running up and around One Tree Hill. I have never carried a chainsaw and I would swear in court that I saw nothing. Up there on One Tree Hill the quiet covers you. On the roads cars chunder at you.

For four or five weeks I will do eight or 10 sprints up the hill every day and then get into endurance running for 50 minutes, work in the gym with weights, cycling, some aerobics. Then gym for the upper body and legs and then the dreaded 150s and Hennie Mullers. I am not sure how the legendary Hennie Muller gave his name to this corner-to-corner field running but, if he invented it, in the nicest possible way I wish him in hell.

The fitness demands are much greater now than when I started with Auckland in 1986. It was a breeze then. The seasons are now insanely longer, the body older. People say I am getting old. They're right. Twelve months older every year. And playing so much more rugby. I become more conscious that because of the requirement for year-round fitness I am depriving myself of things I want to do or like to do. But I accept that commitment. I accept the limitations I must place on myself if it is my choice to play rugby and keep playing it at a level acceptable to me. I have been at top provincial and international level for nine years and as I look through the teams I have played with and against many of the players are no longer around.

I find I am not at my best talking rugby at social events. It is not that I don't enjoy rugby as a talking point but that I don't

Yes, it's true, the boys do like a little drink after the game.

want to be talking rugby all the time – as if it is all I know or enjoy. Players understand that in a sense they belong to the public and that people get a kick out of talking the game through with them. But please, someone, talk to me about the music I like, what restaurants, what my next housing project is going to be and did I really help that guy put the saw into the one tree on One Tree Hill when I was out training.

I know there are players who don't mind. Hey, it's the chance to get your gripes about the ref off your chest. But a discussion on the merits of the 2-3-2 scrum compared with "the shambles out there today, son," or the shoulder-to-shoulder lineout or the zig-zag defence or what about that knock-on, Zinny? Pardon my wandering eyes. And everyone wants to know about your leg. The year I broke my ankle I had a shirt printed up: "Thank you, my ankle's fine." But meet me after a game and talk stocks and shares and dollar-values and property investment and I'll talk to you all night. You want boredom? I can give it to you. In spades. Or is that not politically correct?

185

14

Life And Death

I looked up and saw all these pale little faces looking down at me, open mouths, dark eyes and woolly hats. I thought, "God, is this the way it all ends?" There was a despair I could never describe. Minutes earlier when I felt the bang in my leg and went down there was an uncanny flashback. Almost instantaneously, I had this picture in my mind of JK in plaster, Pontypool, 1989, telling me it had felt as if someone very big and very angry had whacked him in the back of the leg with a piece of 4-by-2. Same joker, JK. Same piece of timber. Same six months off? Or was it 12? Eighteen? Whatever, goodbye World Cup and goodbye career.

So you're 30. You've played 70 games for the All Blacks, 28 tests. You've had your fair crack of the whip, Zinny. Haven't you? No way. I need to get to the World Cup. I want to tour South Africa next year. I want to be part of what I feel in my bones is a rugby revolution – in the playing of the game and in the paying of the game. I have never more desperately wanted anything than these things as I lie on the stretcher at Rugby Park, Hamilton, April 16, 1995.

What have I done? I am in this pretty jersey, playing for the Harlequins, which is the shadow New Zealand team, against Waikato. Next week the test against Canada. Everything is building up nicely. The training camps and the road show have seen the building of the All Black spirit as I have not known it since World Cup 1, but maybe now even closer, warmer. Young players have been pulled into the whole show as equal partners and they're contributing to it all, the rugby ideas, the humour, the feeling that this is a team on the move.

We Harlequins have been doing unto Waikato as we would never have them do unto us when there I am, with the ball in hand running for space and linkage. I am grabbed by the jersey, which always pisses me off a bit. I mean, grab me by all means, even where it hurts most, but leave my pretty gear alone. Then I am grabbed by the left leg, which I reckon is a more reasonable way to go. I try to push out with my right leg and as I go down I hear the bang and I feel JK's piece of 4-by-2. Then there is the sensation of an intense jet of ice and, under the ruck, I try to move the leg and I yell a brief word not unknown in *Once Were Warriors*. Fitzy looks shocked but I think it's because I've told him I need a stretcher.

As they carry me off I see the kids' open mouths and the dark eyes staring down. As they carry me into the dressing-room I shout that word again. Doctors climb all over me and I am saying to myself, "Don't be broken. Don't be broken." They have trouble getting the tape off my ankle it's so tight. But it has probably saved the achilles from a complete break. Then Ali is there at my head and she looks stricken. They turn me over, put on the ice bag and Doc Mike Bowen is saying, "Zinny, this may hurt for a second." He grabs the back of my leg and squeezes. It hurts like hell. Mike says, "It's not broken." Bazza Donaldson, the physio, is there and he stares at me and says, "Mate, you're going to the World Cup. Keep believing that." Ali squeezes my hand, which is much less painful than everyone squeezing my leg.

In the plaster room at the hospital a specialist says, "Zinny, this may hurt for a second" and he has his squeeze and proves it still hurts like hell. He says, "It's not broken." They immobilise the achilles.

That evening all the guys are in to watch me eating apple pie and ice-cream. Bazza comes in, looks at the plaster and says, "What the hell is that thing?" He is not impressed and wants to know how the hell he can start work on the leg with all that gunk over it.

He talks quickly with Mike Bowen. He cuts the plaster off and puts ice on the leg. He says he is going to give me some acupuncture, turns me over and jabs five needles into me. Every now and then he gives them a tweak. Then he ices me again. I feel like a demonstration model.

For the next 48 hours the leg is to be iced, every hour for the first 10 hours and then every two hours for 20 minutes each

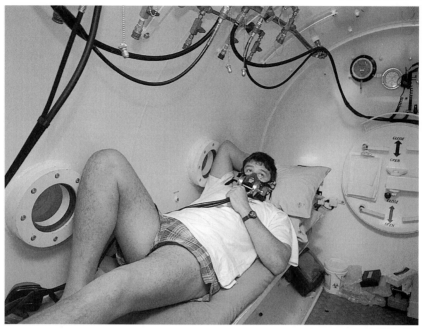

Decompressing...extreme measures at Devonport Naval Base.

change. Ali sets the alarm and for two nights gets less sleep than I do. She is my bodyguard, my ice-person, my first-aid person, my protector from the telephone, my soother and comforter. She is everything. She is a tranquil lady, revitalising when I'm down, there to pick up the pieces and put them together when things seem to be falling apart.

One day Doc John Mayhew orders me not to laugh. Then he tells me about treatment in the decompression chamber at the Devonport Naval Base. Pressure while under pure oxygen increases the circulation-rate and pumps the blood through to the injury. I laugh. Yeah, doc? You sure of this?

Actually I'm very excited about it and we settle on 20 treatments of two hours. After four or five I'm looking for something less boring, like a quick read of *War and Peace* in the original Russian, but make do with backgammon with the medical staff. When I am not there I am at the gym working on body-strength, in the pool working on stamina, making sure that a busted leg is not going to mean an unfit body. Bazza sweats over me faithfully. My determination is real but so are my periods of depression. Backing me up all the way, encouraging, giving me every minute and every second to recover are Laurie, Pinetree and BJ. One discouraging word from any of them would have been lethal but the message is clear: I have until the death-knock to convince them, not that I will be fit for duty at the opening of the World Cup but that all the medical signs say I will be right for action as the campaign gets serious.

Came the day and the final test. It is at the East Coast Bays stadium and my task is to run for 10 minutes. It is the hardest 10 minutes I have ever been through, conscious there is still mending to do, trying not to limp, trying to flow through. But I get through it and they say in a week I will be able to run 50 minutes. I am happy to take them at their word. I am going to the World Cup. A month ago I was going nowhere.

With their great gift for accentuating the negative many New Zealanders had me in a pine box long before the leg injury. Radio, in the absence of any accurate information, diagnosed an old problem of mine as a serious heart condition which had forced my admission to the coronary unit at Greenlane Hospital. My imminent death distressed a lot of people, not least my mother who heard the report on radio and went to pieces. It was the result of a deep-throat big-mouth at Greenlane adding two and two together and making a calamity out of the answer, seven. He rang the media and tipped them off that Zinzan Brooke was in deep strife.

In 1986, in the days when I believed eating a meal before a game was over-loading the legs and draining the stamina, I was playing for New Zealand Colts against the Australians. It was not unusual on my ill-advised match-day starvation regimen for me to become light-headed during a game. This day light-headedness and a climbing pulse-rate took me on a flight straight to the dressing-room. I took several minutes to come around. I have been on medication ever since for an irregular heart-beat. The heart at full throttle may go up to 170-180. Mine may go up to 220-230, fluttering so quickly it is not pumping the blood. I feel faint, I induce hyper-ventilation, slow the rate down and drop-kick another goal.

I must say that when I went to Greenlane early this year I was under a lot of pressure. I had so much on my plate. I had All Black camps and I was involved in a developing professional rugby scheme through my employer, Sky Television. I was doing promotional work, visiting schools, getting to gym, training in the evening, putting time in at the pool and into my housing project. I would go to bed with my mind bounding around at 100 miles an hour I sometimes woke with my pulse racing.

I rang John Mayhew, the former All Black doctor, who had known about the problem from day one. I went to have the thing checked out and the tests showed my recovery rate to be disgustingly normal. The day the media leaped into action I was on a routine visit to the coronary unit for some tests which would bring up the heart-rate artificially so my recovery could be monitored. When I got home the cameras were there. TVNZ told me they had been tipped off from Greenlane though later, when the heat was on, they had an incredible or convenient lapse of memory and could not recall anyone from Greenlane calling them. They had, they now said, "heard it on the grapevine".

I was angry but courteous and I told this TVNZ guy he could interview me immediately after training. I wanted it over and done with, to try in some way to repair the damage which had already been done and to strangle what I anticipated would become wild conjecture. As we were going out on to the paddock for training he grabbed me and virtually demanded to do the interview first. So bloody insistent. I told him the arrangement was for after training and that was what I intended to do. He persisted so I told him to go away, using the expression no Kiwi can refuse.

They had their interview after training but I wish now I had wiped the whole arrangement. This was a personal thing I had kept to myself for nine years. I had not told the family because I didn't want my parents worrying themselves to bits every time I went out to play. Now it was public property, compliments of the Greenlane turkey.

Anyway, I should have it so good. A torn achilles and a playful heart. Chickenfeed in the broad picture of life. The Coca-Cola Road Show taught me that. I heard a former rugby administrator sneer at the road show. He called it a showpiece for a bunch of prima donnas. Pig-ignorance, of course. Straight for the jugular, no thought to what it was all about, no consideration of the thousands of kids in a dozen small towns and along the country by-ways who swarmed to meet us. That was what it was all about. The kids were excited not just about us as All Blacks but about rugby.

It was at Oamaru that we jumped off the bus at the local centrepoint. A lady came to me and asked if I could take a little

With Clinton Mains in Oamaru…so what's a torn achilles?

time to meet her son who was very ill with muscular dystrophy. I asked all the players to autograph one of the road-show jerseys and went in her car to her home. Clinton, was an avid fan. When I walked into the bedroom he was lying there, frail and colourless. But his eyes lit up and he smiled when he saw me. I stayed for half-an-hour chatting.

Four days later, on February 13, Clinton died. His father wrote, "When I came home from work (after your visit) Clinton had some of his old sparkle in his eyes and he couldn't wait to tell me about your visit. This letter is very difficult to write, Zinny, because Clinton passed away a few days after your visit. He died in his sleep, no doctors, no hospital, no pain. My wife and I know your visit made him feel really good and he was tremendously

191

Waisake Sotutu...gamebreaking option.

proud of his jersey and of having you visit him."

A torn achilles and a playful heart? As I said, chickenfeed. The road show a showpiece for prima donnas? What small-minded, fault-finding, nit-picking pygmies there are out there. There was a fair bit of criticism, too, of the extent of the World Cup build-up: there was no need for the final trial, no need for the spin-off matches, no need for the summer camps. The whole programme was worthwhile because it gave every player in the squad the last ounce of opportunity to make the team. The players knew they had to deliver the goods at a certain time of the year. If they didn't, they were told to get themselves right for the next phase or they were out. As the build-up campaign went on there developed greater understanding of just how dedicated Laurie Mains was.

At the time of the final selection I disagreed with three positions. I would have had Waisake Sotutu because he gave us more attacking options with the strength to stand in the tackle, burst tackles and tackle big. He is in the mould of the game-breaker. In Jonah Lomu you have the ultimate game-breaker. In Sotutu there is someone very close to him.

I thought Stephen Bachop was very unlucky, such a skilled

192

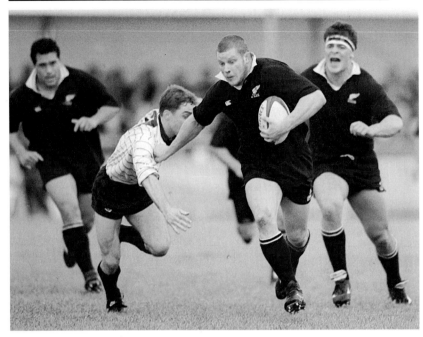

Bull Allen...had the business.

player. Obviously, they opted for two specialist goalkickers and that was the end of it for Bachop. My preference would have been to take Bachop for Simon Culhane and rely on Jeff Wilson and Glen Osborne as the second goalkicker. Bachop had hardened up his defensive attitude and in South Africa, on the hard grounds, he could have played the game as he likes to play it – running the ball and probing with those long, raking kicks.

The third player, and the one I felt for most, was Bull Allen, the Taranaki prop. I think of the things he does probably better than any other prop and which he continued to do well in a thoroughly beaten pack in the final trial. Bull drives with great body position, always seems to take bonus yardage through tackles and sets up the ball better than any of the others. He can really do some stuff with his hands on the ball. For the game we were looking to play Bull had the business and no one can tell me he is less than capable in scrum and maul.

These things were judgements of the time and now, after the event, I still believe Sotutu, Bachop and Allen would have thrived over there. But the reality is that the players who went did the job they were selected for. Simon Culhane is a very good player,

193

well balanced, unfazed by occasion. There's an essentially South Island low-key "togetherness" about him. I watched him at training and his skill-levels with the ball on the foot are astonishing. He's test-young but no boy and would have been a very safe bet were Mehrtens injured.

The other point of debate leading up to the selection of the Cup squad was whether Michael Jones should be carried through the Sunday matches. Looking forward to the agenda of this World Cup my vote would have gone against taking Michael. I am sure you cannot afford to have a player sitting out the truly crucial games. It cuts back options too severely in a campaign of this sort. Everything else being equal you would select 15 Michael Joneses if 15 were available, but Michael's convictions about play on Sunday created too much inequality for this campaign.

As it eventuated we found we had something extra special in Josh Kronfeld. I had my reservations about Josh's physical capacity until the build-up spin-off match down the West Coast when he was non-stop devastating. He is not Michael Jones. Michael is incomparable even though he may not be quite the lightning bolt of old. But nor is Michael Jones Josh Kronfeld. They are their own sorts of players and Josh's World Cup was a remarkable triumph for a new international.

I should confess, too, that after the tests against France in 1994 I wanted someone with the authority to go to Jonah Lomu and talk to him about his position in rugby, to help him overcome any doubt that still existed in his mind as to his future, as wing or blindside flanker. But in whichever position, that long ago I believed he could win the World Cup for us. My strong preference, however, was that he should be placed in the care of Alan Whetton for as long as it took and trained in the disciplines of blindside flank for I saw him there as a towering prospect. I found it scary that he was training sometimes with the forwards, sometimes with the backs. I was impatient for his future to be designated so there was no confusion in his mind, so that he could take up the single challenge and turn his awesome potential into awesome reality.

That he stayed with the wing after the bollocking he took out of the French tests, that he worked so single-mindedly on his defence, whether confrontational or turning to recover, demonstrates the boy's character. He brought to the World Cup a dimension of wild excitement far, far beyond the scope of any other player.

15

...And That's The Truth

Conversation piece: Hey, bro, did you see that Zinzan Brooke? That drop-kick? Choice! Seventy metres easy. And, hey, what about that monster-pass to Big J? Juu-*rassic*, man!

Well, thanks anyway. I wish one drop-kick and a monster-pass made a World Cup triumph. I would be fooling no one, least of all myself, if I claimed to have had a great World Cup. I didn't even jump at the end of the haka and that was a first. I have set my own standards and no one knows better than I that I did not achieve them in South Africa. It may be that the drop-kick and the pass and a this and a that will be what most people will remember about my World Cup. As against those things, they will also remember, and vividly, that I dropped the Stransky up-and-under which led to the scrum which led to the drop-kick which won the World Cup for South Africa.

As a critic of myself I know I played below my capacity. For all the work I did and all the pain I went through to get myself ready for hard, concentrated rugby, at the end of the campaign I could look back and weep. Physically, I was never right. Maybe right enough to hold my own but that is not the measure I apply to myself and it is not the measure I expect others to apply to me. Things I know I can achieve I could not achieve. I could not rid myself of doubt about my leg, could not free my mind of the consequences if the achilles fell to pieces again. It was clear to everyone I was not getting around the paddock as I normally do. At training runs I am usually one of the more dominant ones in talking the team up and backing that up with the right action. At the World Cup I was not offering that. I was wrapped up in a restrictive, maybe a protective, shell of my own, desperate to emerge but not quite able to call up the power to do so.

My career has been a patchwork for the last few years. In 1990 I broke my ankle; in 1991 my own World Cup was not too bad; in 1992 there was Laurie's silent treatment, but once that barrier was broken I played well; in 1993 I let myself down playing with the sciatica problem, was dropped and then selected again; 1994, the French tests lost, but my own form riding as high as ever it did; 1995, perhaps the greatest year of my life in prospect, and turned to dust. I knew that given an injury-free run I could carry my 1994 level through 1995 and I dreamed of contributing to a World Cup victory. It was the fiercest ambition I have known. I wanted to bury memories of 1991.

But a week before I took the field against Japan for my first World Cup match I was on the point of throwing in my hand and coming home.

In South Africa my day started at 7am with a 20-minute shower to warm up the leg, stiff from yesterday's work-out. Stretches under the hot water, stretches outside, breakfast, physio for 90 minutes, ultrasound, acupuncture, massage, strapping, suppository, 25 minutes to get myself in a condition to run. Suppository? An unspeakable medication to numb the leg without deadening it. Then, after the work-out, tape off, ice-pack, back to the hotel, get the leg up, ultrasound, ice every couple of hours...that's the way it was for six weeks.

So who was fooling whom? How did I get through to South Africa? What I know now is that the specialist in Auckland never really let on how serious the injury was. He has told me that when I went to him after the Harlequins match he gave me no show of getting to the World Cup, that the injury was severe, the achilles nearly snapped and the calf muscle damaged. Laurie Mains was aware the injury was serious but not of its real severity.

We trained for the Ireland game at the Wanderers ground. All I had to do was sprint across the field. The cameras were there. It was as if a thousand media guys had their binoculars trained on my leg and they were all saying, "I told you so." I said to Bazza, "It's no good, mate. I can't do it. I just can't do it." He said, "You're bloody-well going to do it. You're not going to break it. Just keep running. Get through the pain barrier. Now do it." When I broke into the sprint it was excruciating.

Bazza told me he had spoken to Laurie and I was on the

dreaded FPH call. First Plane Home if I didn't front up against Wales for the next match. Both Rob and I were to play against Wales. From the time we arrived in South Africa we felt like specimens under a microscope. We were aware of debate back home about us even being there, both recovering from injuries. We were "the Broke Brothers" and while we knew the team and the management were behind us there was a nagging guilt-thing ripping at my insides. Or maybe it was fear. I used to agonise through the nights, asking myself what the hell I thought I was doing here, anyway. Just a couple of days before Wales I said to Rob, "Look, I just can't go on like this. It's not fair to anyone. I'm going to pull out of the whole show."

Rob tried to dissuade me from going home. If I must pull out, he said, why not stay on with the Coca-Cola support tour, drink some booze, socialise. Like hell. I wasn't going to set myself up as some sort of social butterfly when I wasn't fit enough to be on the paddock doing the job.

So Rob and I knew just a couple of days before the Welsh game that I was finished. That was it. As the Afrikaners say when all the cards have been played and the outcome is clear, "Finish and klaar." And the day before the Welsh match Rob was within a hairsbreadth of joining me.

I gave myself no choice. I would try to guts out the match, play mind games on my body, and that would be it. The day before the match, during light training, we both tweaked our calf muscles. "Tweak" was a convenient word for the media. Mine felt like a tear but I ran on it anyway, just kept running, desperately running, remembering old-timers like Pinetree saying that in their day if they pulled a muscle they got on with it and ran it off. I knew the calf would seize up that night. It did, and late at night I went to Bazza and told him if I played the next day I would let everyone down.

Twenty-four hours later, at the stroke of a wand, both Rob and I were out of the woods. I trained and I ripped two big pieces of scar-tissue free of the muscle. Rob, goaded by Bazza and Mike Bowen, got on the treadmill, ploughed through the pain barrier, wrenched scar-tissue free, and was away laughing. We both experienced much the same emotional release. For Rob it was total relief. For me it was now coping with something I regarded as a familiar enemy, something I could deal with – the stiffness at the achilles but without the spin-off pain through the calf.

Playing Japan was a celebration for this 'broke' brother.

Playing in the Japan game was a celebration. My objectives were simple: to do my basic job efficiently and to get around the track in attacking support and in defence. Nothing riotous about that. But here we were, a team of starving reserves and recovering crocks with the mind to put New Zealand rugby on display in such a way that the "big match" boys would know we were breathing down their necks. The team was alight, bristling. Norm Hewitt wanted Fitzy to know there are no sure things; Simon Culhane had a very sharp message for anyone who cared to read it; Marc Ellis was going to bury the hated second-string tag; Alama Ieremia was as pumped-up as I have seen any player...and so it went, right through the team.

Laurie asked me if I would captain the side. At any other time I would have been rapt but here it would have been dishonest. In my first match I wanted to concentrate on my job and on getting my leg through the game. Captaincy was outside that concentration. It was not a game where you could really target yourself on anything because it opened out into an every-direction display of running and try-scoring; but at the end of it I had achieved what I needed, Rob had played a ripper and all the players, quite magnificently, had shot off their messages to the glamour-boys.

I have dwelt on the Japan game because it was something special. Above any other game it illustrated just what sort of squad this was because it showed that the spirit and the skill ran right through the team, that whatever players might be for their provinces in home surroundings, here, as All Blacks, they were all imbued with this free-flow philosophy and had the hands and feet to express it. It was an expression of the excitement New Zealand injected into what would otherwise have been a very run-of-the-mill World Cup.

That we tripped at the last fence while striving to play much the same sort of rugby was, of course, shattering to the team. I take the risk of being charged with sour grapes when I say that with 15 fit players we would have beaten South Africa. It is surprising to me that journalists who demand the truth because the truth – the facts – is supposed to be the lifeblood of their existence, also set themselves up as selective judges of it. When Laurie Mains talked of his sick players he was accused by the South African media of sour grapes, of being a bad loser. Had he lied and said we had no sick players or that we would have lost anyway, he would have been hailed as a true sportsman.

Laurie took it a stage further by saying pointedly it was too much of a coincidence that most of the party came down with food poisoning 48 hours before the final. On the Thursday morning before training some of us could not drink the water in our drink bottles. It tasted sour. And it was at lunchtime that Buncey said to me, "this food tastes like crap," and I agreed with him that there was a funny, artificial taste to it. I will not say the food was spiked. There is no evidence it was. I will say that had we been free of its effects our error-rate would have been significantly lower, our concentration and our dynamism significantly higher and that we would have beaten South Africa.

All the pressure South Africa might have placed on us would not have been enough to stop us. We had been virtually error-free in so many games but with players thinking about whether they were going to be able to make it through the game there were going to be lapses. It has been said we left too much magic on the field against England. Fit, there was enough left to cope with South Africa. The players know it and, though it may seem to be an unlikely source of support, some of the British media knew it and said it. On a level playing field we had more bullets to shoot than South Africa, more fire-power and more resilience.

It is the truth, too, that we did not have a happy relationship with the cook at our Johannesburg hotel. It is the truth that when our management tried to have our Cape Town cook brought through to Johannesburg there was indignant resistance. You would agree vomiting, diarrhoea, dehydration, sleeplessness for 48 hours is something less than an ideal preparation for a rugby test. You might agree, at least, it would be a contributing factor to a sub-standard performance. If you do not agree you are nuts or a South African.

Had this not been a World Cup final, had it been any other match in the tournament, several of our team would not have been playing on the grounds of sickness. Mehrtens, Wilson, Dowd and Loe were only four who would not have been allowed near the track.

Having said all that, there is a case for criticism that, having estimated South Africa's strategy, old-fashioned basic that it was, we should have varied our own. I am not sure at what stage of such a tightly strung game it should have happened but when it was clear our error-rate was higher than we would have expected and the South Africans were drifting their defence cleverly to have Jonah pincered, the option may have been to have Walter and Buncey target Hennie le Roux for the crunch in midfield, then the drive over the top and the release with Jonah uncrowded and with the chance of taking on James Small with room. However, there is less merit in the suggestion we should have approached the final with a much more restrictive policy than we had been playing all along. We saw England try change in 1991. From having played it tight and close they bent to pressure to spread their game wide and played directly into Australia's hands.

I will go further with the truth and say that England was a better team than South Africa and had England played the final it

Final haka, final game…

would have won. And I suggest you disregard the England performance against France in the third-fourth play-off. They played like men suffering from a prolonged hangover; some of them like men still ever so slightly pissed, which may not be far from the truth, either. It might have been the worst game of rugby I have seen and if it was an example of how England is aiming to fix itself it is going to be a long, long process. But in a battle of the conservatives, England, when not suffering from a hangover, was better at it than South Africa.

The English were a very well balanced team. Had they appreciated the broader range of their capabilities they would have been an even better team. Having been shell-shocked to smithereens by our onslaught in the semi-final they came back, out of desperation gave the ball air and scored tries. That should be the lesson of the World Cup for England. Guscotts and Carlings and Underwoods do not grow on trees. It is a sin that for so much of their careers England's closed-door mentality reduced them to numbers on a field.

Rob Andrew, who carried the can for what was a rigid coaching and on-field leadership policy, wrote: "We should aspire to a game that they (New Zealand) play, of keeping the ball alive." And

Stuart Barnes, the former Lions flyhalf, said New Zealand and England were fairly matched in pace and power but the difference was in ambition and vision.

We were more worried about the English than about the South Africans. It was not that we were unprepared for the Springboks' true grit, nationalistic fervour and hunger to win the World Cup for Nelson Mandela's brave new one-South Africa. We expected all of that. But England loomed as the greater threat for its power forward and its control behind the pack.

The All Blacks' preparation for the England game was the most clinically focused in my experience. We studied them in every way. We watched videos of their games, scrutinised every individual, sorted out their tendencies as well as their compulsions. And ever in our minds was the awful option of a play-off for third. Bugger that. Six of us had been there in 1991 and we told the others it was a deeply depressing experience. By then our style had captured the minds of the public and the media and we were not ready to pack it up and take it home. There was never a suggestion at any stage of the tournament, including the final, that we should so alter that style that we would compress ourselves into another sort of team. We had the players to play that sort of footy, forwards with the skills of backs, quick, athletic men no matter their shape.

England had a powerful front row, magnificent lineout depth through Bayfield, Johnson, Clarke, Rodber and Richards, and much bigger loosies. We were not going to kick the ball out for an England lineout benefit. We were going to keep them moving and guessing. The reverse kick-off by Mehrtens was the beginning of it and it never stopped. The only man outside the All Blacks who knew the kick-off was going to be a special was the referee, Steve Hilditch. We warned him because we didn't want him getting in the way.

The Jonah-factor was huge. In fact, *The Times* of London covered Jonah versus England and quoted Carling as saying Jonah was the difference between the teams, a view it endorsed in an editorial. The difference between the teams started in the minds of 15 players and their coach and was expressed physically by 15 players. Jonah, with his awesome arsenal of qualities, was the most dynamic expression of that difference – as Carling said, a freak. That was the second time Will had been graphically correct in the space of a few weeks, the first being his impeccable judgement

The Jonah-factor was huge.

of his administration's old farts.

My own part in the England game was much more than I could have hoped. I felt caught up in the game's movement and purpose and played quite a full hand in the game as it developed. The drop-kick, its gift-wrapped presentation, its shameless opportunism and its unpromising flight-path I have described. The pass which sped Jonah on his way for his second try came from a breakdown-maul after Jeff Wilson had thrust down the right touchline. The ball popped out, I grabbed it and expected someone large and singing *Swing Low, Sweet Chariot* to crunch me into touch. I glanced behind and saw no one there and then far out to the left I glimpsed a hungry-looking Jonah with Glen Osborne lurking. They seemed a likely pair so I let it go off my left hand, Os gathered it about 35 metres wide and sent Jonah one-on-one against Rob Andrew. For Rob it was a mismatch masterminded in Hell.

England should have had the courage to play their own Kronfeld, Neil Back. As it was, in Rodber, Clarke and Richards they had three players of an identical type. They needed a flyer to create some sort of mischief in our ranks.

In any other climate the final would have been judged to be a boring game of rugby. Its excitement was generated by anticipation of it, by the occasion and by the tension of close scoring. The only enjoyment from it for a player was in the challenge it presented to create the winning break out of jail, to turn the game on its head. But as a match compared with many others it was a throw-back to closed-ranks rugby which, I admit, presented its challenge to us to come up with a game-breaking alternative.

Quite a lot was made of Ed Morrison's whistling-up as a forward pass the transfer from Walter which had Jonah haring off at full-bore, a try for the taking and probably the match for the winning. But I was there in a perfect position, probably better than Morrison's, and the pass was definitely forward. Had Walter sent it on just a fraction earlier it would have been sayonara Jonah. As I write this, several weeks after the event, I have not watched the game. I think maybe I am scared to watch it, that there are things there I do not want to see. I am conscious that even now I have not felt the full impact of the loss. Though we were all broken at the end of it I know that for me there is worse to come and that I am shielding myself from it for as long as I can. Realisation of it will come when I watch the video. But I am still excited about the rugby the All Blacks played over there and about the future of the game as it will be played by our young guns.

We knew that in extra time we had to set ourselves up down there in the right-hand corner, get the ball off the top, drive it, bang it out to midfield for the drop-kick. But when we directed our attack deep down there it came back with interest so that we were always trying to advance from inside our own territory. Even when Stransky missed the penalty shot with South Africa leading 15-12 I still believed we could win it. There was, too, criticism that after that kick we did not drop-out long. But that wouldn't have made any sense. It would be delivering the ball to the Springboks for them to tie it all up as they liked. So we called the "sevens" move where Bachop runs to the 22, tap-drops, passes through his legs to me, I pass and we run it for our lives. My pass was on the way to Walter Little when Jamie Joseph's head popped up and did a neat soccer job on it. That was the ball game. That was the World Cup.

The Springboks were aggressive and orderly but their skill levels as a team were average. There are players with fine natural ability like Andre Joubert, like Joost van der Westhuizen, Joel Stransky himself. The key forwards were Mark Andrews and Ruben Kruger. But the forwards played with a sort of robotic adherence to their specialised positions. The locks pushed in the scrums and went after lineout ball. The props were scrummagers. Beyond that sort of existence they offered little other than commitment. Yet even though they stacked their lineout by turning Andrews into a No 8 we were able to call lineout ball to Ian Jones as a matter of almost-smug confidence because compared with Hannes Strydom he was an eagle to a clipped-wing pigeon.

It was important for us to pull together as a team afterward. We were still in a state of shock at the formal dinner when, in that endearing, subtle little way of his, Louis Luyt scraped emery paper across the wounds with his assertions of South African superiority, past, present and, by implication, always. Louis, who was a graduate of the same charm school as Attila the Hun, later tried to buy back our respect with a paid-up holiday, another subtlety straight out of chapter 3 of the charm school curriculum. Mike Brewer and Paul Henderson fronted him and gave him unmistakeable messages. I was impressed with the English team.

Louis Luyt...same charm school as Attila the Hun.

Before walking out they gave Louis a standing ovation with cries of, "Oh, jolly good one, Louis. Great speech, Louis. Piss off, Louis" – all delivered with the understated, aristocratic sarcasm only the English command.

I don't know what can be done about Louis. He seems to have the South African Rugby Union by the pubes and he owns the Transvaal Rugby Union. I understand that at the roots of the giant ruckus with the Transvaal World Cup players, led by Francois Pienaar, were his promises of rewards if the Cup was won and which he then failed to deliver on. At least he gave us something to focus on the next morning when, in the process of getting gloriously smashed, we all drank many toasts to him. I am sure he would have been impressed by our subtlety, too.

Our message from the World Cup is that we must not now fall off the pace we have set. In a way, we established a new

206

character for New Zealand rugby. What we have achieved in attitude and in practice in the last couple of years may not have been consistent enough to be totally convincing to everyone. But we have gone a long way toward changing the face of rugby not only here but in other parts of the world, too. It was one of the great rewards from the World Cup campaign that others picked up on the gospel according to the All Blacks and carried it back with enthusiasm.

Now that there is massive entertainment sponsorship to satisfy, demands on top players everywhere will be even more intense. Frighteningly so. The danger of player-burnout becomes very real. As it stands at the time of writing, we would be playing the Springboks five times next year, the Australians twice, Scotland here, say twice, plus two tests on a northern tour plus the international provincial championship plus-plus-plus...much bigger squads of international players will be needed to fulfil that sort of programme. What has to come is a top level of professionalism in the way the game is marketed, presented and played. In the playing that professionalism has to embrace entertainment through the running game.

During the World Cup campaign the England manager, Jack Rowell, said in a rather disparaging reference that the All Blacks' rugby was a bit like league. I doubt that he would accept he was paying a compliment to league. It was the great Australian league player Laurie Daley who said recently that so much of the league played in the Winfield Cup was boring because coaches could not see past the no-risk five run-ups, five play-the-balls and delivery to the backs to kick so the opposition could have five run-ups, five play-the-balls and delivery to the backs to kick. That sounds uncannily like English rugby. After England had been beaten by France in the play-off at the World Cup, Rowell was more generous: "England must play more dynamically. New Zealand have taken the game to another level since last year." More accurately, New Zealand had restored the touch of their 50-point defeat of Scotland and added zest to it.

One of the most heartening analyses I have read since our match against England was by Kate Battersby in London's *Daily Telegraph*. She wrote, "Perhaps the most shocking part was the bloodlessness of it. For all their huge unstoppability, the All Blacks' play was not brutal. You could not call what happened carnage. They did not bludgeon their way to victory. They did it with a lightness and grace that was eerie. It was like some hammy episode of *Star Trek* in which Captain Kirk and his crew encounter aliens from another planet possessed of the ability to win wars by power of thought alone…"

That sort of comment emerging from Britain may be the most startling expression of what has been achieved because it is in such stark contrast to what they had been saying about us less than a year before when they were as much obsessed with our "brutality" as they were with the "magnificent winning way of English rugby".

As I have said, the injection of players like Mehrtens, Kronfeld, Lomu and Osborne has been a tonic to older players. They have lifted our hopes and our hearts. I see in Mehrtens a blend of Foxy and Wayne Smith. Foxy himself has taken a strong hand in Mehrtens' development and is impressed by his head for the game technically and by his vision. Pinpoint accuracy in field-kicking of the sort Foxy established will come. There is a quickness about him – Smith's pace, Smith's quick eye for the gap, Smith's quick communication. There is also an engaging quirkiness about him. At training early in the South African campaign he went to Laurie and said very audibly, "Look here, Laurie. I need to talk to you about something very serious. I think you and I have a personality clash to sort out." Laurie looked stunned. Then, if you can look wary with an open mouth, he suddenly looked very wary, then grimmish and, just as the words were about to spill out, Mehrtens swivelled, punched the air and yelled, "Gottim!" He had played just one test match. Had I done that to Grizz after my first test against Argentina he'd have taken my head off.

Osborne has the instinct. He is a natural, a humorist, a player for the times. He has a little way to go in belief in himself but there must be no effort to close his mind to the breadth he brings to New Zealand's attacking options. In some of the things he does, mostly related to his balance and the suggestion he plants that he is going to do one thing while drifting off a tackle to do another, he reminds me of old film I watched of Bob Scott, the great All Black fullback of the '40s and '50s. Silky rhythms and timing.

As I have said, Jonah was the World Cup sensation. I watched him and was so impressed with what he had done for himself and what he had absorbed from others. But I also watched him with concern. He is going to come under pressure which may become

Andrew Mehrtens...new-age All Black.

unbearable from a public demanding juggernaut performance from him every time he plays. At the World Cup he set standards beyond any normal player's scope, not just through his strength and speed but through his astonishing agility for such a big man. He set himself standards, too, notably in defence. I will never forget one shattering tackle he made running in from the wing to bury Ben Clarke. He was so pumped up about defence against England. The Underwoods had gone public on it to the extent that they threw doubt on Jonah's "untested" one-on-one defensive ability against speed and agility. There was a hilarious little scene after he had scragged Tony Underwood and chucked him yards over the touchline. As he walked backwards for the lineout play Jonah, on fire, eyeballed Tony and gestured toward himself. He was saying, "Hey, Tony. That was me. Come on, Tony. You want some more of it?"

From what I know now about contracts and the volume of

209

Glen Osborne...a player for the times.

pressure-rugby and the commitment that will be required from players to do promotional work there will be burn-out. It is inevitable. Jonah will be more vulnerable to it than any other player because there will be huge demand for him. That, on top of the public expectation of him as a player, will be a heavy, heavy burden and he will need protection from it. He needed protection in South Africa as the demands for interviews and appearances went wild. They were telephoning from anywhere in the world at any hour to get him on the line for bizarre questions and for questions he had already answered a hundred times.

Nick Farr-Jones took a pretty crass stance in a newspaper column by complaining that the New Zealand camp had put Jonah in wraps, that the whole mad media circus had not had open access to him. Jonah would have learned from the experience, he said, and so would the media. I am surprised Nick could not make an intelligent guess why Jonah, still an unsophisticated boy, was not public property in that last week after the grilling he had already had and the crazy rush of telephone calls through the nights.

Jonah has such exciting times ahead of him as a player in whatever field he chooses. I want him to pick up again on his aspirations, to take everything he played for in the World Cup and use it as his platform to relaunch. I do not want to watch big money softening his ambition and drive; that would be a tragedy for him and for rugby because rugby needs Jonah as it drives into the whole new ball game of entertainment based on professionalism.

The All Black capacity to run the ball was comprehensive...a running fullback, a first-five who could dash, a halfback in the best form of his life, depth in top wings, a pair of centres who were exciting, innovative. Walter Little and Frank Bunce were the best centre combo in the tournament by far. They created uncertainty tending to sheer nervousness in opposing midfields. Walter was a magnificent player, attacking and defending, and Frank responded to criticism last year that he was now too slow by playing his sharpest rugby ever without losing an ounce of his tackling velocity. Late in the final he was the player still searching through the Springbok defence.

The forwards set a great base and Ian Jones and Rob, having coped with comparative giants in other lineouts, were far more athletic and mobile in field play. I would sort out Blair Larsen because I see in him a player of wonderful potential, bigger than Rob and just as athletic, but lacking the confidence in that big-framed body to have it work for him with aggression. He needs hardness of mind to lift him into greatness. I hope it happens because at the base of him there is a super player.

While setting guidelines for players like Mehrtens, Osborne and Lomu, Laurie has told them that if they sensed the chance outside those lines to go for it. That must not change as coaches

Sean Fitzpatrick...nurtured and sustained team spirit.

change. Laurie has achieved wonderful rapport with all the players. As he chilled-out after the first season or two there was a readiness to accept the means through which we all would pursue his vision for the game. It became our vision, too, and senior players were as excited about it as the youngsters. He has carried Fitzy along with him and the bond between captain and coach became one of the great strengths of the All Blacks. Loyalty begets loyalty and Fitzy has been able to nurture and sustain team spirit of a sort which was beyond the understanding of the class of '91. He himself would say his attitudes have changed since those days when false values ruled. He became a captain for _all_ players, not a select band of players and, through that, the team has prospered.

It was in the hearts and minds of the players to express that prosperity to New Zealanders when we came to undertand how they had come in behind us even as we were losing the World Cup. The opportunity was there in home-and-away Bledisloe Cup matches and we approached them knowing that we needed to win them both for the supporters and for ourselves. So, the Bledisloe Cup was valuable silverware – priceless, in fact. Without it, we emerged from a campaign of high hope with little but frustration and a place in history which was eminently forgettable. The public knew one measure: the Wallabies had lost in their World Cup quarter-final to England; the All Blacks had taken England to pieces in the semi-final. Therefore, the All Blacks should fall upon the Wallabies and beat them to a pulp. I think that's what they call a metaphor.

The build-up was difficult. Many of the players had played little rugby since the World Cup. The Aussies had played their twin interstate matches and the message coming through was that they were primed to restore the reputation they had carried into the World Cup. So it was an intriguing stage we played on.

The conditions for the first match constricted the intentions. Yet the feeling was that even in the rain we had set a fair foundation for a cracker of a match given decent conditions for the return in Sydney. We came off Eden Park 28-16 winners and there was no intention of coming away from Sydney as one-week wonders. Mehrtens suffered criticism from those who could not read that he was deliberately missing touch as a consideration of the Australians' massive lineout strength. It was part of the game plan. Kicking out for them to throw in was not a clever option.

Bob Dwyer made the right sort of strategic noises about playing us at a running game but then dropped his open-side flanker David Wilson and went for size in his back three with Tim Gavin, Willie Ofahengaue and Daniel Manu. Josh Kronfeld had the legs and the lines to get to the ball ahead of Manu and Mike Brewer and I set ourselves up to knock over Daniel and Willie when they ran.

The fairy-tale of playing us at the running game was further exposed in the dry at Sydney. We went into the game intent on running the tripe out of the Wallabies knowing that we had a gun with an endless supply of bullets. We could run from so many sources and when we ran from inside our 22 there was no hope of the Australian loosies getting out in cover. So the excitement was generated and Jonah magnificently displayed the unearthly

213

Jonah...saved for rugby and for the All Blacks.

range of his powers. It was so good that he did, so good for rugby, so good for Jonah himself for he was to suggest to us it could be his last game for the All Blacks. That was a saddening event and it came as we were all contemplating our futures in the game. What eventuated, of course, was that from the crazy roundabout of offers and counter-offers Jonah was saved for rugby and for the All Blacks. I will always see Jonah with his right hand in Joe Roff's face, his right foot held fast by Jason Little on the ground and his left hand guiding the ball into a position to flick a backhand pass to Frank Bunce coming around outside him. It showed spectacularly that he was not just the barnstormer but a player of rare skill and with vision.

Playing with the young guns was exhilaration enough, lifting all of us into their new-age groove. That sort of uplift became even more so when you add to it the experience of playing with a centre-pairing which is so completely the best in the world. There is no place for runners like these to go if the front five are not performing and, as Frank Bunce said, the confidence of the backs was built on the shoulders of the tight five. A nice way with words has Buncey.

And just a plug for the family: It may be that this year was the first that Robin Brooke ceased to be oh yes, Zinzan's brother and that Zinzan became oh yes, Robin Brooke's brother. He has my proud admiration for what he has become to the All Blacks.

16

Come The Revolution

By the time this book is published rugby as we have known it will be history yet, within its new professionalism, its survival as the game New Zealanders wanted to identify with through the All Blacks has been secured The contest for the players' allegiance, the battle of the bucks, has been won and lost and won again after a frantic few weeks of revolution following the sale of rugby television rights for an astonishing 10 years to the Rupert Murdoch empire.

The pace of activity during the early part of 1995 was bewildering in a sport which by tradition has treated change, except in the law book, as an invasion of its privacy. From the time my employer, Sky Television, emerged as the first player in the game, long before the development of a super-league incidentally, rugby moved into a turmoil of temptation as offers, counter-offers and counter counter-offers landed in the players' laps. Sums of money which one week were considered to be unbelievable became believable the next week as rumour of colossal counter-offers leaked out. There was truth in some of what appeared in the media though much of it was merely nudging at the facts, more concerned with questioning the players' integrity and only rarely touching on the serious concerns the players had about the direction in which the game was heading.

We saw the Kerry Packer-driven World Rugby Corporation as something much more significant than some sort of free-pass to Fort Knox. We saw it as a truly global expression for the game with protection for the players at all levels and, in our particular sphere, for players in the Pacific islands. What will happen, for instance, to Western Samoa rugby now that the "big three", New Zealand, Australia and South Africa, will play their tri-series and their International Provincial Championship? Rugby needs the Western Samoans, the Fijians and the Tongans. Outside the contract-world their players became wide open to league-raiders.

After the World Cup players' representatives in several countries maintained contact, no one of them making significant moves without the knowledge of the others. It was like a military exercise with strategies firmly in place but flexible in day-to-day tactics. Yet it was to be a breakdown in this communications network, with the South Africans falling into total disarray, which was the beginning of the end of the WRC. With the South African segment falling flat on its face the WRC lost its momentum. Then when Jason Little very publicly opted for the Australian Rugby Union and Jeff Wilson and Josh Kronfeld for the New Zealand union the WRC lost the heart for the contest.

The week after they returned from the Cup New Zealand players had distinct reservations after listening to what was called a "presentation" of the conditions for the Rupert Murdoch-backed circus with its tri-series with Australia and South Africa and the international provincial series. The first "presentation" was half-baked, sketchy in detail vital to the players, an amateur blackboard session where, considering the time there had been to prepare adequate material, we looked for a professional package, something to take away, study and debate. Although the New Zealand Rugby Union noted the "satisfaction" of the players there was not much satisfaction in the reaction I saw or heard or felt. Instead, I am sure it served to harden the players' conviction that they were still pawns in the game.

While this was happening Ross Turnbull, fronting the WRC charge, was talking money beyond the dreams of most players. While Richie Guy was talking a base-rate of $150,000 for All Blacks, going much higher for individuals judged to be "market-place" attractions, Turnbull was into the business of $US900,000 over three years for 900 players in regional, national and international championships in eight countries. It was inevitable these figures would leak out by accident or design and because they have I feel free to talk about them.

The New Zealand "market-driven" policy stuck in the throats of some players. I think it is some sort of bullshit to talk in rugby of one player in a team being worth more than any other. The fact is you have 15 players and the opportunity for tryscoring "stars" to be born usually depends on the ball-winning sweat and toil of the "non-stars" who, in their specialist capacities, are as good at what they do as the glamour boys at what they do. Who is to say, for instance, that Craig Dowd or Robin Brooke, Bull Allen or Ian Jones are not worth as much as Jonah Lomu or Glen Osborne, Jeff Wilson or Andrew Mehrtens? Or, if you like, would a "maker" of tries like Frank Bunce or Walter Little be worth less because he does not actually score them?

The professional feeding-frenzy of these past few months is the direct result of many years of comfortable idleness by rugby administrations which, generation after generation, have plied the players with more responsibilities than they could fairly be asked to cope with as "amateurs" and with no meaningful proposal to see them right – either under or over the counter. Oddly, under-the-counter payments were most common where protestations of pure amateurism were at their loudest. It was little wonder, then, that the yen, the lira and the franc were becoming increasingly attractive to players and that rugby league sensed the growing dissatisfaction and mounted drive after drive on rugby's top players.

It was fear rather than conscience which motivated the big move in rugby as league invented super-league and went out into the marketplace with bottomless wallets. However, Sky Television moved long before the super league was heard of and with the right sort of concern for all the players, not just the internationals. The New Zealand Rugby Union, under Eddie Tonks and Rob Fisher, moved in firmly behind Sky and the players were in consultation when the ball-game changed dramatically.

When I was called in by Sky executives Nate Brown and Peter Scutts that September 1994, day, it was to react to their plan not, as I thought, to hear some sort of pointed suggestion I should be spending a little less time on my rugby commitments and a little more in my Sky office. I was enjoying my work with Sky. They pulled me into their marketing and management meetings and into their advertising and promotional programmes so that I was getting a broad education in the whole process.

Sean Fitzpatrick and I listened to the outline of a scheme which would pay a basic rate of $50,000 but with the capacity through promotional work to treble that. It was an exciting concept not only for what it was offering the top players but for what it offered those who would never be All Blacks and whose service to rugby was immense. The player Nate and Peter used as their role-model in this was the Otago captain and hooker, David Latta. What was there for Latta after serving the game magnificently for a decade and more? Another house to build in an Otago frost. The scheme would significantly redress that.

It was when they presented that element of the scheme that I thought back to London, 1991, when half-a-dozen All Blacks, having been booted out of World Cup contention by Australia, were taking in the big city's sights, sounds, pubs and restaurants. We dined at a restaurant which looked affordable; modest appearance, modest menu. We were hacking at our steaks when we noticed this guy washing dishes out the back in a shabby kitchen. He looked familiar to me. Joe Stanley knew immediately who it was. He went out there and, sure enough, it was an All Black, a loose forward – and a very good one – of comparatively recent vintage. Joe asked what the hell he was doing in a dump like this and he said, "It's a job. It's all I can get." It was as if, having passed his use-by date as an All Black, he had been spat out the other end of the grinder and told to find his own way in the world. It was a depressing end to the night.

Fitzy and I agreed John Hart was the ideal man to front the Sky programme and he was brought in immediately. He had the right mix of brilliant communication, a successful background in corporate affairs and high credibility as a rugby man. He was quickly identified by the media as "the mastermind behind the Sky proposal", which rather overstated his initial input and understated that of Nate Smith and Peter Scutts. Though the game has moved on since Sky's first thrust the company is still involved, philosophically behind any move which will encourage players below the international level to stay in the game and top players to have the means to attract them to stay with the game in New Zealand. The WRC proposals had much the same effect.

I thought the most incisive comment on the professional development came from Laurie Mains. Laurie had already come in behind the players. He had said to me that the players were all-important and that with all the behind-the-scenes machinations there should be no possibility that opportunist fringers were creaming-off the system. Now, as others were bumbling about, concerned about the outrage from other IRB members, trying to rationalise it as being something other than professionalism, contradicting themselves almost day to day in an effort to deny outright professionalism, Laurie said succinctly, "Let's do it and the IRB can come on board if it wants to. It's time to be first."

So it was time to be first and if being first meant defying the IRB then that was OK, too. The risk, after all, was minimal. Would the IRB chuck us out? With the same gesture would it chuck out Australia? South Africa? To be consistent would it chuck out France, the prime amateur pretender for years? It would have been a tattered old international scene had all countries which had toyed with the amateur ethic for years been chucked out.

The New Zealand Rugby Union chairman, Richie Guy, probably had serious political reasons for saying forthrightly one week that professional rugby was the only way to go…"It has been our attitude for a long time that we would like the game to go professional – we are talking about players getting paid to play"….and a couple of weeks later denying professionalism had ever been a priority or a proposed policy of the New Zealand Rugby Union.

The widening gap between the ideals, however cynically observed, of English administration and the reality for its players was clearly illustrated by the published outrage of Dudley Wood, the Rugby Union secretary, with what was happening in the Southern hemisphere and the almost simultaneous statement of Tony Underwood: "The goalposts have moved, and today amateurism is being flouted throughout the world. The IRB should not be looking how to maintain an amateur game, but how to usher in this new phase so that some semblance of control is kept over our sport, and soon." "Soon" was already too late. Had Tony's warning been issued 10 years ago and had the IRB acted on it then matters would never have reached the state of revolution of June-July, 1995.

In a statement which was a direct contradiction of Woods' claim of paranoia over league in Australia and New Zealand Will Carling said: "The most negative aspect of rugby's development since the 1991 World Cup has been the corrosive and unnecessary amateurism debate which should have been sorted out a long time ago. If the Rugby Football Union doesn't sort things out soon and work with the players properly, looking after them from the top down, rugby will get blown out of the water by other sports, or by people within the game who will just leave because they get so fed up…there's no point in us wasting time clinging to

219

every vestige of amateurism. It is arrogant to think that the Murdoch-rugby league alliance is not a threat. It is. You can't just sit there and lose all your best players and think the sport will survive intact..."

Immediately after the World Cup Carling was even more explicit: "The next time we run on to the field we will be doing so with a contract. When we play South Africa in November there is no way we can take the field as we have done in the past. They will be paid to play, and so will we."

Just before the World Cup, even as England was announcing a handsome new sponsorship aimed at player-payment beyond anything New Zealanders were receiving – but, of course, "within the guidelines of amateurism" – there were still writers who were sneering at southern hemisphere "greed". Eddie Butler in *The Observer:* "Apparently you only have to whisper Super League to an Australian or a Kiwi and their executives hold an emergency meeting and put a few more noughts on the figure for which southern union will prostitute itself in order to remain amateur".

"Prostitution" of that sort is a much older profession in England than in New Zealand – and, apparently, even older in Eddie's home territory, Wales. After turning to league with St Helens last year Scott Gibbs, the very good Wales and Lions centre, resented being called a "rugby prostitute", saying, "The Welsh are the worst in Britain when it comes to upholding amateur status. The hypocrisy of it all sucks. Players and officials keep on covering up what is going on in union...whatever way it is done – cash bonuses for wins, 5000 quid and a car plus match payments to join a club – clubs in Wales are paying their players."

"Prostitution" comes in many forms other than between the sheets or in the front seat of a BMW. Before our England test in 1993 each England player received an allocation of five tickets plus the right to buy at face value 15 more. These they pooled and sold-off, at the going rate for a packed Twickenham, at anything between 250 and 500 pounds sterling each. Just a tidy nest-egg within the guidelines of amateurism, of course. Like Wales, England has become comfortable with the position that if it can conceal its professional pregnancy its purity before the high priest of amateurism will stand intact. Being "only slightly pregnant" has become an art-form.

As I was starting work on this book there was a "coup" at the top of New Zealand rugby. There had been ready acceptance by the players that Eddie Tonks, as chairman of the New Zealand Rugby Union, and his deputy, Rob Fisher, were assertively leading the way toward international agreement that the contribution of the players had to be recognised by realistic monetary support – pay, if you like. It seemed to the players to be a bizarre time to be having an eruption at the top of the game's administration when continuity was vital. There was concern whether power-plays by administrators were going to supercede the business in hand. What we knew was that a successful businessman with the players' interests at heart had been ousted by what we with agricultural backgrounds might call "a cow-cocky" from Waipu.

And when in his first television appearance Richie Guy looked as grim as only old props can and made a slighting reference to the marketing of the Warriors league team, players winced and thought maybe the Warriors' frontman Ian Robson was right when he said that on the day of the coup daylight saving went back one hour and rugby went back 30 years. But what happened, of course, was that in partnership with the Australians Richie Guy, backed by the expertise of Rob Fisher, moved aggressively into the payment for players negotiations and the process accelerated and then, with the entry into the marketplace of Rupert Murdoch, exploded. It was a sound which reverberated around the rugby world until it was overpowered by the WRC nuclear explosion.

The process of the sale of television rights to Murdoch and the proposed distribution of the takings could not have been better designed to convince the players that their position in the market was of a commodity – and you don't consult with commodities. You juggle them and move them around and they don't talk back. It was this fait accompli thing which bit us because it showed that what had been at the very source of discontent for so long had not really changed at all. And it was clear to most of us "commodities" that a 10-year deal for $828 million was a dangerously long period without the right of renegotiation, say, every three years. It was a deal which would have had Rupert Murdoch celebrating a commercial coup.

The players were approached on the WRC proposal straight after the World Cup final in South Africa. Former All Black great Andy Haden was the principal mover and shaker. He worked through our own "legal eagle," Eric Rush who was a sort of legal liaison between the WRC and the players. Rushy's involvement was in the setting-up of a meeting for the Monday night after the final.

All the players met in Fitzy's hotel room and he and Mike Brewer, who had been briefed that morning, explained the detail of the Packer proposal. We were told the South African and French players had already been signed up. The next meeting followed the parliamentary reception to the team in Wellington. Geoff Levy, the package-carrier and negotiator for WRC, had contracts ready for signing. He went through the whole picture and told us to take the contracts away, have them legally scrutinised, think about them and make a decision within a fortnight.

Most of the guys seemed keen but there were those with league offers to consider and those with individual endorsement contracts to sort out. Some contract clauses were re-written, some modified, all tailored to individual situations. On the Sunday before the first Bledisloe Cup match at Eden Park those of us from the north met in Eric Rush's office and there was a conference call with the others all around the country. We met again after the match. Levy was pressing for contract agreements and signatures. Fifteen were signed up and ready to go. The demand was for 22 of the World Cup squad of 26.

It was a very difficult position for some of the players who were reluctant to see their All Black status placed at risk. Levy gave us until the Monday after the second Bledisloe Cup match but emphasised that was deadline time, no reservations, 22 signatures.

The New Zealand Rugby Union by now had wind of the WRC campaign. They assigned Brian Lochore, Jock Hobbs and Rob Fisher to talk to us. BJ talked of the game's spirit and traditions and of the ramifications for the game should there be a total breakdown between players and traditional administration. Jock spoke of the legal pitfalls and consequences should the Packer deal fall over. Their message was that there should now be a clean slate. Everything that had gone before would be wiped. We would start talking on a level playing field. There was in this the indication that the whole show had been mismanaged by the NZRFU and that they were desperate to patch-up the ship.

We met again as players and gave a lot of consideration to what BJ and Jock had said. We did not discard it out of hand for much of what they said had merit and covered some of the serious reservations players already had.

Again conflicting statements hit the headlines. One had Richie Guy saying the players faced a lifetime ban should they opt out of the system. Then that was contradicted by Richie, who said it was far too soon to be making that sort of threat. It was puzzling. The volatility of the situation was such that nothing which was achieved or attempted one day necessarily held good the next. The WRC organisation quickly sniffed out changing patterns, including substantially increased offers from the NZRFU, and mounted an even more urgent demand for signatures. Levy demanded signed contracts before the second Bledisloe Cup match. Players' representatives met him on the Friday night in Sydney. Levy was insistent. He knew the NZRFU would be presenting new contracts to the players Saturday night and he was trying to anticipate that offer.

We were just as insistent we did not want the players involved that close to the game. We left the meeting on the promise there would be another immediately after the match. Straight after the game we were taken miles out of the city to the home of a Packer executive. We had a very short time before we had to go back for the Cup dinner. We met a group of executives and 24 players acknowledged their commitment to the WRC and Walter Little, Frank Bunce and Glen Osborne had been saved for rugby union. Part of the contract with the WRC was that there would be a substantial payment for each player on November 22. Following the switch back to the New Zealand Rugby Union some of us sent a letter through legal representatives here forfeiting that payment provided there was no legal action over our contracts.

As events had unfolded publicly we knew there would be repercussions, that some would see us as the wreckers of establishment rugby and find our action unforgiveable while giving little consideration to the motives behind it. Andy Dalton, much admired as a New Zealand captain, said he was "appalled" by what he alleged were "standover tactics" by older All Blacks to influence the younger and was disturbed about older players looking at the dollars before the game. I have to say it was not only inaccurate and exaggerated, but surprising coming from the captain of the rebel Cavaliers of 1986, whose levels of payment can only be guessed at. There were no standover tactics and the younger players would endorse that. This was a group of players, young and older, who had become very close during the World Cup campaign and to suggest some players would brow-beat others betrayed blind ignorance of that. Andy was not the only old player to climb in. I suggest to him and to others that given the circumstances of modern rugby they, too, would have been engaged in a battle for the best deal for players openly designated as professionals but blocked-off from consultation on their destinies. The players love the game. Probably they love it a great deal more than the people who will condemn them and certainly as much as old players who resented what was happening. We all want the best for the game but the world of the players has changed, too. It is senseless to sneer at the reality that the administrators of the game through the years have made it impossible for players at the top level to commit themselves to the professional agenda while not making the professional money. The point was going to be reached when the players cried enough.

Now much has been achieved. The NZRFU is very conscious of the need to have the players as working partners rather than as lackeys in the big new professional world. Three players will join three councillors on a special committee to consult on tour schedules and more effective administration of the All Blacks.

Even as the battle for the players raged Graham Lowe was crossing the Tasman to buy rugby union players for Australian league. He was confident he would do it, too. The policies which have invited the league raids on rugby's carefully nurtured stars through the years may by now be destroyed in the upheaval. Have the Olympic Games lost their heart? Even tighter than rugby the Games were bound to amateurism. But the Olympics have become open slather with sports-millionaires becoming sports multi-millionaires by competing at what was the source of amateurism. The awful ultimate, professionalism, has saved the Olympic Games from becoming a nondescript event for inferior athletes and, inevitably, from death. It may be it is doing precisely the same for rugby by removing its players from the reach of league.

I never wanted to lose contact with the heart of rugby. I always wanted to be able to meet my old club-mates over a pint and swap exaggerations of the tries we scored and the goals we kicked. For all that has happened, I believe rugby's pride in tradition is preserved. We will not have that change because we are now paid servants of the game. The heart of rugby will still be in Puhoi where the kids scramble to be first into the stream to retrieve the ball. I could never have dreamed as I was finding my way through rugby that one day, near the end of the road, I would be in the middle of a revolution in the game, an event of such magnitude that traditional administrations world-wide would be embroiled in a contest for the players' allegiance and that the players would be looking at payments beyond the imagination.

All this, and all I ever wanted to be was a shearer.

Statistics

Zinzan Brooke First Class Career

(to August 25, 1997)

Team	Games	Tries
Auckland	132	91
New Zealand	95	41
Auckland Blues	22	8
NZ Maori	22	12
NZ Colts	8	1
NZ Trials	7	
North Zone	4	1
North Island	1	1
North Maori	4	1
NZ Marist	1	1
NZ Barbarians	1	
NZ Harlequins	1	
	298	**157**

1985

Team	Versus	Venue	Result	Tries
Marist Presidents XV	Condors XV	Auckland	30-26	(1)
NZ Colts	Horowhenua	Levin	43-3	
NZ Colts	Wanganui	Wanganui	12-3	
NZ Colts	Manawatu	Palmerston North	15-9	
NZ Colts	Australian U21	Auckland	37-21	

1986

Team	Versus	Venue	Result	Tries
Barbarians	Auckland	Auckland	18-36	
Auckland	Fiji	Suva	15-10	
Auckland	New South Wales	Auckland	34-15	
Auckland	Queensland	Brisbane	16-25	
Auckland	Wellington	Auckland	26-10	
Auckland	Taranaki	New Plymouth	43-18	
Northern Maori	Southern Maori	Dunedin	24-3	(1)
NZ Maori	Southland	Invercargill	28-17	
NZ Maori	East Coast	Ruatoria	54-9	(2)
NZ Maori	Wairarapa Bush	Masterton	41-9	
NZ Colts	West Coast	Greymouth	61-13	
NZ Colts	Nelson Bays	Nelson	62-3	(1)
NZ Colts	Wellington	Wellington	6-52	
NZ Colts	Australia U21	Sydney	11-35	
Auckland	Counties	Pukekohe	18-0	

1987

Team	Versus	Venue	Result	Tries
Auckland	New South Wales	Sydney	19-18	
Auckland	Queensland	Auckland	43-18	
Auckland	Fiji	Auckland	68-7	(3)
New Zealand	Argentina	Wellington	46-15	(1)
Auckland	Wanganui	Auckland	59-6	(2)
Auckland	Otago	Dunedin	34-6	(2)
Auckland	Canterbury	Christchurch	24-15	

Auckland	Hawke's Bay	Auckland	56-18	(1)
Auckland	East Coast	Auckland	72-0	
Auckland	North Auckland	Whangarei	25-6	(1)
Auckland	Bay of Plenty	Auckland	43-3	(1)
Auckland	Taranaki	Auckland	49-6	(4)
Auckland	Waikato	Auckland	34-11	(2)
Auckland	Wellington	Auckland	33-18	(1)
Auckland	Counties	Auckland	48-9	
New Zealand	Japan	Osaka	74-0	
New Zealand	Japan	Tokyo	106-4	(4)

1988

Team	Versus	Venue	Result	Tries
Auckland	New South Wales	Auckland	38-19	(1)
Auckland	Queensland	Brisbane	39-10	(2)
Auckland	Wellington	Auckland	58-0	(1)
Auckland	Canterbury	Christchurch	26-15	(2)
North Zone	Central Zone	Rotorua	68-6	
Auckland	Fiji	Suva	27-7	(3)
North Zone	South Zone	Timaru	28-21	
Auckland	Waikato	Hamilton	18-3	(1)
New Zealand	Western Australia	Perth	60-3	(1)
New Zealand	NSW Country	Singleton	29-4	(1)
New Zealand	ACT	Queanbeyan	16-3	(2)
New Zealand	Queensland	Brisbane	27-12	
New Zealand	Queensland B	Townsville	39-3	
New Zealand	NSW 'B'	Gosford	45-9	(1)
New Zealand	New South Wales	Sydney	42-6	
New Zealand	Victorian Invitation XV	Melbourne	84-8	
Auckland	King Country	Te Kuiti	28-0	(1)
Auckland	Taranaki	New Plymouth	41-13	
Auckland	North Auckland	Auckland	43-15	(1)
Auckland	Counties	Pukekohe	18-7	
Auckland	Wellington	Wellington	17-12	(1)
Auckland	Hawke's Bay	Napier	62-9	(2)
Auckland	Bay of Plenty	Rotorua	28-22	
Auckland	North Harbour	Auckland	39-12	
Auckland	Manawatu	Auckland	59-3	
Auckland	Otago	Auckland	27-17	(1)
Auckland	Canterbury	Auckland	31-10	(1)
NZ Maori	NZ Universities	Auckland	37-19	
NZ Maori	Italian Barbarians	Rome	57-9	
NZ Maori	Littoral Selection	Toulon	22-9	
NZ Maori	Pyrenees Selection	Rodez	10-10	(1)
NZ Maori	Languedoc Selection	Narbonne	25-31	
NZ Maori	French Army XV	Castres	20-16	
NZ Maori	French Barbarians	Mont de Marsan	31-14	(2)
NZ Maori	Spanish Selection	Seville	22-12	
NZ Maori	Rosario Selection	Rosario	88-12	(2)
NZ Maori	Tucuman	Tucuman	12-3	

1989

Team	Versus	Venue	Result	Tries
Auckland	Wellington	Wellington	51-3	(4)
Auckland	Canterbury	Auckland	33-15	(1)
Auckland	Queensland	Auckland	24-15	(1)
Auckland	New South Wales	Sydney	11-16	
Auckland	Fiji	Auckland	72-9	(1)
North Zone	Central Zone	Wanganui	45-11	

North Zone	South Zone	Takapuna	25-19	(1)
Possibles	Probables	Hamilton	25-31	
Auckland	North Harbour	Takapuna	9-9	
Northern Maori	Southern Maori	Gisborne	40-17	
Auckland	Hawke's Bay	Napier	50-12	(1)
Auckland	Argentina	Auckland	61-6	(1)
Auckland	North Auckland	Whangarei	48-3	(1)
New Zealand	Argentina	Wellington	49-12	
Auckland	Thames Valley	Paeroa	58-7	(2)
Auckland	Taranaki	Auckland	44-15	(1)
Auckland	Otago	Dunedin	13-3	
Auckland	Mid-Canterbury	Ashburton	66-0	(1)
Auckland	Canterbury	Christchurch	15-6	
Auckland	Counties	Auckland	84-3	(1)
Auckland	Bay of Plenty	Auckland	34-21	(2)
Auckland	Waikato	Auckland	22-9	(1)
Auckland	Wellington	Auckland	29-6	
New Zealand	British Columbia	Vancouver	48-3	(2)
New Zealand	Pontypool	Pontypool	47-6	
New Zealand	Neath	Neath	26-15	(1)
New Zealand	Newport	Newport	54-9	(1)
New Zealand	Leinster	Dublin	36-9	(1)
New Zealand	Munster	Cork	31-9	
New Zealand	Ulster	Belfast	21-3	(1)
New Zealand	UK Barbarians	London	21-10	(1)

1990

Team	Versus	Venue	Result	Tries
Auckland	Canterbury	Christchurch	36-12	(2)
Auckland	Wellington	Auckland	49-9	(2)
Auckland	New South Wales	Auckland	55-13	
Possibles	Probables	Palmerston North	25-39	
Auckland	Fiji	Suva	21-8	
Northern Maori	Southern Maori	Auckland	32-7	
NZ Maori	Auckland	Auckland	9-22	
NZ Maori	NZ Universities	Rotorua	63-9	(3)
Auckland	King Country	Auckland	58-3	(4)
Auckland	Waikato	Hamilton	21-12	
Auckland	Wellington	Wellington	40-12	
Auckland	Australia	Auckland	16-10	
New Zealand	Australia	Christchurch	21-6	
New Zealand	Australia	Auckland	27-17	(1)
New Zealand	Australia	Wellington	9-21	
Auckland	Taranaki	New Plymouth	31-9	
Auckland	Poverty Bay	Gisborne	42-3	(1)
Auckland	Bay of Plenty	Rotorua	26-9	(2)
Auckland	Southland	Auckland	78-7	(2)
Auckland	Otago	Auckland	45-9	(3)
Auckland	North Auckland	Auckland	41-21	(2)
Auckland	North Harbour	Auckland	18-9	
New Zealand	Lanquedoc	Narbonne	22-6	(1)
New Zealand	French Barbarians	Agen	23-13	
New Zealand	France	Nantes	24-3	
New Zealand	French XV	La Rochelle	22-15	

1991

Team	Versus	Venue	Result	Tries
Auckland	Fiji	Auckland	36-6	
Auckland	Hawke's Bay	Napier	49-18	(2)
Probables	Possibles	Rotorua	24-25	

228

Auckland	Bay of Plenty	Auckland	29-18	(1)
Auckland	North Harbour	Takapuna	21-12	
New Zealand	Rosario	Rosario	81-9	(1)
New Zealand	Cordoba	Cordoba	38-9	
New Zealand	Buenos Aires	Buenos Aires	37-9	
New Zealand	Argentina 'B'	Buenos Aires	22-6	
New Zealand	Mar del Plata	Mar del Plata	48-6	(1)
New Zealand	Argentina	Buenos Aires	36-6	(1)
Auckland	Counties	Auckland	27-0	(1)
Auckland	Manawatu	Auckland	52-4	
Auckland	North Auckland	Whangarei	18-9	
New Zealand	Australia	Sydney	12-21	
New Zealand	Australia	Auckland	6-3	
Auckland	Taranaki	Auckland	55-9	(1)
Auckland	Waikato	Auckland	40-12	
Auckland	Wellington	Auckland	31-21	
New Zealand	England	London	18-12	
New Zealand	Italy	Leicester	31-21	(1)
New Zealand	Canada	Lille	29-13	(1)
New Zealand	Australia	Dublin	6-16	
New Zealand	Scotland	Cardiff	13-6	

1992

Team	Versus	Venue	Result	Tries
Northern Maori	Southern Maori	Tauranga	17-33	
NZ Maori	King Country	Taupo	27-6	(1)
NZ Maori	NZ Presidents XV	Rotorua	30-11	
Auckland	Wellington	Auckland	33-12	(2)
Auckland	Ireland	Auckland	62-7	
Auckland	Waikato	Hamilton	20-13	
New Zealand	South Aust Invitation	Adelaide	48-18	
New Zealand	ACT	Canberra	45-13	
New Zealand	Victorian Invitation	Melbourne	53-3	(1)
New Zealand	Queensland	Brisbane	26-19	
New Zealand	Australia	Brisbane	17-19	
New Zealand	Australia	Sydney	26-23	
New Zealand	Natal	Durban	43-25	
New Zealand	Junior South Africa	Pretoria	25-10	
New Zealand	Central Unions	Witbank	39-6	
New Zealand	South Africa	Johannesburg	27-24	(1)
Auckland	Otago	Auckland	21-16	
Auckland	Hawke's Bay	Napier	40-9	
Auckland	King Country	Taupo	42-15	
Auckland	North Auckland	Auckland	49-3	
Auckland	Canterbury	Auckland	47-38	
Auckland	Counties	Pukekohe	24-19	
Auckland	North Harbour	Auckland	25-16	
Auckland	Waikato	Auckland	21-27	

1993

Team	Versus	Venue	Result	Tries
Possibles	Probables	Rotorua	19-20	
Auckland	Transvaal	Johannesburg	17-20	
NZ Maori	British Isles	Wellington	20-24	
Probables	Possibles	Pukekohe	18-15	
Auckland	Hawke's Bay	Auckland	69-31	(1)
New Zealand	British Isles	Christchurch	20-18	
Auckland	British Isles	Auckland	23-18	
New Zealand	British Isles	Wellington	7-20	
New Zealand	British Isles	Auckland	30-13	

229

New Zealand	Western Samoa	Auckland	35-13	(1)
Auckland	Taranaki	New Plymouth	48-19	(1)
Auckland	North Harbour	Takapuna	25-9	
Auckland	Otago	Dunedin	21-25	
Auckland	North Otago	Oamaru	139-5	(2)
Auckland	Canterbury	Christchurch	39-13	
Auckland	Wellington	Auckland	51-14	
Auckland	Waikato	Auckland	6-17	
Auckland	King Country	Auckland	97-3	(1)
Auckland	North Harbour	Auckland	43-20	
Auckland	Otago	Auckland	27-18	
New Zealand	London-S.E. Division	London	39-12	
New Zealand	Midlands	Leicester	26-10	
New Zealand	England South West	Redruth	19-15	
New Zealand	England North	Liverpool	27-21	
New Zealand	England A	Gateshead	26-12	
New Zealand	South of Scotland	Galashiels	84-5	(4)
New Zealand	Scotland	Edinburgh	51-15	(1)
New Zealand	England	London	9-15	
New Zealand	Barbarians	Cardiff	25-12	

1994

Team	Versus	Venue	Result	Tries
NZ Maori	Vaal Triangle	Sasolburg	119-3	
NZ Maori	Orange Free State	Johannesburg	16-16	(1)
NZ Maori	Griqualand West	Kimberley	21-30	
NZ Maori	Eastern Province	Johannesburg	24-26	
Auckland	Bay of Plenty	Rotorua	39-33	
Auckland	Waikato	Auckland	27-10	
Auckland	Western Samoa	Auckland	13-15	
Auckland	New South Wales	Sydney	19-22	
Auckland	Natal	Durban	12-24	
Probables	Possibles	Gisborne	31-54	
New Zealand	France	Auckland	20-23	
New Zealand	South Africa	Dunedin	22-14	
New Zealand	South Africa	Wellington	13-9	(1)
New Zealand	South Africa	Auckland	18-18	
New Zealand	Australia	Sydney	16-20	
Auckland	Wellington	Wellington	52-30	
Auckland	Otago	Auckland	46-30	(1)
Auckland	Counties	Pukekohe	18-15	
Auckland	Waikato	Hamilton	37-15	
Auckland	Otago	Dunedin	33-16	
Auckland	North Harbour	Takapuna	22-16	

1995

Team	Versus	Venue	Result	Tries
Auckland	Canterbury	Auckland	27-22	(1)
Auckland	Tonga	Nuku'alofa	37-25	
North Island	South Island	Dunedin	55-22	(1)
Harlequins	Waikato	Hamilton	96-25	
New Zealand	Japan	Bloemfontein	145-17	
New Zealand	Scotland	Pretoria	48-30	
New Zealand	England	Cape Town	45-29	
New Zealand	South Africa	Johannesburg	12-15	
New Zealand	Australia	Auckland	28-16	
New Zealand	Australia	Sydney	34-23	
Auckland	North Harbour	Takapuna	11-12	
Auckland	King Country	Auckland	46-15	(2)
Auckland	Otago	Dunedin	25-21	
Auckland	Southland	Invercargill	21-19	(1)

Auckland	Counties	Auckland	59-24	(1)
Auckland	Canterbury	Christchurch	35-0	
Auckland	Waikato	Auckland	26-17	
Auckland	Counties	Auckland	60-26	(1)
Auckland	Otago	Auckland	23-19	
New Zealand	Italy	Bologna	70-6	(1)
New Zealand	French Barbarians	Toulon	34-19	
New Zealand	France	Toulouse	15-22	
New Zealand	France	Paris	37-12	

1996

Team	Versus	Venue	Result	Tries
Auckland Blues	Wellington Hurricanes	Palmerston North	36-28	
Auckland Blues	Canterbury Crusaders	Christchurch	49-18	
Auckland Blues	ACT Brumbies	Canberra	34-40	
Auckland Blues	Western Province	Auckland	48-30	
Auckland Blues	Waikato Chiefs	Auckland	39-31	(1)
Auckland Blues	Queensland	Brisbane	13-51	
Auckland Blues	New South Wales	Auckland	56-44	(1)
Auckland Blues	Transvaal	Johannesburg	22-34	
Auckland Blues	Natal	Durban	30-23	
Auckland Blues	Northern Transvaal	Auckland	48-11	
Auckland Blues	Natal	Auckland	45-21	
Presidents XV	NZ Barbarians XV	Napier	72-18	
New Zealand	Western Samoa	Napier	51-10	
New Zealand	Scotland	Dunedin	62-31	(1)
New Zealand	Scotland	Auckland	36-12	(1)
New Zealand	Australia	Wellington	43-6	(1)
New Zealand	South Africa	Christchurch	15-11	
New Zealand	Australia	Brisbane	32-25	
New Zealand	South Africa	Capetown	29-18	
New Zealand	South Africa	Durban	23-19	(1)
New Zealand	South Africa	Pretoria	33-26	(1)
New Zealand	South Africa	Johannesburg	22-32	
Auckland	Wellington	Wellington	44-33	(1)
Auckland	Otago	Auckland	50-23	
Auckland	Waikato	Hamilton	27-7	
Auckland	North Harbour	Auckland	69-27	(1)
Auckland	Otago	Auckland	59-18	
Auckland	Counties	Auckland	46-15	

1997

Team	Versus	Venue	Result	Tries
Auckland Blues	Waikato Chiefs	Albany	26-16	(1)
Auckland Blues	Queensland	Auckland	49-26	
Auckland Blues	Canterbury Crusaders	Pukekohe	29-28	
Auckland Blues	ACT Brumbies	Auckland	41-29	
Auckland Blues	Gauteng Lions	Auckland	63-22	(2)
Auckland Blues	Natal	Auckland	39-17	
Auckland Blues	Otago Highlanders	Dunedin	45-28	
Auckland Blues	Wellington Hurricanes	Auckland	45-42	(1)
Auckland Blues	New south Wales	Sydney	34-20	(1)
Auckland Blues	Natal	Auckland	55-36	(1)
Auckland Blues	ACT Brumbies	Auckland	23-7	
New Zealand	Argentina	Wellington	93-8	
New Zealand	Argentina	Hamilton	62-10	
New Zealand	Australia	Christchurch	30-13	(2)
New Zealand	South Africa	Johannesburg	35-32	
New Zealand	Australia	Melbourne	33-18	
New Zealand	South Africa	Auckland	55-35	
New Zealand	Australia	Dunedin	36-24	

- Currently 157 tries – highest of any current player
- New Zealand record for tries by a forward
- First holder of the Kel Tremain Trophy as the NZ Rugby Personality of the Year, 1994
- Selected for the All Blacks before playing an All Black trial
- NZ Sevens rep for 5 years – captain in '90, '91, '92
- The only player to have scored 4 tries in a match 3 times for Auckland
- Twice scored 18 and twice scored 17 tries in a season for Auckland
- Kicked the first conversion for Auckland Blues in Super 12 Rugby
- His 4 tries scored against the Springboks equals the most by any player – a record jointly shared with JJ Williams (British Isles 1974) and Jeff Wilson
- Shares with Sean Fitzpatrick, Olo Brown and Frank Bunce the unique record of 9 victories over the Springboks
- His 2 dropped goals were both kicked in South Africa

AUCKLAND APPEARANCES

196	H.L. White
189	G.J. Fox
178	G.W. Whetton
158	A.M. Haden
151	S.B.T. Fitzpatrick
149	A.J. Whetton
141	J.J. Kirwan
139	M.A. Herewini
137	J.T. Stanley
135	T.J. Wright
132	B.G. Williams
132	**Z.V. Brooke**

AUCKLAND – MOST POINTS

Player	Games	Tries	Convs	Pens	D Goals	Total Points
G.J. Fox	189	25	613	441	31	2746
T.J. Wright	135	112	17	11	3	531
A.A. Cashmore	38	13	91	66		445
J.J. Kirwan	141	104				436
R.R. Dunn	73	11	63	76	10	428
S.L. Watt	61	1	53	102	1	419
S.P. Howarth	53	42	63	28	3	418
Z.V. Brooke	**132**	**91**				**378**

AUCKLAND – MOST TRIES

112	T.J. Wright
104	J.J. Kirwan
91	**Z.V. Brooke**

RANFURLY SHIELD – MOST GAMES

57	G.J. Fox
56	G.W. Whetton
56	S.B.T. Fitzpatrick
53	J.J. Kirwan
52	T.J. Wright
50	**Z.V. Brooke**

RANFURLY SHIELD – MOST POINTS

Player	Games	Tries	Convs	Pens	D Goals	Total Points
G.J. Fox	57	3	233	140	8	923
R.G. Deans	23	11	60	56		332
T.J. Wright	52	53	6	1	2	240
J.J. Kirwan	53	44				187
Z.V. Brooke	**50**	**44**				**180**

RANFURLY SHIELD – MOST TRIES

53	T.J. Wright
44	J.J. Kirwan
44	**Z.V. Brooke**

NEW ZEALAND APPEARANCES

133	C.E. Meads
126	S.B.T. Fitzpatrick
117	A.M. Haden
113	I.A. Kirkpatrick
113	B.G. Williams
102	B.J. Robertson
101	G.W. Whetton
96	J.J. Kirwan
95	**Z.V. Brooke**

TEST MATCH APPEARANCES

91	S.B.T. Fitzpatrick
66	I.D. Jones
63	J.J. Kirwan
58	G.W. Whetton
55	C.E. Meads
54	**Z.V. Brooke**
51	M.N. Jones
51	F.E. Bunce

- 48 test appearances as No.8
- 5 test appearances as openside flanker
- 1 test appearance as blindside flanker

TEST MATCHES AT No. 8

48	**Z.V. Brooke**
34	M.G. Mexted
24	B.J. Lochore
22	W.T. Shelford

MOST TEST MATCH TRIES BY A FORWARD

17	**Z.V. Brooke**
16	I.A. Kirkpatrick
13	M.N. Jones
12	S.B.T. Fitzpatrick
11	C.J. Windon (Australia)
11	J.J. Jeffrey (Scotland)

HIGHEST TRY SCORERS IN NZ FIRST CLASS RUGBY

199	J.J. Kirwan
177	T.J. Wright
171	B.G. Fraser
157	**Z.V. Brooke**
145	R.A. Jarden
137	B.G. Williams
136	K.R. Tremain

HIGHEST TRY SCORERS FOR NZ IN TEST MATCHES

35	J.J. Kirwan
21	J.W. Wilson
20	F.E. Bunce
19	S.S. Wilson
19	T.J. Wright
18	C.M. Cullen
17	**Z.V. Brooke**

HIGHEST TRY SCORERS IN ALL MATCHES FOR NZ

67	J.J. Kirwan
66	B.G. Williams
50	I.A. Kirkpatrick
50	S.S. Wilson
49	J. Hunter
49	T.J. Wright
46	B.G. Fraser
45	G.B. Batty
42	M.J. Dick
41	**Z.V. Brooke**

Has played against 24 of the 27 Unions in NZ. Those he has yet to play: Buller, Marlborough and Wairarapa bush. Yes he has played against Auckland – in fact he played against Auckland before he had played for Auckland – 13/3/86 for Barbarians – and later for NZ Maoris on 19/5/90.
He has scored against 20 of the 27 unions. Virginal Unions are Auckland, Buller, Horowhenua, Manawatu, Marlborough, Wairarapa Bush and West Coast.